WILHELM RÖPKE

ECONOMICS OF THE FREE SOCIETY

ECONOMICS OF THE FREE SOCIETY

by

WILHELM RÖPKE

*Professor at the
Graduate Institute of International
Studies—Geneva*

Translated by

PATRICK M. BOARMAN

HENRY REGNERY COMPANY
Chicago, 1963

The assistance of the Intercollegiate Society
of Individualists, Philadelphia, in the publication
of this book is gratefully acknowledged.

First Published in Austria in 1937
Die Lehre von der Wirtschaft
(Julius Springer, Vienna)

Translated from the 9th German Edition
Published in Switzerland in 1961 by
Eugen-Rentsch Verlag
Erlenbach-Zurich

PREFACE

This English translation of my *Die Lehre von der Wirtschaft* is based on the 9th German edition (Eugen-Rentsch Verlag, Zurich, 1961). The appearance of the work in the United States some twenty-five years after its original publication in German may be the proper occasion on which to relate its rather tumultuous history. The original draft was composed during a period of exile in Turkey in 1936 and was published in Vienna (Julius Springer Verlag) shortly before the National Socialist takeover of Austria. It was a publication which properly should have excited the deepest suspicion of the agents of the brown totalitarians. Nevertheless, it managed for a time to avoid outright proscription and enjoyed a modest clandestine circulation in certain areas where the swastika flew. Ultimately, the Gestapo, with its sure nose for intellectual contraband, broke into the cellars of the Vienna publisher and confiscated the remaining copies. Thus the book, like its author, was forced to emigrate and had the good fortune to be adopted by a Swiss firm. A Czech and an Hungarian translation were prepared, but before they could be published the political upheavals which followed in the wake of Nazi conquests silenced this antitotalitarian voice.

A better fate was reserved to the French translation which was published in 1940 in Paris (Librairie de Medicis) under the title *Explication économique du monde moderne*. Perhaps "published" is not quite the right word to describe what happened to the book. Arrangements for its distribution had been completed by May of 1940, but shortly afterwards Paris capitulated to German troops. This appeared to doom the book, particularly since a very frank foreword and final chapter had been prepared for the French edition wherein the description of the "ère des tyrannies" left little to the imagination. Luckily, however, the book had received the imprimatur of the French authorities prior to the German invasion. Secured with this flimsy document, the courageous and inventive directress of the Paris publishing house managed to sell it under the very nose of the Gestapo on the pretext that it was of no concern or interest to the "Kommandantur." No doubt she had also counted on the German censor's regarding it as a completely harmless economics textbook, like so many others of its kind, and failing to note the concentrated poison of antitotalitarian resistance which was concealed within it. This expectation proved to be well founded, although to anyone familiar with the French version, the perpetration of such a deception over a period of years must appear miraculous. Despite the fact that the book, understandably, could not be advertised or promoted in any way, the publisher's initial supplies were quickly exhausted. The probable explanation of this miracle is that the German censors were too uneducated to understand the book, while those Germans who understood it were civilized enough to rejoice at such a discovery and not to betray it. There were, indeed, many Germans who reported in later years of how happy they were during their Paris sojourn to come upon the book. *Habent sua fata libelli.*

* * *

The need for a book such as this, it seems to me, is a twofold one.

There is, first, the pedagogical need of a coherent description of the whole of the economic process. Such a description should be scrupulously scientific. But it should also be adapted to the understanding, interests, and experience of people of average education. Certainly one cannot complain today of a dearth of substantial economics treatises for the advanced student. What had been lacking, however, when I decided to write this book more than thirty years ago, was a text on the elementary level which, while avoiding superficiality, would reveal to the reader all those complex relationships which make up the ordered whole of economics and which would at the same time provide him with the incentive and the means for continuing his investigations. Whether there is still such a vacuum and, if so, whether the present work fills it, I would not venture to say. My efforts, in any case, were directed wholly to this end. It was my intention to write a book such as I would have liked to have had available in my own student days, the kind of book which, in later years, I would have liked to recommend to my students.

The second need I had in mind results from the general condition of our age, a condition so obvious that it may be described in a few words. For years the economic and social structure of the West have been in a state of severe crisis; and in this crisis traditional economic teachings have been shaken violently from their moorings, have been increasingly called into question. What, really, is left of economic science? And what services can this science render us at the present time? Various answers may be given to these and similar questions but under no pretext can they be ignored. Clearly, there is urgent need of presenting to the lay reader a sort of accounting of economics, of examining and weighing with great care the intellectual heritage which has come down to us, and of bringing it to bear upon the burning questions of the present. This also is one of the aims of the book.

While the book is primarily intended to be an introduction to economic science for the intelligent layman, it could also serve as a principal or supplementary text for an introductory college course in economics. To this end, each chapter is followed by notes which pursue certain questions raised in the text beyond the elementary stage and suggest ways of making a more intensive study of them.

I hardly know how to express adequately my thanks to my good friend Professor Patrick M. Boarman who, at the sacrifice of postponing some of his own scientific work, has devoted his great talents both as a scholar and a stylist and accomplished linguist to the translation of the present book. Although English is not my mother tongue I have the impression that he has done a most admirable job.

I owe a particular debt to Professor Glenn Saxon who, both by his sympathy with my ideas and by his constructive criticism of the original text of the present book, has been highly instrumental in bringing about its American edition. I want to use this occasion to express my sincere gratitude to him. I am grateful also to my American publisher for his abiding interest in the English version of this book.

Geneva, 1962

WILHELM RÖPKE

TRANSLATOR'S PREFACE

It was in 1946, as an American exchange student at the University of Geneva, that I first heard expounded the economic principles and the economic philosophy which are set forth in this book. Listening to Wilhelm Röpke was a revelation; his lectures and seminars, presented in an elegant and dramatic English, were small masterpieces of economic wisdom and wit. But they were more than just exercises in economic analysis, for they were infused with Röpke's own deep humanity, his vast learning in the sources of Western culture, ancient and modern, his passionate devotion to the grand principles of liberalism in the best sense. It is in gratitude for the inspiration received from a great teacher and a great economist that this English translation of *Die Lehre von der Wirtschaft* was undertaken.

Since the book first appeared in Austria in 1937, nine Swiss [German] editions of it have been published, manifest testimony to its continuing popularity and influence in central Europe. Successive translations into French (1940), Swedish (1946), Italian (1949), and Finnish (1951) expanded the book's readership far beyond the confines of the German-speaking countries.

Through the years, the author has continually revised and updated his book; all of these revisions and additions have been incorporated into this English translation. In particular, it is necessary to note the introduction of new material especially for the American edition. Section 3, Chapter VIII, "The Impact of Keynesianism", is newly added; it is based on two separate essays by Röpke, "Keynes und unsere Zeit" (1946) and "Was lehrt Keynes?" (1952), both of which have been reprinted in the anthology of Röpke's articles, *Gegen die Brandung* (Zurich: Eugen Rentsch Verlag, 1959). New also is Sec-

ix

tion 3, Chapter IX, "The German Experiment in Noninflationary Market Economy." Finally, references to German works in the "Notes" have been replaced, where possible, by English translations of such works, or have been supplemented by references to similar works in English. Except for these changes, the present English text conforms to the revised German text of 1961.

My especial thanks are due to Dr. Russell Kirk who read an early draft of the translation and whose encouragement contributed to its ultimate publication.

Bucknell University
Lewisburg, Pennsylvania, 1962

PATRICK M. BOARMAN

CONTENTS

Chapter I

The Problem

Chapter II

The Basic Data of Economics

Chapter III

The Structure of the Division of Labor

Chapter IV

Money and Credit

Chapter V

The World of Goods and the Flow of Production

Chapter VI

Markets and Prices

Chapter VII

Rich and Poor

Chapter VIII

Disturbances of Economic Equilibrium

Chapter IX

Structure of the Economy; Economics and the World Crisis

CHAPTER I

THE PROBLEM

"Grasp the exhaustless life that all men live! Each
shares therein, though few may comprehend: Where'er
you touch, there's interest without end."
GOETHE (*Faust,* Prelude on the Stage)

1. *Ordered Anarchy*

On the threshold of every scientific speculation about the universe
(as the Greek philosophers taught us long ago) is inscribed the word
"wonder." Before explaining anything, we must first feel that it
needs explanation; before answering questions, we must first learn
how to ask them. Science cannot progress where men take the world,
their own existence, for granted. If our knowledge of these phenomena is to increase, we must see them naively, with the eyes of
children. Unfortunately, if understandably, the more the familiar
and commonplace is a given fact, the less does it excite the sensation
of "wonder." Is there anything, for instance, more familiar or more
humdrum than economic life? What is so usual, even banal, as the
housewife's daily marketing, the farmer's sale of a calf, the working-
man's weekly pay check, the sale of a share on the stock exchange?
Still, it needs but a moment's reflection to discover behind these
banal occurrences something unexplained, even mysterious. Once
we have made this discovery, we have already taken the first steps
onto the terrain of economics.

Despite the power of the human imagination, it can only feebly
picture the economic life of our age in all its variety and complexity.
If only we might at this moment have the gift of omnipresence, what
an unimaginable number of activities, mutually interacting with and

1

determining each other, we would behold. We would see millions of factories in which thousands of different products are being manufactured; people sowing somewhere, somewhere reaping; a thousand boats and trains hauling to the four corners of the earth cargoes of fantastic variety; shepherds tending flocks in Australia and New Zealand; miners digging copper ore in the Congo or in the American far West and starting it on its way throughout the whole world; the Japanese spinning silk, the Javanese gathering tea—all swelling an unbroken stream of goods flooding across the land into warehouses and factories and from thence into millions of shops. We would see a still finer network of little streams going from the shops into countless households, rivulets of food and clothing and all the other things required by an army of billions: laborers, office workers, clerks, businessmen, farmers—the very ones whose work has created the mighty river of goods. Simultaneously, we would see another current of goods (machines, tools, cement, and similar products not intended for direct consumption) supplying the factories in city and country—the auxiliary goods needed to keep the first stream of consumption goods flowing. And still the panorama would not be complete, for in every direction we would see a host of services being performed: a surgeon beginning an operation, a lawyer making a plea, an economist endeavoring to explain the economic system to a circle of unknown readers. And more than this: we would behold the bewildering moment-to-moment fluctuations of the money market and the securities market—phenomena which we sense are contributing in a mysterious fashion to the movement and progress of our economic system. Finally, our attention would be drawn to small and large ducts labeled "taxes" and "exercises" debouching at all stages of the economic process and serving to divert part of the flow of goods to the state for the maintenance of the army, the administrative agencies of the government, the schools and the courts.

Today, we are witnessing a rapid decline in the number of individuals who satisfy their wants independently of the outside world. The modern farmer manages to retain in a greater degree than any other class the independence of the self-sufficient man, although even he satisfies a growing share of his needs by selling his surplus produce in exchange for the things he does not raise. The rest of mankind, however, is almost completely dependent upon this indirect method of want-satisfaction. Indirect production, in turn, is based upon the principle, familiar to everyone, of the *division of labor,* but it presupposes, nonetheless, a harmonious coordination of the divided elements of the economic process.[1] Who in the countries of the free world is charged with this coordination? What would happen if no one were in charge?

Consider, for a moment, the problem of the daily provisioning of a great city. Its millions of inhabitants must be provided with the basic necessities, to say nothing of the "luxuries" which cheer and brighten existence: so many tons of flour, butter, meat, so many miles of cloth, so many millions of cigars and cigarettes, so many reams of paper, so many books, cups, plates, nails, and a thousand other things must be daily produced in such wise that a surplus or deficiency of any particular good is avoided. The goods must be available hourly, monthly, or annually (according to the kind of good in question) in exactly the quantities and qualities demanded by a population of several millions. But the people's demand for goods is necessarily dependent upon their purchasing power (money). The existence of purchasing power presupposes, in turn, that the millions who appear in the market as consumers have previously as "producers" (whether employees or independent proprietors) so adjusted their output, both in quantity and quality, to the general demand for goods that they were able to dispose of their stock without loss. Now the highly differentiated modern economic system encompasses not alone a single city, however great, not alone a country however vast, but, in a way to which we shall give our particular attention later, the whole terrestial globe. The craftsman in an optical instrument factory makes lenses for export to the most distant countries, which in turn supply him with cocoa, coffee, tobacco and wool. While he is polishing lenses he is also producing, indirectly, all these things more abundantly and more cheaply than if he produced them directly. This immensely extended and intricate mechanism can function only if all its parts are in such constant and perfect synchronization that noticeable disorder is avoided. Were this not the case, the provisioning of millions would be immediately imperiled.

Who is charged with seeing to it that the economic gears of society mesh properly? Nobody. No dictator rules the economy, deciding who shall perform the needed work and prescribing what goods and how much of each shall be produced and brought to market. Admittedly, people today must perforce accept a great deal more dictation from authorities of all kinds than a few decades ago. Yet by and large the world outside of the Communist bloc—the "capitalist" world, to use a popular if vague expression—still adheres to the principle that decisions about production, consumption, saving, buying and selling, are best left to the people themselves. *Thus, the modern economic system, an extraordinarily complex mechanism, functions without conscious central control by any agency whatever.* It is a mechanism which owes its continued functioning really to a kind of anarchy. And yet capitalism's severest critics must admit that all of its parts synchronize with amazing precision. Political anarchy leads invariably to chaos. But anarchy in economics, strangely, produces an opposite result: an orderly cosmos. Our economic system may be anarchic, but it is not chaotic. He who does not find this a wondrous phenomenon and thereby deserving of the most patient study cannot be expected to take much of an interest in economics.

The order which is immanent in our economic system compels recognition even by those who are far from finding it perfect. Indeed, even those who radically disapprove of this kind and degree of order and who wish to replace it with a system of conscious and centralized control (socialism) cannot deny that it exists. Order there is in our economic system; we have a centuries-long proof of it; it is a fact which is beyond debate but which is at the same time compatible with every political faith. Honesty compels the admission that the existence of ordered anarchy is cause for astonishment, that it is something which urgently requires explanation. Further reflection, moreover, must occasion serious doubt as to whether an enormously complicated and differentiated process such as is represented in the economic systems of the advanced industrial nations could be "commanded" in all its details from on high, after the fashion of an army or a factory, without the direst consequences. The existence of order in spite of anarchy—"spontaneous order" if we wish—is not alone an astounding phenomenon in itself. The processes peculiar to economic life in a free society make evident the fundamental superiority of the *spontaneous order* over the *commanded order*. Spontaneous order is not just another variety of order, albeit one with the surprising ability to function, if need be, even without command from on high. For if the organization of the economic system of a free society can be shown to differ fundamentally from the organization of an army, there is reason for believing that a spontaneous economic order is the only possible one. Notwithstanding, our enthusiasm for spontaneous order will be tempered by the realization that as measured against any given ideal, it may leave much to be desired.

2. *Other Enigmas of Economics*

Once we have become aware of the element of the mysterious and the problematical in the economic process in which we ourselves are engaged, we are alerted as well to the enigmatic aspects of all the individual parts of the process. Once we have begun to ask questions and have sloughed off the naive unconcern of the unphilosophical man who regards all these things as "given," our intellectual curiosity pushes us ever deeper into the thickets of economics. What about "interest," for example? Here is one of the biggest conundrums of economics and one which will no doubt appear as disconcerting at first sight to the modern tenderfoot as it did to the writer in his own youth. Or again: how many are there who regard money as something self-evident, something on which it is unnecessary to waste much discussion? They know what money is in its concrete form of coin and bank note and that one must have it to survive, but that is the end of the matter for them. It requires a serious monetary disturbance, such as the inflationary crises which developed in some countries after both World Wars, to bring home to people what irreplaceable services are rendered by a healthy monetary system, what fecund and also destructive forces lie hidden in those pieces of paper and those small discs of metal which are passed so nonchalantly from hand to hand. Then, even the uninitiate can see some point in reflecting on the meaning of money. And when once this act of reflection has commenced, how quickly comes insight into and appreciation of the mysteries and the problems which lie hidden here. It is then that the realization comes that money is not something natural and self-evident, but a human invention, and as such an historical phenomenon which acquires significance only at a certain stage of economic development, namely, that of an advanced society founded on the market and the division of labor.

Let us take a step further, leaving aside for the moment the broader interrelationships of economic life (whose problematical aspects are really not so difficult to discern) and confine our attention to a single banal fact, selected at random. Assume that we have a pencil costing $.05 and a watch costing $50. Whence comes this difference in price? There are three possible explanations. *First:* the two prices are simply the result of chance. Chance, clearly, plays a role in the formation of prices as anyone will attest who has ever attended an auction or paid some exorbitant price in an Eastern bazaar. And there is little doubt but that on most of our imperfectly organized markets the formation of prices takes place within a more or less wide range of indeterminacy. Yet no one would seriously maintain that price formation is governed only by the capricious play of chance. It would, at any rate, be difficult to make such an assertion about the pencil and the watch. There is too great a difference between the two prices and too little likelihood of supposing an inversion of the prices. Experience proves that, in reality, prices of all commodities are coordinated in a single system in which each individual price tends to remain stable for a considerable period of time, varying only within relatively narrow limits; a marked change will occur only for good and sufficient reasons.

A *second* explanation is that prices are arbitrarily set by the public authorities. It will be at once evident that this explanation does not apply in our case nor to our experiences, though we are all familiar with a few instances in which the authorities have fixed prices. In wartime, of course, the exception becomes the rule and an elaborate apparatus of price control is set up by the government to prevent a rise in the prices of vitally needed commodities (ceiling price policy). Even in normal times, there are many prices which are fixed (institutional prices). Examples are theatre tickets, taxi fares, etc. But it is precisely our wartime experiences with price control which have made at least one thing clear: a government which fixes prices too far below the level they would have reached in the absence of the official regulations will encounter increasing resistance, ending in complete defiance. It is well to remember that even in these instances of compulsory price fixing, the fixing is linked to factors which have nothing to do with compulsion or chance. It is these factors which provide the *last* and most satisfactory explanation: prices are formed in accordance with inherent social necessities. The elucidation of such price formation is one of the chief tasks of economics.

3. Marginal Utility

The preceding examples, which were intended to give us some idea of the tasks of economics, have turned our attention from the narrow confines of our personal experiences to a consideration of the larger fabric of society with which they are mysteriously interwoven.

It is as if, all this time, we had been unconcernedly and thoughtlessly drawing water from a brook for our own private needs when, of a sudden, we look up and perceive that our brook is, in reality, a broad and majestic river stretching away upstream into illimitable distances. A recognition of the existence of the great social problems is a long step forward on the road to an understanding of economics.

But we would be traveling, ultimately, in a wrong direction were we not to consider another circumstance which leads us back to ourselves and to our own individual experiences. For it is imperative that we keep clearly in mind that the economic system is not an objective mechanical thing which functions whether we will or no, but a process to which we all contribute in the totality of our reflections and our decisions. At bottom, it is the millions upon millions of subjective events taking place in the mind of each individual which form the substrata of economic phenomena. It is the feelings, judgments, hopes and fears of men which are manifested objectively in such things as prices, money, interest, prosperity and depression. But around what axis do these movements of the human psyche revolve? An answer to this question will provide us with the key to an understanding of all the objective events of economic life—to an understanding, in brief, of the "phenomena of the market."

The meaning of all economic decisions and actions can be summed up in the word *economize*. When we have only a limited quantity of an important or useful commodity, we invariably tend to husband the inadequate supply. When we cannot have as much as we would like of a thing, there must be a certain order in our use of it if "waste" is to be avoided—if we wish, that is, to forestall our acting in an uneconomic manner. Unhappily, we do not live in Cockaigne; there are only a few goods of which there is an inexhaustible supply (free goods). Under normal circumstances, the air of our atmosphere is a free good, though it is at the same time the most essential commodity we know. A calisthenics addict may fill his lungs to bursting with air and no one will label him a glutton. But if he continues his exercise too long, a glance at the gymnasium clock and his own increasing fatigue will soon alert him to the fact that at least two things do not exist in unlimited quantities: time and physical strength. These things must be husbanded. However important and useful breathing exercises are, they cannot be kept up indefinitely without neglecting even more important things. Because time and physical strength are limited in quantity, they are not free goods, but *economic goods.* We are forced to economize them no matter how little importance we attach to life's other activities.

Economic goods and not free goods determine our behavior. Our whole life is made up of decisions which seek to establish a satisfactory balance between our unlimited wants and the limited means at hand to satisfy them. To say that economic goods are limited in quantity is simply to say that the existing stocks of such goods are unable to satisfy the total subjective demand for them. It is important to note that this is not the same thing as objective scarcity. Rotten eggs are, happily, scarce, but even so, there are too many of them, economically speaking (Robbins). Not only do we not want them, but energetic efforts are made to see that as few as possible come into existence. They have no value for us, indeed, they are an inconvenience, which is to say that they have a negative value. On the other hand, an economic good which is not objectively scarce can increase infinitely in value, if life itself depends upon its possession. So the sorely-beset hero of Shakespeare's *Richard III* feels compelled to offer his kingdom for a horse. The scale of values of things encompasses, then, all values from minus (negative value) through zero (free goods), through a range of finite values (economic goods) to infinite values (meta-economic goods). The place of any good in this scale of values is determined ultimately by the strength of the subjective demand for it.

Air and water are ordinarily ranked very low on our scale of values, though they are essential to life. On the other hand, a diamond is valued very highly, though it is not in the least an object of vital importance. This circumstance leads us to a further important concept which is indispensable for an understanding of the subjective foundations of economic life. Our preceding discussion has made tacit use of this concept; it behooves us now to give it the most careful scrutiny.

When it comes to assigning a good its place on the scale of values, the determining factor is utility—not a general utility based on the degree of the good's vital importance, but the specific, concrete utility of a definite quantity of the good. The larger the supply of a good at our disposal, the smaller is the amount of satisfaction procured by its individual units, and hence the lower is such a good ranked on our scale of values. The reason for this is that with increasing satisfaction of a want, the utility (satisfaction or enjoyment) furnished by each successive dose diminishes. Moreover, take away any one of a number of identical units and the loss of utility or satisfaction will be the same as if any other had been taken away. It follows that the minimum utility of the last dose or increment determines the utility of every other unit of the supply and therefore the utility of the whole supply. The value we attach to water is not determined by the infinite utility of the single glass of water needed to save us from perishing of thirst; it is determined by the utility of the last dose used to bathe ourselves or to sprinkle the flowers. We call the utility of this last dose *final* or *marginal utility*.

We may now affirm the following theses: (1) marginal utility diminishes with increasing supply, that is, with the increasing possibility of satisfying a want; (2) marginal utility determines the utility of all other units of the supply; (3) as the quantity of a good is increased, there is a corresponding fall in its place on our scale of values, providing our taste (scale of preferences) has not changed in the meantime; (4) the utility of the whole supply (total utility) increases as quantity increases, but at a decreasing rate due to the absolute decline of marginal utility. In fact, if marginal utility diminishes faster than quantity increases, total utility may decline absolutely.

Now it is readily apparent that marginal utility will fall at a different rate for different commodities. Oddly enough, the rate of fall is greater the more vital the commodity. Let us reconsider the example of water. Each of us can remember a long walk on a hot summer's day when we had only one thought in mind: water. We at least reach a spring and, consumed by thirst, fling ourselves down to drink. The first mouthful of water is swallowed greedily, but with the second there is an abrupt lessening of satisfaction. Finally, we bathe our faces, we refill our canteens, and then forget both thirst and water to stretch out on the grass in leisurely contemplation of the countryside of which "we can't get enough." We will observe that as the result of the extremely rapid fall in the marginal utility of water, its total utility can easily become negative. Those unfortunates who, during the Middle Ages, were tortured by forceful infusions of water, could have furnished convincing proof on this point. Or consider the proverbial discontent of the farmer with the weather. He complains as often that it rains too much as that it rains too little—a further proof that water is characterized as much by the urgent need we have for it, as by the extremely rapid fall in its marginal utility.

From the concept of diminishing marginal utility may be deduced still another: *elasticity of demand*. In general, the elasticity of demand for a good varies inversely with the urgency (intensity) of the demand for it. Later, we shall see how this principle underlies important phenomena of the price structure, especially on the markets for agricultural goods. With low elasticity of demand (rapid rate of fall in marginal utility), the total utility of a supply may decrease absolutely, as illustrated in the well-known fact that the income derived from grain production in a given year may be smaller for an abundant harvest than for a lean one.

The meaning of "rapidity of fall in marginal utility" and of "elasticity of demand" will become clearer if we apply these concepts to certain considerations of a practical nature.

Remembering that elasticity of demand varies for different commodities, it is obvious that individuals will tend to consume more nearly the same amounts of a given commodity the less elastic is the demand for it—and this despite differences in income. And inelasticity of demand, we will recall, is the greater, the more essential to life is the commodity in question. Another outcome of these relationships is this: the smaller is one's income, the larger is the share of it which is expended on foodstuffs. This fact was first demonstrated by the Prussian statistician Engel in 1857 (Engel's law). Somewhat later, another statistician, Schwabe, arrived at identical conclusions for housing expenditures (Schwabe's law). We may conclude, therefore, that taxes on basic consumption goods hit the poor more severely than the rich.

A closer scrutiny of the expenditures of the rich will show that the notion of the rich gluttonously stuffing themselves is inexact, the stomach capacity of most individuals being approximately the same. Of course, the larger is a man's income, the greater will be his consumption of luxury goods, such goods having a high elasticity of demand (slow fall in marginal utility). But even such luxury wants are not sufficiently elastic to absorb the whole of a very large income. The result is that the unspent portion of the very large income is saved. This gives us an inkling as to how important is the function of the rich in the formation of capital. It follows that very little can be expected from a redistribution of the large incomes among the poorer classes. For if the rich spend for their vital needs but little more than the poor, the poor will hardly be benefited by such redistribution. Moreover, the amount of money which the rich spend on luxuries is relatively insignificant, in spite of what the lay mind imagines. The rich are so few in number that the amount they expend on luxuries is trifling in comparison with the total expenditures of the rest of the citizens. (For example, of the 58,701,000 individual income tax returns filed in 1958 in the United States, only 236 showed incomes of $1,000,000 or more; only 115,000 income units earned $50,000 or more [*Statistical Abstract of the United States for 1961*]) . As for that part of the large income which is saved, it cannot figure in any scheme for the redistribution of the wealth since the cessation of saving will invite general economic decline. It should be remembered that the wealth of a Henry Ford consisted not of money but of factories which were built with his savings, factories which even a Communist state would have built had it the necessary means. Looked at in this light, people like Henry Ford are really public servants who administer our productive resources after the manner of trustees and who, if their trusteeship is bad, undergo the immediate and heavy punishment of financial loss. The problem, then, is not whether the fate of the poor will be appreciably better in a society where there are no rich. The problem is, rather, whether it is preferable to put state functionaries in the place of private entrepreneurs and to convert private enterprises into state enterprises; and further, whether the economic, social, and political power wielded by the rich is such as to result in economic evil or social injustice.

Let us clarify this point by still another illustration. Let us suppose that a poor street cleaner wins first prize in a lottery. How will he dispose of his sudden wealth? We see at once that it is the elasticity of his wants which will play the decisive role. Obviously, he will first satisfy his pressing needs for food, clothing, and shelter. But it is soon apparent that for these inelastic needs the point of satiety is quickly reached. The larger the winnings from the lottery and the richer the individual before his winnings, the smaller will be the percentage of his total income expended on inelastic or vital needs. However, while it is certain that all men will spend a part of their incomes for the basic subsistence goods, we cannot predict how they will distribute the remainder of their incomes among other wants. People will consume more nearly the same amounts of a given commodity the more inelastic is the demand for it. The more elastic is the demand for a commodity, the more probably will its consumption vary with the fluctuations of individual taste. It has been shown, for instance, that during the years 1926-27 the percentage of national income spent for food in Canada, Switzerland, and England was, surprisingly, the same (30-31 per cent), while expenditures on other items varied considerably among the three countries.

If it is now the whole population instead of the street cleaner which is enriched, the same sequence of cause and effect will be operative. The percentage of income expended on food (inlastic demand) diminishes, while other needs assume increasing importance. This means that the relative importance of agriculture will ultimately diminish, and that within the agricultural domain itself grain production will become relatively less important than the production of more highly valued foods (milk products, meat, eggs, fowl, vegetables and fruit). Similarly, non-agricultural branches of production satisfying "luxury" wants of a still higher type ("tertiary production") will increase in importance as the general standard of living rises. Trade, transportation, tourism, motion pictures, radio, television, the legitimate theatre, books, art works, concerts, etc. absorb an ever-larger share of the national income as the standard of living rises. Otherwise expressed, rises in living standards go hand in hand with increased production, in the agricultural domain, of butter, meat, fruit, etc. As incomes rise still further, the ultimate stages in the developmental process—urbanization and industrialization—are attained. Our own age clearly reflects this evolution.

Thus far we have sketched the broad outlines of the principle of marginal utility, a clear apprehension of which will show it to be almost a commonplace. But as the above examples indicate, it is a commonplace which is indispensable to an understanding of economics. Indeed, it is upon this principle that the whole edifice of modern economic theory has been built. It is to a group of economists who initiated their researches within the last fifty years that we must assign the credit for this accomplishment.[2]

4. Choice and Limitation: the Essence of Economics

We have now reached a point in our inquiry where we can begin to grasp the fundamental nature of economics. On every hand we are hemmed in by scarcity: by scarcity of goods, scarcity of time, scarcity of physical strength. We cannot fill one hole without opening another somewhere else. In this world of scarcity we are faced with a twofold task. In the first place, we must choose from among our several wants those which are in most urgent need of satisfaction. In the second place, since marginal utility decreases with the increasing satisfaction of a want, we are compelled to interrupt this satisfaction sooner or later. We are under the continual necessity of achieving some kind of balance between our unlimited wants and our limited means. This we do by making a *choice* from among our wants and by *limiting* the extent to which any one of these wants is satisfied.

On what basis shall we make these decisions? It is certain that we shall arrange our purchases in such fashion that the satisfaction procured by the last increment of one commodity will be approximately equal to that afforded by the last increment of any other commodity. This is the abstract explanation of what is, in reality, a very simple process, something we do at every hour of the day without waiting on the proper formula. A very clear illustration of what is involved here is to be found in the otherwise trivial act of packing one's bag for a journey. Since we cannot take all of our possessions with us, we first decide upon the things which we most urgently require (choice). At the same time, we proceed to balance a plus in shirts by a minus in shoes, a plus in books by a minus in suits, in such a way as to arrive at a reasonable proportion among the several items (limitation). Silly as it may sound, it is really true that the traveling bag is ideally packed when the marginal utilities of suits, shirts, socks, handkerchiefs, shoes and books are at the same level and higher than the utilities of the things left behind.

Our example may be objected to on the grounds that it omits the possibility of taking along more and bigger bags. This complicates our problem somewhat, but changes nothing with respect to the principle involved. For how would the size and number of bags be decided on unless by all sorts of utility comparisons between more and bigger bags? Those to whom such an objection occurs have only to consider the plight of the soldier in the field who is restricted to one haversack and consequently must take very seriously indeed the operations of "choosing" and "limiting." Who would have thought that the whole of economic activity is only an endless series of very complicated variations on the simple and fundamental theme of packing a bag? Our whole life is made up of an immense number of similar decisions serving to balance continuously means with wants. Choice, limitation, equalization of marginal utilities—these are the concepts to which we must repeatedly return. They determine how we use our incomes, how we direct our businesses, how we organize production, how we divide up our time between work and leisure, and even between sleep and wakefulness. The utility we renounce constitutes the "costs" of the utility we realize in our private economy as well as in the national economy. *To economize is simply to be constantly making a choice from among different possibilities. Economics is at bottom nothing other than the science of alternatives.* Choosing and limiting are the eternal functions of every human economy, whatever its organization, be it the isolated economy without exchange or our highly developed market economy founded on the division of labor and the circulation of money.

NOTES

1. (p. 3) *A Glance at Economic History*

It is universally agreed that the division of labor in modern times has been extended and refined to a degree unknown in previous history. Completely self-sufficient economies of the Robinson Crusoe type are practically unknown today. Indeed, it is doubtful whether a wholly exchangeless economy of this kind, ambiguously termed *natural economy* (ambiguous because the term is also applicable to a moneyless exchange economy), could have existed at any period in history in pure form and on a large scale. The contention that, for instance, the early Middle Ages were characterized by such natural economies has been refuted by contemporary historical investigation. See A. Dopsch, *Naturalwirtschaft und Geldwirtschaft in der Weltgeschichte* (1930).

Economic historians have attempted to trace through the course of economic history the red thread of a principle labeled "development." This has produced the so-called *theories of economic stages,* the earliest of which we owe to Friedrich List in his *National System of Political Economy* (1841; Eng. trans. by Lloyd, 1885). More scientifically accoutered statements of the same theory appear in Bruno Hildebrand's *Die Nationalökonomie der Gegenwart und Zukunft* (1848). Hildebrand distinguished three stages of development: the natural economy, the money economy, and the credit economy. K. Bücher's *Die Entstehung der Volkswirtschaft* (tr. under the title of *Industrial Evolution* by S. Morley Wickett from the 3rd German ed., New York, 1901) distinguishes the stages of (1) the search for food by individuals, (2) the closed household economy (isolated economy without exchange,) (3) the urban economy of the Middle Ages (with its emphasis on production for individual consumers of "custom-made" goods), and (4) the modern market economy (production of goods which are supplied by middlemen to an anonymous circle of buyers). G. Schmoller and many others have enriched the literature devoted to this theme and it remains the object of intensive study by economic historians. As it turns out, the idea that economic history can be reduced to a series of developmental stages was much too arbitrary and required doing more or less violence to the facts. The basic error was to conceive of this "evolution" as progressing in a straight line—an echo of the eighteenth century's faith in linear progress. Recent researches have shown that the ancient world, and in particular the Roman Empire, reached an astonishing degree of economic development. The ancient world too, it appears, had its capitalism and its world economy. For information on this point, the reader is referred to M. I. Rostovtzeff's magnificent work *Social and Economic History of the Roman Empire* (New York, 1926).

A theory which has enjoyed a considerably longer life is the one made popular by Bücher, viz., that from the Middle Ages onward, economic life evolved directly from more primitive to more complex forms, up to the present worldwide division of labor. To this theory are joined more or less romantic and idealized notions of the idyllic characteristics of medieval economic life and medieval economic thought. The writings of Sombart, especially his voluminous work *Der Moderne Kapitalismus* (three volumes: I, II-1902; III-1928, Berlin), have given currency to these ideas among a wide circle of readers. Here too, recent investigation demonstrates the need for thorough revision of received opinion. We know now that even in the Middle Ages there was an intense degree of economic activity and that it is legitimate to speak of a "world economy of the

Middle Ages," an economy which was not by any means confined to the exchange of luxury-type goods. We have evidence also that the individuals engaged in this economic activity—and this should not surprise—exhibited a pronounced propensity for business enterprise. What is particularly significant is that this highly developed economic system of the Middle Ages crumbled at the beginning of the modern era, to be succeeded by a less differentiated type of economy in the period which saw the rise of mercantilism and of national territorial states. Like the world economy of antiquity, the world economy of the Middle Ages fell in ruins, together with the political system which supported it. It is a story with special relevance to our own age. See F. Rörig, *Mittelalterliche Weltwirtschaft, Blüte und Ende einer Weltwirtschaftsperiode* (Jena, 1933). In his *Die Grundlagen der Nationalökonomie* (6th ed., 1950, tr. into English as *Foundations of Economics*, London, 1950), Walter Eucken offers a fundamental criticism of the evolutionary interpretation of economic history and a convincing analysis of the relations between economic history and economic theory. See also: Ludwig von Mises, *Theory and History, An Interpretation of Social and Economic Evolution* (New Haven, 1957).

2. (p. 12) *Marginal Utility: Foundation of Modern Economic Theory*

The significance of the marginal utility principle was recognized quite early, for example, by Gossen in 1854. Later, it was further developed and established as the foundation of modern theory by three scholars working simultaneously but independently: the Austrian Carl Menger (1871), the Englishman W. Stanley Jevons (1871), and Leon Walras, a Frenchman who was then teaching in Switzerland (1874). The most important stages in later development of the principle are indicated by the following works: Friedrich von Wieser, *Theorie der gesellschaftlichen Wirtschaft* (1914; English tr. *Theory of Social Economics* by A. F. Hinrichs, New York, 1927); E. von Böhm-Bawerk, *Positive Theorie des Kapitals* (1889; there are several versions in English, the earliest being that of William A. Smart in 1891 and the most recent being that of George D. Huncke and Hans F. Sennholz, *Capital and Interest,* South Holland, Illinois, 1959); Alfred Marshall, *The Principles of Economics* (London, 1890); V. Pareto, *Cours d'économie politique* (Lausanne, 1896/97); M. Pantaleoni, *Principii di economia pura* (Florence, 1889; English tr. *Pure Economics,* London, 1898); J. B. Clark, *The Distribution of Wealth,* (New York, 1899); Philip H. Wicksteed, *The Common Sense of Political Economy* (London, 1910; newly edited by L. Robbins, 1933); K. Wicksell, *Lectures on Political Economy* (2 vols.; London, 1934; published originally in Swedish in 1901); G. Cassel, *Theoretische Sozialökonomie* (1918; English ed. *The Theory of Social Economy,* 1923); Ludwig von Mises, *Nationalökonomie, Theorie des Handelns und Wirtschaftens* (Geneva, 1940; an amplified version of this work in English is Mises' *Human Action,* New Haven, 1949). These works are truly the pillars upon which reposes all of modern theory. In spite of their differences of perspective and of opinion on many individual matters, they form a unified body of thought which the serious student of economics cannot afford to neglect.

In some quarters, the marginal principle is contemptuously dismissed as a *plaisanterie viennoise* and nothing more. But it cannot be too strongly emphasized that the whole of present-day economic thought is inconceivable outside the framework of this fundamental concept. Even those economists who expressly deny the usefulness of the marginal utility theory are heavily dependent upon it, nevertheless. An especially typical example of this is supplied in the book cited above by the Swede Gustav Cassel. Cassel, if the truth be known, is largely in debt to Walras and his school, though he never once refers to this source. By putting Walras' involved theories into intelligible form and by enriching them with his own valuable ideas, Cassel performed a most useful service and contributed greatly to the advancement of economic science, especially in Germany after World War I. But there is no doubt that he is a product of the general tradition of modern economics.

Pantaleoni's observation (1897) that there are really only two schools of economists, those who understand economics and those who don't, is worth recalling. If limited to pure theory, the statement is by no means the joking exaggeration it might appear to be. This is evident in the theoretical developments of recent decades. Thus, the three schools which simultaneously discovered the principle of marginal utility (the Austrian school of Menger and Wieser, the Lausanne school of Walras and Pareto, and the Anglo-American school of Jevons, Marshall and Clark) have shown a convergent evolution. The Austrian and Anglo-American movements agree much more than they disagree (especially as a result of the strong emphasis on and persistent investigation of objective cost factors by the Anglo-American school). The Lausanne school, however, is distinguished from the others, firstly, by it emphasis on synthesis rather than analysis. With but brief attention to the motives underlying individual economic behavior, it attempts by means of mathematical formulae to arrive at a method for determining when a state of *total* economic equilibrium exists. Secondly, the Lausanne theory is more a functional theory (one, that is, which *describes* mutual dependencies in a state of equilibrium) than a genetic-causal one (which explains *how* and *why* the factors work toward a given equilibrium).

The Lausanne school teaches a general and doubtless more comprehensive truth, but this is of little help in solving individual problems. Granted the necessity of dwelling, even at some length, on the more general and more comprehensive truth, the Lausanne theories are too abstract for significant practical application, entirely apart from the forbidding and not altogether necessary mathematical formulae in which the theories are expressed. In spite of the respect which it rightly inspires, the work of the Lausanne school seems somewhat like a mathematical castle in Spain. Its divorcement from reality gives it a patently static character and this is precisely what renders it of little use in solving the most important concrete problems of the economic system, viz., those arising from *disturbances* of economic equilibrium. On this subject, the reader should consult: Hans Mayer, "Der Erkenntniswert der funktionellen Preistheorien," in *Wirtschaftstheorie de Gegenwart* (vol. 2, 1932; in this memorial to Friedrich von Wieser is to be found perhaps the most comprehensive survey of modern economic theory; an excellent supplement is the anthology published under the auspices of the American Economic Association entitled *A Survey of Contemporary Economics*, ed. H. S. Ellis, Philadelphia, 1948; a critical review of the most recent trends in economic thought is furnished in the essay by Murray N. Rothbard, "Toward a Reconstruction of Utility and Welfare Economics" in the "Festschrift" for Ludwig von Mises *On Freedom and Free Enterprise*, New York, 1956). It is clear from the foregoing that the differences among the schools are not differences between true and false but differences of presentation and emphasis, and even these have lessened with the passage of time.

Modern marginalist theory must be understood against the background of the so-called classical theory which it overthrew. The fathers of classical theory were Adam Smith (*An Inquiry into the Nature and Causes of the Wealth of Nations*, 1776), David Ricardo (*The Principles of Political Economy and Taxation*,

1817), and Thomas Malthus (*Essay on the Principle of Population*, 1798). Classical theory was further refined by J. B. Say, J. H. von Thünen, Senior, Hermann, J. S. Mill, and others. One of its last representatives was J. E. Cairnes, whose book, *Some Leading Principles of Political Economy* (London, 1874) still makes enjoyable reading and was published, piquantly enough, in the same year which saw the birth of modern theory.

A fact which, of course, did not escape the classical theorists was that utility is somehow connected with value. Obviously, a thing which is good for nothing can have no value, but does utility determine value? For the classicists, the case of water and diamonds seemed to prove that utility might well be one of the conditions, but not the cause of the value of a good. Because they had not grasped the *specific* character of utility (marginal utility), they reasoned that so soon as a thing possessed any utility whatsoever, its value (price) was determined by quite other factors. Unfortunately, the classical economists, in spite of their acumen, did not succeed in reducing these value factors to a homogeneous formula. In fact, from their early gropings, *three distinctly different theories* emerged. They began by distinguishing two kinds of goods: scarce goods, whose quantity could not be increased by production and goods which could be "produced at will." The value of the first would be determined solely by the degree of their scarcity; the value of the second by their costs of production, thus by something objective. Onto this classification, the classicists grafted a distinction between a normal price (natural price) and a market price which oscillates around the normal. The normal price was supposed to be determined by the costs of production whereas the market price was determined by supply and demand.

The existence of three different explanations of the same phenomenon was unsatisfactory enough. But the classicists, in addition, became ever more entangled in the internal inconsistencies of their concepts the more they sought to get to the bottom of things. Of what do the "costs of production" consist? How can cost factors be reduced to a common denominator? Up to the very end, the classical school struggled vainly to find an answer to these questions. (See A. Amonn, *Ricardo als Begründer der theoretischen Nationalökonomie*, 1924). It became increasingly clear, too, that a cost-of-production theory was of no help at all in explaining a variety of important phenomena (monopoly price, prices of jointly produced goods, international price formation).

The labored disputes of the classical economists were brought to an end with the simple discovery that their too hasty examination of the utility concept had led them to confuse *general* with *specific* utility. From this time on, the objective-technical explanation of value was supplanted by the subjective-economic emphases of modern theory. It is to be noted also that the marginal utility concept makes the labor theory of value, which constitutes the theoretical base of Marxism, wholly untenable. In fact, the purely economic basis of Marxism must be regarded today as merely an intellectual anachronism. Specifically, a suit is not eight times as valuable as a hat because it requires eight times as much labor as a hat to produce. It is because the *finished suit* will be eight times as valuable as the finished hat that society is willing to employ eight times as much labor for the suit as for the hat (Wicksteed). It is upon this discovery that the remaining parts of Marxist theory (surplus value, capitalist disintegration) have foundered. This certainly does not mean that socialism can be dismissed as mere foolishness, but simply that it cannot be scientifically established upon a Marxist base.

Notwithstanding, it would be an error to believe that classical theory is a collection of sterile fallacies. On the contrary, modern theory itself remains heavily in debt to the spadework of the classical school. There is no difference in the approaches of the classicists and the moderns to the fundamental issues of economics, a fact which, as the "Methodenstreit" (conflict over methods) has demonstrated, flows from the internal logic of things. Moreover, there is no great difference in the conclusions arrived at by the two schools, even though their underlying premises are, in part, quite different (e.g., with respect to the law which causes prices, under competition, to fall towards the costs of production). In several instances, indeed, classical theory anticipated the basic notions of modern theory (e.g., in international trade theory). The acumen which enabled the classical school, in spite of its false foundation and its tortured constructions, to come to useful conclusions deserves admiration. Where modern theory showed the greatest advance over the classical school was in the practical sphere. The stiff classical machinery of "natural laws" has been made so much more flexible that economics has gotten closer to reality, become more capable of adaptation, and more largely human. Purified of the premature economic policy conclusions professed by the classical school (laissez-faire liberalism), modern theory has not only become less partisan politically, but in virtue of that very fact has developed into an indispensable instrument in the solving of current problems of economic policy. Classical theory was philosophical in character while modern theory is primarily instrumental in character.

An extended analysis of the principle of marginal utility will raise difficulties too numerous to be dealt with here. Then too, the process of analysis in this instance is itself subject to the law of diminishing marginal utility, that is, as economic analyses are increasingly refined, they tend to produce less and less interesting results. Much of the criticism of the marginal utility principle is, upon closer inquiry, seen to be aimed at such exaggeratedly long and psychological marking of time at the point of departure. The same impression, indeed, is created by the true, but otherwise not very helpful intellectual architectonics found at the other extreme in the mathematical equilibrium models of the Lausanne school. At all events, these are difficulties which must one day be resolved.

A good survey of the relevant discussion on these matters may be found in the article "Value" in the *Encyclopedia of the Social Sciences* and in D. H. Robertson, *Utility and All That* (London, 1952). To bewail such clarification would be just as unintelligent as to let ourselves be irritated by the footnotes in a book. (Though he who believes he can skip the footnotes is quite at liberty to do so). On the other hand, a book should consist of something else besides footnotes. If this point of view were more widely adopted, many a sterile dispute over the principle of marginal utility would be avoided.

CHAPTER II

THE BASIC DATA OF ECONOMICS

"Je ne connais que trois manières d'exister dans la
société: il faut être mendiant, voleur ou salarié."
MIRABEAU

1. *The Moral Foundation (the Business Principle)*

The struggle against scarcity (deficiency of means) is the eternal basis of every human economy. It characterizes all ages, all climates, all social systems. The forms which this struggle assumes, however, show the greatest diversity. We may divide them into two principal groups: the individual forms and the social forms. The *individual form* of this struggle is exemplified in the isolated, exchangeless economy of a Robinson Crusoe with which we are here not concerned. We shall give our attention, therefore, only to the *social form* of the struggle against scarcity.

The *social form of the struggle* is manifested in the different methods men use to obtain those things which nature has not freely supplied. There are, in principle, three such methods, as a result of which we see three kinds of struggle. There is, first, the *ethically negative method* of using violence and/or fraud to procure for ourselves, at others' expense, the means of overcoming scarcity. The second method is the *ethically positive* one of altruism, thanks to which goods and services are supplied to us without our being required to give anything in return. The third method does not lend itself easily to such brief description. It is not founded on egoism, if this implies that individual well-being is achieved at others' expense. Neither is it founded on a selfless altruism, if this implies that individual well-being is neglected in order that others may benefit. It is, rather, an *ethically neutral* method by which, in virtue of a con-

20

tractual reciprocity between the parties to an exchange, an increase of one's own well-being is achieved by means of an increase in the well-being of others. This method, which may be termed "solidarity," means that an increase in my well-being is achieved in a way which not only does not deprive others of well-being but which yields them, as a by-product of my gain, an increase in their own well-being.

In concrete terms, I may obtain the wherewithal to live either: by selling adulterated butter (first method) ; or I can be the object (or subject) of a gift of butter (second method) ; or, by following the axiom "honesty is the best policy," I can acquire a fortune by attracting more and more customers with butter of irreproachable quality, kind and courteous service, finding out where I can buy butter cheapest, keeping a neat and attractive shop, etc. (third method). Whereas people are "handled" in a public facility such as the post office, in our shop they are "served." In this last case I obtain the means which allow me to satisfy my needs neither by violence, exploitation, fraud, nor illicit profit, nor by accepting alms or gifts, but through the supplying of an equivalent service or good (performance principle). It is this method, based on the principle of reciprocity, of value given for value received, which is commonly referred to as "business." It is the business method which characterizes that form of the struggle against scarcity which is based on exchange and the division of labor. Regarding the economic system in this way, however, raises several important questions and it is upon these that we must focus our attention.

In the first place, the three methods are by no means rigorously separated, but, on the contrary, overlap to a degree. Plainly, there is an essential distinction between defrauding your neighbor in the struggle for survival and accepting a charitable gift from him for the same end: the first and second methods are incompatible and cannot be employed simultaneously. But it is possible to combine the first method (fraud and/or violence) with the third (business), and also the second method (altruism) with the third. "War, trade, and piracy—an inseparable trinity," declares Goethe's Mephistopheles (*Faust*, II, 5) , and, in truth, the history of the trading and colonizing nations is a history of invasions, piracies, and oppressive exploitation. It offers us a depressing demonstration of the truth that when left to our own devices, we tend to choose the first method and return nothing in exchange for a service received. Only the powerful influences of religion, morality, and law appear able to induce us to adhere scrupulously to the third method.

There are a variety of procedures for avoiding the rendering of a service equal to one received. Leveling a revolver at someone is one of the quickest but also one of the riskiest ways of getting something for nothing. Much safer and more efficient are the devices of special privilege and monopoly for they can be tricked out in ideological trappings which may make them seem not only innocuous but even beneficial to the general interest. The modern problem of monopoly can ultimately be defined in no other way than as a distortion of the principle of equivalence or reciprocity in exchange effected by means of the method of exploitation. Solving the monopoly problem, therefore, means nothing other than finding a way to eliminate this distortion.

If, as unfortunately happens, the method of "pure business" is often combined with fraud and exploitation, it is just as frequently commingled with elements of altruism. Indeed, business in the real world is not as ethically neutral as we at first supposed. There are businesses which embrace more or less an element of self-sacrifice (and, therefore, of uncompensated "giving") and of genuine service. The medical profession is one example. Then, too, we expect of the scholar and of the artist that they put devotion to their vocations before mere gain, and that in practicing their profession they be not motivated by the principles of the delicatessen-owner. In these cases, the pure business principle is subordinated to a certain moral standard which we may call professional ethics. Members of such professions frequently have or are expected to have a strong service instinct. Expressions such as "trade" or "business," applied to the professions of medicine or law, are felt to be out of place and demeaning. But even the pure businessman who adheres unbendingly to the principle of exact reciprocity in exchange does not, by so doing, remain completely neutral in an ethical sense. His unbending conduct, and the conduct of those with whom he does business, is at bottom conditioned by the acceptance of certain ultimate principles, for the lack of which the business society itself will in the long run founder. It is, therefore, of great importance not to forget the moral reserves which nourish the prosaic and in itself ethically neutral world of pure business, and with which it stands or falls.[1]

The proportions in which the three methods are found and in which they are combined determine in the final analysis what we call the *economic spirit* of an age. The evolution of our own times can be better understood in the light of the double moral standard which has for so long prevailed: a sterner code is applied within the narrow circle of our own family and friends (internal morality) and a laxer one is employed in our dealings with strangers (external morality). For a soldier to steal from his bunk-mates is regarded as a low form of treachery, while to practice the same theft upon the occupants of a neighboring barrack passes for a feat of cunning. And let the same soldier return laden with loot taken from the citizens of a conquered country and his mates will give him a hero's welcome. The evolution of the last few centuries can then be regarded as a process in which *the domain of internal morality has been continuously enlarged while its content has been simultaneously diluted*. In the Middle Ages, trade among the small group of provincial guilds was rigidly circumscribed while a large place was reserved to charity—a natural outgrowth of the deeply religious spirit of that time. But beyond these confines there was much unscrupulous and unrestrained exploitation. In the course of the development which saw the rebirth of ancient morality (humanism) and the secularization of the substance of Christian morality, the principle of sacrifice lost much of its force, even among members of the same family. In its stead appeared a new principle, and one which served at the same time to reduce the practice of violence and exploitation to negligible proportions, viz., the selfsame business principle we have been discussing.[2]

Not all of the consequences of this development were happy ones. "Business" has occasionally lain its cold and impersonal hand on the family, requiring children to pay their parents for room and board; and science, art, even religion itself, have become commercialized to a lamentable extent. On the other hand, the general use of the business method has had the effect of narrowly circumscribing the area in which violence and exploitation can be profitably employed and of enlarging the sphere of activities yielding equal benefits to the participants.

A proper appreciation of the differences among the three methods aforementioned will prove helpful in dispelling a double confusion met with today at almost every turn. On the one hand, there is the common mistake of attributing to the third method (business) acts which properly should be put to the account of the first (fraud, exploitation, etc.). Some of us still cling tenaciously to the belief that business is nothing else than a shameless picking of other people's pockets, especially so when it is a question of as abstract and mysterious a business as the modern stock exchange. Just as deeply ingrained is the habit of describing business operations in terms suited only to acts of the first category. People speak of the "conquest" of markets and of the "imperialist exploitation" of foreign countries without realizing that they are confounding two entirely distinct categories of acts.[3] The myth that the employer always necessarily exploits his employees is another of the same series of errors.

On the other hand, the second and third methods (altruism and business) are also frequently confused. It is a confusion deliberately encouraged by a certain breed of businessman who desires to have people see in him the devotee of self-sacrifice and disinterested service, though in reality he is motivated solely by business considerations. He speaks of "serving the customers," he puts himself "at their disposal," he bids us "be at home," as if, like St. Francis of Assisi, he had nothing in his heart but the disinterested love of his fellow man. Each shop, each factory, becomes a kind of "studio" where work, relieved of its grosser motivations, is carried on on a higher and nobler plane. Cloaking ordinary business operations with such pious phraseology serves not only as effective advertisement, but is in the vanguard of the democratic instincts of our time. There is still, perhaps, unconscious resentment of the old contempt attaching to "people in trade," and it is comforting if the illusion can be created that one is not simply working out his life within the drab business framework but that he is a dedicated being, a member even of a superior class. The "canonization" of business, if we may use the term, is particularly noticeable in the United States (witness the emergence of the peculiarly American doctrine of the "social responsibility" of business). It is accompanied by a tendency to relegate to a lower class all the professions which do not originate in business (scholars, civil servants, artists, career military officers). It is a process which has been made easier by the commercialization of these professions and the consequent perversion of the true hierarchies of rank and value—a grave American malady and one of which Europe, too, is beginning to exhibit the symptoms.

This complex of problems is one which properly should be of the greatest concern to economists. Indeed, before we pursue our inquiry any farther, it is necessary to stress the artificiality and extreme fragility of the pure reciprocity principle (business principle). "Business" is a product of civilization and it cannot exist for long in the absence of a specific constellation of conditions, chiefly moral, which support our civilization. The economic ingredient in the constellation is, as we shall see, free competition. But free competition cannot function unless there is general acceptance of such norms of conduct as willingness to abide by the rules of the game and to respect the rights of others, to maintain professional integrity and professional pride, and to avoid deceit, corruption, and the manipulation of the power of the state for personal and selfish ends. The big question of our time is whether we have been so heedless and unsparing in the use of our moral reserves that it is no longer possible to renew these vital props of our economic system and whether it is yet possible to discover new sources of moral strength.

2. What Are Costs?

The perpetual tension between means and wants (scarcity) at once explains the meaning and fixes the goal of our economic system founded on exchange and the division of labor (business principle). Since we possess only limited means of satisfying our unlimited desires, we are compelled, as we have seen, to make a rigorous selection from among many competing wants and to limit the satisfaction of any one such want in order to make the best use of the means at hand (economic principle). Some will say that this view of economic behavior is quite appropriate to the conduct of the housewife who must hold her expenditures within the limits of a fixed sum of money (use of income, *economics of consumption*), but that it does not apply either to individual economy insofar as it is *economy of acquisition* (procuring of income), nor to the *national economy* since, in these two cases, the means are not fixed but may be increased by production.

Further reflection shows, however, that production changes nothing with respect to the need for practicing economy in the use of means, but that it simply results in the transfer of the problem to a higher level (or levels). Why, for instance, do we not produce as much chocolate or paper as we can consume? Why is production stopped at a certain point—which in our business economy is determined by profitability—when there is still a large and unsatisfied need of paper and chocolate? Is this the result of a stupid organization of our economic system from which socialism will deliver us? Such questions do not merit serious reply, for it is clear that production is tied to "costs." But "costs of production" mean simply that while the quantity of a given consumption good may be increased by production, we encounter a scarcity of certain ultimate factors of production whose quantity cannot be so increased. Ultimately, we are compelled to acknowledge the harsh facts that our capacity for work and our time are strictly limited; that the location and the fertility of the soil are immutable data of Nature; and that even tools and machinery cannot be increased in quantity according to our good pleasure. In using these ultimate factors of production for the production of one good, we thereby renounce the use of the same factors for the production of another good. When we draw a coverlet by one end, the other end does not become longer. We have, then, no other alternative but by means of choice and limitation to allocate the factors of production to the producing of the kinds and quantities of goods which will procure the maximum advantage from the available means.

It follows that the need to make the most economical use of a given supply of means is not the less urgent simply because we can increase this supply by production. The process of equating means and wants takes place in this case merely on a higher level. It is distinguished from the simple process of determining what use is to be made of a given supply of means in the same manner as the traveler's estimation of the relative utilities of taking more and bigger bags on a journey is distinguished from the case of the soldier who must pack his sack with foreknowledge of exactly what articles he must get into it. In the case of the traveler, more trunks and suitcases are taken along only "at the cost" of other pleasures of the trip. Just so, the costs of production are nothing more, in the final analysis, than a faithful reflection of the utility that the factors of production would have furnished had they been otherwise employed—a utility which we renounce in favor of the one we have chosen. *The costs of production, in sum, owe their existence and their amount to the competition of alternative uses for the factors of production.*[4] They stand for utilities which escape us at some other point in the national economy.

This is a principle of such overriding importance that it is worth dwelling on it in some detail. Suppose, for example, that it is planned to build a bridge. What are the problems that must be faced here? The first order of business is, generally, for technicians and engineers to calculate the costs of building a bridge of a given type and quality. These costs are subsequently compared with the traffic needs of the projected bridge site on the one hand, and on the other, with the possibility of financing the bridge out of the public purse. That is to say, we take into account the urgency of *other* public needs as this urgency is reflected in the possibility or impossibility of diverting a part of current tax revenue to the construction of the bridge or of increasing taxes in general. Taxes, on their side, represent the personal utility which the taxpayers must renounce in transferring a part of their purchasing power to the state. Thus we see that the "costs" of building a bridge are simply an indication that for the land which must be preempted, for the workmen who must be hired, and for the steel which must be used (including all the resources required in the making of the steel), there are still other uses. And it is the intensity of the competition among these alternative uses which determines the costs, greater or less, of the aforementioned factors of production. The process of production then, analyzed to its foundations, clearly shows the alternative nature of costs. In fine, the construction of the bridge will be justified from an economic point of view if it can be shown that it will result in the best possible use being made of the given means with relation to the national economy.

Our example—the building of a bridge—makes clear the important difference between the economic and the technical (or engineering) point of view. The job of the economist is to decide, first, whether the bridge should be built at all; secondly, whether it should be built on one site rather than another. For the economist the total quantity of means is fixed; his task is to discover the best use that can be made of them. The job of the engineer, on the other hand, is to achieve a given end—in our example, the construction of a bridge of a given quality in a given location—with the least means (technical principle). Here, differently than in economics, the end is given, while the means must be found. The successful solution of the technical problems involved in building a bridge does not in the least imply that its construction is justified economically. Economic justification follows only after costs have been entered on the ledger; only, that is, after the proposed use of means is compared with alternative possible uses and a satisfactory balance established among them. For all of this, confusion of technical with economic problems remains a tenacious undergrowth in the economic thought of our time. Fallacies stemming from it are particularly rife in the field of foreign trade (which is a fertile breeding ground for error in any case).

It is almost an *idée fixe* of contemporary economic policy to see economic advantage for the nation in the exploitation of technical discoveries and inventions and to support the production of synthetic foods or raw materials, even though the synthetic product costs more than the imported natural product and requires special measures to make it "competitive." Apparently, only a minority comprehends that the same reasoning which is used to defend the production of synthetics can be used to justify cotton growing in the Arctic Circle so long as the engineers can supply the necessary greenhouses and artificial heat. Although the manufacture of synthetic materials has registered some notable successes and shows promise, in some cases, of even greater success in the future, the role of costs in this field cannot be ignored. Every so often, the complaint is heard that the limitations set on production by costs are the result of our stupid "capitalist" system, a ball and chain which we ought to shake off once for all and thereby win both riches and freedom. Such naive assumptions would quickly wither, were it more energetically made known that *the problem of costs is nothing other than the problem of deciding whether the productive forces of a country will be better employed in one direction than in another.* Here, certainly, is the most elementary problem confronting any economy, whatever be its organization.

3. *Economic Equilibrium: the Possible Systems*

We have now, perhaps, established the truth that in every economic system man is bound by the necessities of choice and limitation. Every economic system consequently must have available to it a device for balancing means with ends. We already have gained some idea of the equilibrium mechanism which is peculiar to our economic system. But for a still clearer apprehension of how this mechanism functions, we must examine briefly the several possible systems of equilibrium:

(a) *System of the queue,* which could as well be called the system of elbowing one's way through the crowd, or the system of first come, first served. It is the simplest and most brutal form of equating supply with demand. It consists in offering the available supply to the public gratis and it invariably results in a more or less violent use of fist and elbow. This system is so unsatisfactory and so little able to guarantee that the most urgent needs of the community will be met that recourse to it is had only in exceptional cases. We are reminded, perhaps, of those occasions on which the beer runs out at "free beer" parties, or of neighborhood get-togethers at which the refreshments set out are quickly devoured by the first wave of guests to the dismay of those who come after. The experiment undertaken by the Soviet dictatorship in its early years is very instructive in this connection. The streetcars and other means of transport were placed at the disposal of the public free of charge. The result, as was to be expected, was such a crush of passengers that the government was soon compelled to return to the "capitalist" equilibrium mechanism (price system). Anyone who has ever tried to watch a parade through the head of the man in front of him knows that the best viewing spots must be preempted well ahead of time. Indeed, when the crowd is very large—as, for example, at the coronation or the funeral of a monarch—it is common practice to resort to the price system for the disposal of the better places. It is to be noted that the system of the queue is the more undesirable the greater the elasticity of demand for a good or service (see pp. 10 ff.). Hence, it will prove easier to put the water of the public fountains at the free disposal of the citizens than to allow them, as in the Russian case, to use the streetcars without paying. The proposal to have free medical services supplied by nationalized doctors should be examined in the same light. The experiences of the British with their National Health Service provide a costly lesson of what may be expected from such an arrangement.

(b) *A rationing system* shows a certain advance over the system of the queue. Here, too, goods are supplied gratis, but equilibrium is obtained by a systematic distribution of the available goods (rationing). It is such a mechanism which would operate in a pure Communist economy. Even in our economic system, however, it is occasionally necessary to have recourse to this method. Every soldier will recall that in the field not only was food rationed, but also cigars, cigarettes and pipe tobacco. The distribution of food did not involve any great difficulties since individual wants were fairly uniform. But the distribution of tobacco, cigarettes, etc., given the pronounced differences in individual preferences, was regularly followed by a lively private exchange where, under a primitive form, the price system again prevailed. This example shows that under a system of rationing (as well as under the queue system), the difficulties increase with the increase in the elasticity of demand for the rationed product.[5]

(c) *The mixed system.* Where prices are introduced, as in a mixed system, the disadvantages of queueing and rationing are somewhat mitigated. Generally, in such cases, the prices are fixed at levels insufficient to balance supply and demand. Nevertheless, the very existence of these prices tends to bring about a certain limitation of demand. What results, therefore, is a mixture of the price system with one or the other of the systems already described. During both World Wars the mixed system, under the names of "ceiling prices" or "price control," was regularly imposed by the belligerent governments on their respective economies. Experience with this system, however, soon compelled abandonment of the queue-price system in favor of a rationing-price system. For it had become apparent that once the maximum prices were established, the equilibrium mechanism of the price system refused to work. When prices were prevented from rising to the point where supply and demand exactly balanced, a part of demand necessarily remained unsatisfied. The people who were ready to pay the maximum price queued up before the shops, but invariably those at the end of the line went away empty-handed. So intolerable did this situation become that recourse was finally had to a system of ration tickets for a list of selected goods.

Ultimately, of course, the disturbances which price controls provoked on the supply side, required government intervention in production itself. Indeed, during World War II, such intervention was universally practiced. The result was that each day that went by saw a further disappearance of the regulating principles of our economic system, ending in a veritable economic muddle. Following World War I, most countries hastened to put an end to the confusion by reestablishing a free economy, i.e., the unhindered price system. And in the post-World War II era, all advanced countries have sought, and rightfully so, to dismantle the system of wartime controls.

Rent controls, the most durable of the wartime price-ceilings, offer a good example of the evolution we have described, beginning with the queue-plus-price system and ending with the rationing-plus-price system. Our experiences with rent control have shown how intolerable in the long run is the situation created by the mixed system. Even in its less noxious form of prices combined with rationing, the marked inferiority of the mixed system vis-à-vis the price system is obvious. This has been publicly acknowledged even in the Soviet Union where the ending of rationing on certain classes of goods was celebrated as an example of progress on the road leading to a more normal situation.

The thoroughly abnormal circumstances of the Great Depression and later of World War II pushed many countries to new experiments with the mixed system. Thus, exchange control is in reality only a variant of the rationing-plus-price system, as is also the control and distribution by government of imported raw materials. The system of ceiling prices was also revived in the foodstuffs markets both under the form of the queue-plus-price system and the rationing-plus-price system. And here again the consensus was that the mixed system is at best only a temporary expedient. The continued repression of a natural force builds up explosive pressures with the result that the price system in one form or another inevitably breaks through the unnatural tensions and rigidities of the mixed system. The greater the amount of unsatisfied demand, the more numerous will be the subterfuges used to circumvent the maximum prices and the bolder will become the disregard for the law. Black markets, under-the-counter deals, illegal currency transactions—a thousand years' experience has shown that these things accompany price control as shadows do the light. Such activities, customarily denounced as "fraud," "smuggling," etc., appear from the objective standpoint of economics merely as corrections of the mixed system by the price system. From the standpoint of ethics these "corrections" are less than edifying and are certainly not the work of the better members of society. Economically speaking, however, they are not always and necessarily harmful.

The United States' experience with Prohibition in the pre-war era and in the postwar period the collapse of the command economy in Germany, Austria, and France prove that the maintenance of economic regulations to which the bulk of the population is opposed in conscience ends by exercising a strong demoralizing influence. A sort of respectability is attached to breaking the law. An economic system which continues to function thanks only to bootleggers, black marketeers, and smugglers becomes a focus of corruption which, little by little, poisons all the arteries of society. Here is a bitter lesson for those who continually petition for state control of economic life out of their moral indignation at the workings of the free economy.

All too often we hear a system of rationing being justified on the grounds that the goods in question are in "short supply" and that their distribution ought not to be left to the working of the price system. The reader is already aware that this point of view rests on a fundamental misconception. All goods which are not "free goods" are "scarce goods," meaning that not everyone can get as much of them as he would like. To say that a "scarce good" is one for which the demand exceeds the supply can have meaning only in relation to a specific price, namely the price which is held by the public authorities below the so-called equilibrium price at which supply and demand are in equality and whose function it is to bring about this equality. Hence, demand can really exceed supply only in those extraordinary situations in which the shortage of essential commodities is so acute that it is considered advisable to ration the available goods equally among the citizens rather than to permit distribution to take place on the basis of the unequally distributed dollars.

Consider, in this connection, the extreme scarcities which prevailed in practically all types of goods during World War II. The plight of the economy is then comparable to that of a besieged fortress whose commander is compelled to ration bread and water with the utmost severity. In such case, everyone will approve the rationing of the vital commodities. But it is extremely doubtful whether this notion of the "besieged fortress" can be validly applied to the economy in peacetime. We should not forget that what we are concerned with in peacetime is not only fair distribution, but an increase in production itself. The *dilemma* inherent in any system of rationing thus becomes clear: in seeking to distribute the available supply as fairly as possible we run the risk of causing a constant diminishment of the amount available for distribution until, in the end, we get a system of rationed poverty, or "poorhouse socialism." The more we depart from the situation of the "besieged fortress," the more necessary it is to recommence production and the more self-defeating, therefore, does a policy of rationing with price control become. Keeping the prices of commodities as low as possible for reasons of social justice discourages their production precisely in the degree to which the price-controlled goods are essential. Such a policy ends by requiring the scarcest goods to be sold at the lowest prices. If the policy is not applied uniformly to *all* goods and services, it amounts to the conferring of a premium for nonproduction of the very goods most needed. The result is that in countries where such a policy is pursued, the stores are filled with the most nonessential and useless goods, the prices of which, precisely on this account, the authorities have left uncontrolled.

From the above it might assumed that a discussion of the mixed system should be reserved for a chapter on economic pathology. But this assumption would be incorrect. For although it is true that this system, when extensively applied, is dangerous and sometimes fatal, in small doses it is relatively harmless. We find it operative in an astonishingly large number of normal economic processes where it appears inopportune, for one reason or another, to use the price system in its pure form. Railroad, bus, and taxi fares, the prices of theatre and movie tickets, as well as many other prices, are ordinarily rigidly fixed, in spite of daily fluctuations in demand (*institutional prices*). The consequence is that these prices under certain circumstances fulfill only imperfectly their equilibrium function; such prices, for all practical purposes, become maximum prices, proof of which is seen in the block-long queues in front of movie houses and theatres where a hit show is playing, in the throngs that pack trains and busses, in the desperate mien of some *paterfamilias* as, homeward bound from vacation with his numerous offspring and equally numerous valises, he stands before the railroad station waving frantically (and vainly) at passing taxis. Even in these cases, there is a tendency for the price system to reassert itself. So we have the perennial ticket scalper, reserved seats on trains and . . . tips. If even these devices fail to correct the disequilibrium in demand, the institutional prices themselves will be changed in the end.

(d) *The price system.* The systems analyzed so far show so plainly the nature of the price system that a long explanation seems unnecessary. Its principal characteristic is that equilibrium (choice and limitation) is attained by leaving prices free to adapt themselves to the market situation, so that there is neither an excess of unsatisfied demand nor an excess of unabsorbed supply (equilibrium price). In the systems previously described, the question of who will bear the costs is distinct from the question of whose needs will be satisfied. In the price system, these elements are fused. The cost of satisfying a given want is imposed on the demanding individual in the price itself. But, as we have already seen, the existence of costs shows that the factors of production which are used for one purpose might have been used with equal advantage for some other purpose. Thus, the price system allocates the factors of production in a way which allows us to perceive, in broad outline, the process by which general economic equilibrium is attained.

Since, in a free price system, costs are necessarily borne by consumers, it is the consumers who decide what and how much shall be produced. Hence, it is the consumers who decide how the factors of production themselves are to be used. This mechanism functions ideally when not an iota of productive resources is employed in a way which yields less utility than if it were used in some other way. The tying of prices to costs, which many regard as one of the stupid quirks of "capitalism," thus assumes a function which is central to any economic system, whatever its organization: the function, namely, of effecting the best possible allocation of the nation's productive resources. This does not in the least imply that our economic system, founded for the most part on the price system, is perfect. For in the price system, only those individual demands count which are backed up by the requisite purchasing power. Even if the price system functioned ideally, the factors of production would be employed in the "best possible" manner only in relation to the existing (and unequal) distribution of income. No one will seriously pretend that our present distribution of income is the best possible. As the result of such unequal distribution a rich cat fancier, to take one example, can buy milk to feed her animals while milk is denied to the mother of a family of poor children because she cannot pay for it. We should not make the mistake of equating the explanation of the price system with a glorification of it, for this would be to fall into the error of the classical school which derived from such explanation premature conclusions with respect to economic policy (laissez-faire liberalism).

When we consider economic history, on the other hand, and in particular the recent history of the Soviet Union, we must conclude that the price system, in spite of all its imperfections and in spite of the situations in which it is inapplicable, remains the most natural method of solving the problem of economic equilibrium. Indeed, its essential irrepressibility is shown in the spectacular failure of the efforts to displace it and to frustrate it. An extremely differentiated society such as our own, resting on an intensive division of labor, is inconceivable outside the framework of the price system. Indeed, if the Communist economic experiment, and the National Socialist economic experiment which so closely resembled it, have proven one thing, it is that the most resolute will to impose collectivism is forced, in the end, to capitulate to the elemental equilibrium forces of the price system.

(e) *The system of collective economy.* To understand this last of the possible equilibrium systems, we must take account of a group of special needs to which none of the systems of which we have spoken thus far can be applied. Up to now, we have tacitly supposed that we were concerned only with the needs of individuals which are satisfied by an act of individual consumption (individual demand). But there are still other wants which are experienced by the members of society collectively (*collective demand*), without it being possible to distinguish the specific utility accruing to individuals from the satisfaction thereof. Some familiar examples are the collectively felt wants for armed forces, for a police force, for protection against epidemics, for street lights. The street light is an indivisible good which cannot be distributed individually to those who declare themselves ready to pay their "share" of the cost. Neither can we deny street lights to the general public because some people, such as lovers or burglars, are annoyed by them. It is the business of the state to satisfy these collective demands. It is the state which assumes the task of choosing and of limiting; it must procure the means of meeting costs in a manner which, contrary to the price system, is completely divorced from benefits accruing to individuals as such. The equity of the procedure resides rather in basing the collection of funds for the given collective demand on the ability of individuals to pay (taxation). All the questions which arise with respect to this collective method of achieving equilibrium belong to the sphere of public finance which is consequently properly studied as part of general economics.[6]

The system of collective economy frequently finds application in cases where collective needs do not actually exist. Although in these cases the other equilibrium mechanisms could be employed, it is regarded as desirable on various grounds to treat the want in question as a collective want. Bridges and roads, for example, are, as a general rule, paid for on a collective basis out of taxes, although there is no reason why the price system would not work equally well in such cases. For proof, we need only recall the practice, common enough in former times and now revived in some countries, of charging tolls for the use of highways and bridges. It is our modern concern for social justice that has resulted in the placing of many hitherto individual needs in the category of collective needs. Primary education, for example, is today almost universally supplied on a collective basis. Other wants have become partly collective, such as secondary and university education, the cost of which is met for the greater part by the state.

The case of secondary and university education is particularly instructive. For in the degree in which the state assumes the costs, there arises a danger of oversupplying candidates for the professions, unless a method of limiting the admission of students is developed to replace the older ability-to-pay criterion (for example, *numerus clausus,* or better, a rigorous examination of students' intellectual aptitudes). Hence, the cheaper higher education becomes, the more necessary it will be to increase the difficulty of examinations.

It should be noted, finally, that a system of complete "Communism" is reached when all needs are treated as collective needs and hence are satisfied in accordance with the system of collective economy ("from everyone according to his capacity, to everyone according to his needs"). The continued enlargement of the collective sector of the national economy, which is characteristic of the economic evolution of the last one hundred years, must therefore be considered as an enlargement of the "Communist" element in our economic system. The continued growth of the public sector (system of collective economy) at the cost of the private sector (price system) must, by the same token, be taken as an indication that an increasing number of economic processes are taking place in accordance with laws radically different from those which regulate the market economy.

NOTES

1. (p. 22) *Economics and Ethics*

Though the business method is in itself ethically neutral, business income may be used for ethically positive (altruistic) ends. The concept "individual increase of well-being" must, therefore, be understood in a broad sense, one which embraces all the possible objectives which the individual fixes for himself, including altruistic objectives. Certain Western peoples are noted as much for their charity and generosity as for their shrewd business insight. Money as an end in itself holds less attraction for them than it does for many Orientals who, while despising Western "business methods," take a miser's joy in accumulating treasure for its own sake. Experience shows that business is only a method of acquiring means which may be then employed for every imaginable object. Even charitable institutions find it necessary to use purely commercial methods to raise needed funds. Heinrich Schliemann, the ingenious discoverer of ancient Troy, amassed a fortune in business with the sole object of paying for the costs of his excavations. On this and related questions see the comprehensive study by P. Hennipman, *Economisch Motief en Economisch Principe* (Amsterdam, 1945). Other significant contributions to the literature on this subject include: L. von Wiese, *Ethik in der Schauweise der Wissenschaften vom Menschen und von der Gesellschaft* (Berne, 1947); F. H. Knight, *The Ethics of Competition and other Essays* (London, 1935); F. H. Knight, *Freedom and Reform* (New York, 1947). The role of ethics in economics is considered in detail in my own book, *A Humane Economy* (Chicago, 1960).

2. (p. 23) *Capitalism and the Economic Spirit*

The question of the origin of the modern economic spirit (spirit of capitalism) is one that has long interested students of economic history. Investigation has shown that the causes are many and complex and that they cannot be reduced to simple formulations, such as those advanced by Sombart, for example. The question can be studied only in connection with the intellectual history of Europe, in particular, the great movements of the Renaissance, of Humanism, of the Reformation, of nationalism, and of the Age of Enlightenment. Max Weber has drawn attention to the especial influence of Calvinism on the growth of the business spirit in his celebrated and still much discussed work, *The Protestant Ethic and the Spirit of Capitalism* (New York, 1930). See also R. H. Tawney, *Religion and the Rise of Capitalism* (London, 1926); A. Rüstow, "Die Konfession in der Wirtschaftsgeschichte," *Revue de la Faculté des Sciences Economiques de l'Université d'Istanbul* (1942, nos. 3,4); for more comprehensive discussion of this theme, see Rüstow's major opus, *Ortsbestimmung der Gegenwart* (Vol. III, Zurich, 1957).

3. (p. 24) *Capitalism and Imperialism*

What has been described in the text as the fusion of the method of exploitation with the method of business is a standard fixture of Marxist theory. Marxists argue that an economic system reposing on the business principle (capitalism) necessarily impels the capitalist countries to expand their political power for purposes of economic exploitation. The truth is that political expansionism undertaken for the purpose of economic exploitation (economic imperialism) is a phenomenon as old as history itself. Moreover, it is precisely such exploitation to which *our* economic system is opposed. Economic imperialism exists today as at every other period in history and as under every other economic system. Nothing would be more false than to regard it as a necessary element of *our* economic system. The causes of imperialism have their locus in quite another world than that of business. Moreover, the theory which seeks to prove that "capitalism" cannot exist without the incessant conquest of overseas markets will be found upon close examination to be untenable. See J. Schumpeter, *Social Classes and Imperialism: Two Essays* (New York, 1955); S. Rubinstein, *Herrschaft und Wirtschaft* (Munich, 1930); R. Behrendt, "Wirtschaft und Politik im Kapitalismus," *Schmollers Jahrbuch* (Vol. 57, 1933); W. Sulzbach, *National Consciousness* (Washington, D.C., 1943); W. Sulzbach, *Capitalistic Warmongers, A Modern Superstition* (Public Policy Pamphlet No. 35, University of Chicago Press, 1942); L. Robbins, *The Economic Causes of War* (London, 1939); W. Röpke, *International Order and Economic Integration* (Dordrecht, Holland, 1959).

4. (p. 26) *Costs as a Renunciation of Alternative Utilities*

The interpretation of costs as a loss of utility ("opportunity cost") sheds light on what has long been one of the most baffling problems of economics. What are the "real" costs behind the money costs which we encounter initially in the market economy? One of the most important and least contested contributions of modern marginal theory was its discovery of the answer to this question. Prior to the application of the marginal analysis—and Marshall himself had held to this view—costs had been regarded as primarily the expression of and the compensation for the pain and sacrifice entailed in production ("pain cost"). This was a conception which found in Marx's labor theory of value its purest and most radical formulation. There is some evidence that this interpretation of costs reflects the moral climate in which the English bourgeoisie of the eighteenth and nineteenth centuries lived, a climate in which every honest gain was thought to require a corresponding sacrifice. This tendency, and the economic errors which developed from it, are especially evident in W. N. Senior's (1790-1864) attempt to describe and to justify the price of capital (interest) as an appropriate reward made to the saver for his sacrifice ("abstinence"). Doubtless, it was this attempt which inspired Ferdinand Lassalle to utter the well-known jest: "The profit from capital is the reward for privation! Admirable maxim, worth its weight in gold! The European millionaires, the ascetics, the penitent Hindus, the stylites perched on one leg on the tops of their pillars, arms outstretched, the body bent over, the face pale, proffering their cups to the faithful in order to collect the reward for their privations! In the midst of them, and overshadowing all the penitents, the penitent of penitents, the House of Rothschild!" The thought expressed here is indeed a disquieting one, for it is obvious that the so-called "sacrifice" of the saver (lender) diminishes with increasing wealth, to the point where saving among millionaires takes place in a quasi-automatic fashion. In due course, we shall see why interest must be detached completely from notions such as "sacrifice" and "reward." The phenomenon of interest is independent of the concept of saving as a sacrifice or a pleasure, just as an author's income from a novel is independent of the pleasure or lack of it the writing of the novel gave him. An author's income is in reality contingent on his writing a good novel and on the fact that good novels are rare. Likewise, interest results from the fact that capital

is at once useful and rare. There is simply not enough capital to supply the
demands of all those who should like to use it. In the level of the interest rate,
which must be entered on the ledger along with the other costs as the "cost
of capital," is reflected the utility of an alternative but rejected use of capital.
What is true for capital costs is true, also, for all other costs. Costs, as reflected
in prices, do not represent a compensation we are compelled to pay for a
sacrifice someone has incurred, for often it is precisely the most laborious work
and the dirtiest which is the least well paid. The function of costs is to compel
us to compare the utility of *our* use of productive factors with the utility of
some other alternative use of the same factors.

The interpretation of costs as a renunciation of alternative utilities involves
a number of difficulties which we cannot deal with here. But it may be observed
in passing that this interpretation is valid only when a means of production
can be used in more than one way ("general" as opposed to "specific" means of
production in Wieser's terminology). These and other aspects of cost theory
are the subject of lively discussion by present-day economists. See F. von Wieser,
Theorie der gesellschaftlichen Wirtschaft, (2nd ed. 1924, pp. 61ff.; published
in English as *Social Economics,* trans. by A. Ford, London, 1927); O. Morgenstern, "Offene Probleme der Kosten- und Ertragstheorie," *Zeitschrift für Nationalökonomie,* (Vol. 2, 1934), 481-522; F. H. Knight, "Cost of Production and Price
over Long and Short Periods," *Journal of Political Economy* (Vol. XXIV, 1921),
reprinted, together with other pertinent material, in Knight's *The Ethics of
Competition* (London, 1935); G. J. Stigler, *The Theory of Price* (2nd ed., New
York, 1953); and finally the extended discussion of these matters in *The Economic Journal,* beginning in 1926 (by Sraffa, Pigou, Shove, Robertson, Robbins,
et al.).

5. (p. 29) *The Pure Rationing System*

The interesting lessons of a pure system of rationing operating under conditions of war, and the economic implications thereof, are presented in detail
in R. A. Radford, "The Economic Organization of a P.O.W. Camp," *Economica* (November, 1948).

6. (p. 35) *Collective Economy—the Basis of Public Finance*

The essential difference between the price system and the system of collective
economy consists in this: in the price system, the equilibration of supply and
demand occurs automatically in the market; in the collective economy, it is
established as the result of conscious political decision. In the price system,
individual preferences are directly manifested; their manifestation in the system
of collective economy involves long and complicated detours. The fact that
some private persons furnish their homes with Oriental rugs must as a general
rule be regarded simply as an expression of their individual preferences. It is
something to which no one can take exception, at least within the context
of the existing distribution of wealth and income. But where the floors of
public buildings are covered with Oriental rugs, we immediately begin to
wonder whether waste or graft is being practiced by our public officials. We
will have in this case grounds (generally good ones) for suspecting that a collective need is being satisfied at the expense of some more important need of
individuals, i.e., of taxpayers. It is obvious that tendencies towards waste are
inherent in a system of collective economy, particularly where, as in our age

of swollen government budgets, the public sector has been continuously expanded. It is in any case difficult to conceive of any alternative method which would enable governments at all times harmoniously to coordinate the satisfaction of collective wants with the satisfaction of individual wants. Further examination of these problems would carry us deep into the intricacies of public finance. See H. Dalton, *Principles of Public Finance* (London, 1923); W. Röpke, *Finanzwissenschaft* (1929); K. Wicksell, *Finanztheoretische Untersuchungen* (1896); M. Cassel, *Die Gemeinwirtschaft* (1925); W. Gerloff and F. Neumark, *Handbuch der Finanzwissenschaft* (2nd ed., Vol I, 1951); O. Pfleiderer, *Die Staatswirtschaft und das Sozialprodukt* (1930); Ursula K. Hicks, *Public Finance,* (London, 1947); R. A. Musgrave, *The Theory of Public Finance—A Study in Public Economy* (New York, 1959).

CHAPTER III

THE STRUCTURE OF THE DIVISION OF LABOR

> "Because it is my social function to supply the world
> as well as I can with a certain thing, therefore I
> dread the world's being so well supplied with it that
> I shall be able to get little or nothing for supplying
> more. It is impossible to exaggerate the importance
> of this consideration, or the penetrating and inti-
> mate nature of its bearing on every aspect of the
> social question."
>
> PHILIP H. WICKSTEED
> *The Common Sense of Political Economy* (1910)

1. *The Meaning of the Division of Labor*

Our economic system is distinguished from its primitive prototypes before all else by its extreme specialization of labor, or what
we call the division of labor. It is this central fact to which we must
return again and again for an understanding of the modern world.
Today, most people are engaged almost exclusively in the production
of goods and services intended not for themselves but for others,
with each one producing always the same goods and the same services.
Except for some sectors of the agricultural economy—and even these
have diminished rapidly in importance—the modern producer personally consumes only a fraction, if anything, of his specialized
output. In some instances, it is true, the small farmer will produce
first for his own needs and then exchange his surplus for other products. But it is difficult to imagine a Ford or a Krupp producing
automobiles and cannon first for themselves and their families and
then supplying to others the surplus which they cannot use. Even
the worker in a shoe factory will buy his shoes, as a rule, in a shop,

41

and it is improbable that he will recognize the pair that he buys as the one he himself has made.

To estimate correctly the role of the division of labor in the building of our civilization is the business of the sociologist and the economic historian. What is important for us to note here is the fact that the division of labor has enormously increased the *productivity of human labor*. The reasons for this are as follows:

(1) The division of labor allows each man to specialize in the kind of work best suited to his capacities.

(2) The division of labor tends to concentrate the production of each commodity in the place where natural conditions are most favorable (the spatial division of labor), a fact which is of great importance in connection with the international division of labor. It is the division of labor alone which brings it about that every type of production, within the national economy or within the world economy, can be established in the *most favorable location*.[1]

(3) It is specialization alone which permits the complete development of professional skill and the acquisition of that experience which distinguishes the specialist from the mere amateur. Thanks to the division of labor, a fund of experience, of knowledge, and of skill can be preserved and increased throughout the generations.

(4) The division of labor avoids the loss of output which ordinarily accompanies the change from one type of work to another.

(5) The division of labor—and here we touch on a most important point—makes possible the use on a vast scale of tools and machines. Because of the large outlays which are required for the purchase of such equipment, it can be profitably used only when it is fully used. It is not worthwhile to make a hammer to drive a single nail into a wall and many a handyman has had to have recourse to the carpenter rather than buy an expensive tool for which he could find only occasional use. Those familiar with farming know that the principal obstacle to the use of farm machinery lies in the peculiarities of agricultural production which prevent maximum use of the equipment. The economic principle in question is this: the use of machines is more limited and thus more dependent on an advanced division of labor, the more specialized are such machines; at the same time, the yield of a machine ordinarily increases with its degree of specialization. The secret of the low-priced automobiles which Henry Ford was the first to put on the market after World War I lay in the huge number of units produced;

for these made possible the mechanization and automation of the entire Ford operation. The specialized machines required for this type of production are extravagantly expensive but they produced, thanks to the volume of output, a car which was at one time the cheapest in the world.

To achieve such high levels of output Ford was required, it is true, to limit production to a single model and to leave this model unchanged year in and year out. Ultimately, the exigencies of public taste forced him to replace the outmoded model by more fashionable ones. To this end, he spent millions for completely new machinery and tools.

A good example of the interrelationships between advanced specialization of the machine and greater output and of the resulting concentration of production in the hands of specialists is the manufacture of automobile bodies by means of special presses. So costly are these tools that only a very large number of orders can yield lower costs and, ultimately, lower prices. The consequence has been the emergence of a special body-building industry serving the automobile manufacturers.

From the last mentioned advantage of the division of labor is deduced an important economic principle. The use of tools and machinery in production means that consumption goods are not produced directly, but via the preceding manufacture of production goods (raw materials, machines, transport facilities, etc.). The more there is of this *roundabout* production and the larger the quantity of capital employed, the more "capital-intensive" will such production become. This introduces a new complication into the division of labor. For, given the difference between consumption goods and production goods (capital goods), it is apparent that a large part of a country's total production serves for the *production of capital goods* and not for the production of consumption goods, and that the production of capital goods must itself become a specialized branch of manufacturing. We must picture the entire process of production as a series of descending levels. At the highest level, raw materials are procured; at a lower level, capital goods are manufactured; and at the lowest level, consumption goods are produced. Just as specialization and division of labor characterize production on any one level *(horizontal division of labor)*, so also we find a division of labor between the different levels of production *(vertical division of labor)*. In other words, there is not only a division of labor between the production of shoes and the production of paper, but also a division of labor between the production of shoes and the production of the fore-products (tools, machines, leather, hides, etc.) which enter into the manufacture of shoes.

2. *The Social Division of Labor and the Role of Money*

The complex ramifications of the division of labor—horizontal as well as vertical—lead us to consider how the various operations occurring under the division of labor are coordinated with one another. There are alternative methods of achieving such coordination, each of which leads to a different form of the division of labor. Consider, for instance, the internal organization of a factory. The management of the factory divides the process of production into various partial operations and assigns these operations to the appropriate workers. Management then sees to the coordination of the whole by means of continuous instructions. This is what we may call the *industrial division of labor*.

Now division of labor exists not only in the interior of this factory, but also between this factory and other factories, between one artisan and another, between a farmer and a physician. We see at once that this kind of division of labor differs sharply from the first. The different operations are here independent and are not submitted to the control of a central authority charged with the coordination of the actions of each individual segment of the total economic system with all the others. We have already seen that it is the process of exchange (the market mechanism) which assumes the task of coordinating the activities of these independent units. We may speak, in this case, of a *social division of labor*.

In our contemporary economic system, the two kinds of division of labor coexist: the industrial division of labor within a plant, a factory, etc., and the social division of labor among the different independent plants and factories. Notwithstanding, it is precisely this social division of labor which distinguishes our economic system from a wholly socialist system. For in the latter system, the industrial division of labor prevails throughout the entire economy, displacing the social division of labor. This characteristic feature of socialism is at the same time a clue to one of its principal weaknesses. It is well known that certain enterprises have attained such excessive size that the managements of these enterprises are no longer able to control and coordinate their operations with efficiency. And many a giant concern has been ruined for not having observed the limitations of size which the requirements of efficiency impose. Imagine the result should the whole economy of a country be transformed into a single huge enterprise!

The concept of the social division of labor embraces most of the essential features of our economic system. It connotes not only the independence of the producer, but also the whole series of rights and liberties associated with such independence: private ownership of the means of production, right of inheritance, freedom of contract, freedom to choose one's occupation, and many others.[2] To think in terms of the social division of labor is to assume that exchange dominates economic life, not the direct exchange of one good for another, but the indirect exchange of a good for money (sale) and of money for a good (purchase). Money, in short, is the indispensable lubricant of a developed exchange economy; and by the same token it is essential to a system founded upon an extensive social division of labor. It is useful to inquire into the reasons why this is so.

Any school boy who has ever swapped stamps with his friends knows that an exchange can take place without money. But he will remember equally well that these primitive exchanges did not take place without some difficulty. He will recall that an exchange of postage stamps could take place only if just the duplicates he possessed were lacking to his friend and *vice versa,* and if the value of the exchanged duplicates was approximately the same. These conditions lacking, the limit of barter (exchange in kind) was reached. The youthful collector was then obliged to do business with a stamp dealer, whose existence is predicated upon the imperfection of exchanges in kind.

By way of further illustration, consider the plight of a butcher who wishes to exchange meat for a chair. Assume that through some ill luck the local carpenter is a vegetarian, and that he wants bread instead of meat for his chair. If we imagine this situation as arising in some period before the invention of money, it is clear that the butcher will be forced to go to the baker and to exchange his meat for bread. Suppose further that at this moment the baker does not require meat but a pair of shoes. Even were we to put a stop at this point to our butcher's travails, this simple example shows that the butcher will be required first to exchange his meat for shoes, then the shoes for bread, and finally the bread for the chair which he originally wanted. He would be required in effect to make an extended detour in order to arrive at his goal. The longer this detour and the longer the associated chain of exchanges, the more difficult does the process of moneyless exchange become until it ends by being completely impossible. During the severe housing shortage which existed in Germany in the inter-war period, there were few persons who were not compelled to participate in a so-called "housing exchange ring"—a chain of exchanges of rent-controlled dwellings which frequently extended throughout all Germany. For the system to succeed, it was necessary that no link in the chain of exchanges be missing, and that the individual who wished to move from Breslau to Hamburg be not seized at the last moment with an attack of appendicitis. The participants in these transactions could never thereafter conquer their instinctive repulsion for the word "exchange," nor could they find enough words of praise for the invention of money which, as a medium of exchange and as a common denominator of the values of all goods, does away at one stroke with the difficulties of exchange in kind. This is, of course, not the only service rendered by money, but it is the earliest and the most important. Money emerges in consequences as an indispensable element in our economic system, one which is inseparable from all economic processes and which gives rise to many special problems. A full discussion of money and of monetary problems is reserved for the next chapter. Our chief concern at this point is to make clear the role of money in the social division of labor.

From my childhood, I recall a strange contract which my father, a country doctor, had concluded with the village barber. Both had agreed not to send bills to each other but instead to pay in kind what one owed to the other. In today's international trade, this would be called a *clearing agreement*. After some time, a prolonged illness of the barber resulted in my father having an excess of credit (clearing surplus). This credit was used up by compelling us children to have our hair cut rather oftener than we liked. The moral of the story is simple: the elimination of money had provoked a disequilibrium of supply and demand. The process of exchange, which if effected by means of money would have extended over many intermediate links, was now reduced to two links only. And this "short-circuiting" of the exchange process entailed a shifting of accustomed expenditures which upset the private mechanism of

choice and of limitation of demand. "Multilateral trade," as it is
called in international economics, had in our case become "bilateral,"
with results which corresponded in small to the results of international clearing agreements.[3] A multilateral exchange without money
is a technical impossibility; a moneyless bilateral exchange is possible, but it is uneconomic in the highest degree. The exceedingly
complex exchange transactions of the present day (which depend
upon money as intermediary) yield us, precisely in virtue of their
multilateral character, the priceless advantages of a rational system
for achieving both national and international equilibrium. To the
extent that it represents genuine economic integration, the world
economy presupposes the existence of multilateralism. But multilateralism requires, in turn, that the international circulation of the
different national monies (convertibility) be not hindered by the
prohibition of convertibility (exchange control).

But rendering multilateral exchange possible is not the only
service money provides. As the common denominator of all goods,
it is an objective unit of measurement applicable to everything
which enters the market. It makes similar, things which are different; and it solves the problem, otherwise insoluble, of adding together apples and pears. Thanks to the continuous exchange of
goods against money and to the social division of labor upon which
such exchange is contingent, prices are formed without which
there can be no rational economic calculation. If we pass the whole
of economic history in review and sift the experiences of every age
and of every locale, we shall find that no economy, however rudimentary, has been able to function without calculation in prices
and money. Year in and year out proposals are made for replacing
calculation in money by some other "natural economic" calculation
(for example, in the form of hours of work or in units of physical
energy). All such schemes must be viewed by the economist as the
mathematician views "solutions" to the problem of squaring the
circle, or as the Patent Department views designs for the construction
of a perpetual motion machine, namely, with a shrug of the shoulders and regret for such vain employment of effort. To resist the
logic of the indispensability of money is simply to indicate that
one has not yet understood that things economic have quite a
different dimension than things physical, technical, and physio-
logical, and that in economics we are not concerned with volumes
or weights or horsepower, but with subjective estimates of value

which assume an objective and measurable form only in an act of exchange accomplished with money.

This is a fact to keep clearly in mind in judging the performance of a Communist system. Where this performance is measured in terms of the increase in production of one or the other commodity, it is unscientific to conclude from the addition of such numbers that the Communist economic system's accomplishments for the welfare of the masses can be even distantly compared with those of the non-Communist (market) systems. The point at issue is not the *physical,* but the *economic* productivity of a system. This can be measured only by means of real prices, and these are by definition excluded in a Communist system. Moreover, increases in genuine economic productivity can only be promoted within a system of genuine prices (market economy) formed according to the processes which are peculiar to the free society.

3. The Conditions Necessary to an Intensive Division of Labor

In order that money may properly fulfill its function of making possible an extended social division of labor it must possess various attributes (which will be considered later in detail), especially uniformity and constancy of value. It is the business of the state to establish a disciplined and stable monetary system so that money will enjoy general confidence and unite the disparate operations of the division of labor in a single payment community. To this is related another condition required for a wide extension of the social division of labor. The great risks implicit in an extreme dependence of all individuals in society upon each other are tolerable in the long run only where an efficiently administered legal system and an unwritten but generally accepted code of minimum moral precepts assure to the participants in the division of labor that they will be able to carry on their activities in an atmosphere of mutual confidence and security. Economic history is a constant illustration of the truth that the intensity of economic activity rises or falls in the degree to which these conditions are fulfilled. Likewise, the spatial extension of economic activity is limited as a rule to the radius within which such conditions, i.e., monetary and legal security, obtain. This is nothing less than the first principle underlying the rise and fall, the expansion and contraction of the economic system itself.

A significant division of labor can develop only in the degree to which the prerequisites of a monetary system, a legal system, and an appropriate moral system are met. History records frequent instances in which these conditions have been maintained for considerable periods within the frontiers of a single state. The intensification of international economic activity, however, has always encountered special difficulties because the creation of an international monetary and legal community has invariably collided with and will in the foreseeable future continue to collide with the unyielding sovereignty of the individual states. This is the chief reason why the progress of the international economy has, even under the most favorable circumstances, lagged behind the development of the several national economies. Because there is no world state, the world economy has lacked a homogeneous monetary system: for such a system depends necessarily upon the existence of a homogeneous international legal order.

It is worthy of note, nonetheless, that the international economy has flourished over the past hundred years in spite of these lacks because substitutes were found for what was lacking. The lack of a uniform international monetary system was offset by the *gold standard*. Scrupulously observed by the principal nations, it resulted in the whole world becoming a single payment community; it banished distrust in the solidity of the monetary foundations of international trade and international capital movements. The obligations imposed on all the participating countries by the scrupulous observance of the gold standard formed a part of the network of written and unwritten rules which made up for the lack of a single international juridical system. The whole world was encompassed in a system of long term agreements based on a universally recognized international law and upon a high degree of accord in respect to the interpretation of such law and of the legal codes of the individual states. International transactions were conducted in an atmosphere of loyalty and fair play in which the disregard of the obligations imposed by the international legal and moral system was regarded as the act of men without honor, honesty, or scruples.

The *actual world crisis* is from this point of view instructive in the highest degree. For the very disappearance of the aforementioned conditions has shown how exceptionally important and necessary they are. The nineteenth century's network of guarantees in respect to security, uniformity, continuity, and fair play, and the adjustment of national policies to the requirements of international order, resulted in an approximate substitute for world government. But all of this was the creation of an epoch, of a state of mind from which the modern world has far removed and from which it in the future may remove still farther.

The foundations of the world economy have been chipped away to the point where the whole structure has become highly unstable. Less and less are nations disturbed by the flaunting of the international proprieties. Almost as a matter of course, governments manipulate their monetary systems for exclusively national ends, block foreign assets, interfere with international payments, practice dumping, expropriate private property, direct the flow of imports and exports now here, now there, at the whim of almost daily changing enmities and friendships, and impose without let or hindrance tariffs, quotas, and prohibitions of all kinds.

The dangerous feature of this process of disintegration is that it is accelerated by its own momentum. In international relations, as elsewhere, "marginal morality" has a tendency to become the dominant morality. If one country can, with impunity, disregard the rights of its neighbors, other countries, unwilling to be dupes, will follow suit. But it is not alone the contagious effects of bad example which foster international disintegration. Every country may legitimately question whether in the light of growing monetary, legal, and moral insecurity it ought not to revise its relations with the world economy. Because there is no world state, the international division of labor, unlike the national division of labor, is a precarious and relatively unstable system. Where a country is significantly involved in the international division of labor, it entrusts a part of its economic life to factors over which it wields only a very slight control and which consequently can cause it disagreeable surprises. In fairness to its own citizens, such a country can adhere to the international division of labor only if the risks implicit in such adherence are reduced to the minimum we have described. During the last hundred years, thanks to the gold standard and to the legal and moral obligations assumed by the gold standard countries, participation in the international division of labor was both possible and profitable. In the changed circumstances of the present, and with the probability of even more radical changes in the future, it has become suddenly obvious that the whole of international trade, with its immense material advantages, depends on conditions which formerly were so taken for granted they were hardly ever mentioned. It is only now, when they have begun to disappear, that the full importance of these conditions is revealed.[4]

It may be assumed that there are few persons today who take the plight of the world economy lightly and who do not recognize the tragic character of the disintegration of the international division of labor, the underlying cause of which has been the gradual weakening of the extra-economic framework of the international society. The true visage of the world economy is now visible: an economy minus its essential monetary, legal, and moral foundations. A genuine restoration of the world economy will prove impossible so long as these foundations are not reestablished. Till then, we must content ourselves with the patchwork aids and *ad hoc* institutional arrangements whose services to this date, it is conceded, have been considerable.

A fact which it is necessary to emphasize in this connection is that the shock to the foundations of the world economy has not been of equal intensity throughout the globe. Thus, the greatest damage has been done where Communist collectivism has swallowed significant parts of the former world economy. This loss is due not alone to the irreconcilability of the political and moral beliefs of the Communist and the free world countries, but to the incompatibility of the dominant economic systems in their respective spheres of influence. Even within the non-Communist world there exists a sharp line of demarcation between the developed countries and the "underdeveloped" countries, due primarily to the fact that the latter countries lack the conditions which inspire the trust so necessary to normal international movements of commodities and capital. In spite of all the disorders to which in our time a country such as Belgium was exposed following its liberation of the Congo, we continue to make available to this country, i.e., Belgium, loans at $4\frac{1}{2}$ per cent interest. We do so because it never occurs to us to doubt the Belgians' word that they will live up to their contracts. But there is no rate of interest under today's conditions capable of opening the private capital markets of the developed countries to the Congo or to most of the other underdeveloped countries. This is the essence of the much discussed contemporary problem of the "underdeveloped countries."[5]

That is the one facet of the situation. The other is that in spite of the defects of the world economy, we can expect some countries which are linked to each other by geographic contiguity and common cultural and political interests and traditions to attain a degree of international "economic integration" which can hardly be hoped for in the world at large. This is the justification and the explanation for the regional economic consolidations of recent years, among which the Common Market and the European Free Trade Zone, are the most significant;[6] these very blocs, however, and their exclusive character, testify to the continuing lack of worldwide coordination.

But the most important and all too frequently ignored international fact of our time is that the unprecedented extension of the division of labor beyond national frontiers over the past one hundred years has been accompanied by an equally unprecedented *increase in the world's population*. A severe contraction of the division of labor would mean, therefore, that millions of people who owe their lives to the division of labor would have the door of life, so to speak, shut in their faces, inasmuch as the conditions which made possible their birth, their existence, and their livelihood, would suddenly have vanished. We are thus bound in this case—to employ a much abused term of speech—to an inexorable destiny which no longer permits us the liberty of glorifying a policy of heroic retreat. Given the immense increase in population of the nineteenth and twentieth centuries (the reasons for which we shall consider presently), we have no alternative—unless we would willingly provoke a frightful catastrophe—other than to maintain the economic apparatus which alone has made possible this growth in population, whether or not this apparatus, for one reason or another, is to our liking. We simply cannot turn back the economic clock to 1700, or even to 1800, without thereby reducing the population capacity of the world to the lowest level of those times. To turn back the clock would be tantamount to ordering the destruction of millions of lives.

4. The Division of Labor and the Number of Men (the Population Problem)

The relationship between the division of labor and *population movements,* which we have just touched upon, is so important that it merits closer investigation. This relationship is a reciprocal one: the extension of the division of labor increases productivity, thereby augmenting the capacity of the economy to absorb population increases. But the converse is equally true: an increase in population permits, in turn, the attainment of a greater degree of division of labor. As Adam Smith has shown in a celebrated passage of his *Wealth of Nations* (Book I, Chapter 3), this reciprocal relationship is clear from the fact that the division of labor is inevitably limited by the extent of the market *(law of the extent of the market)*. The division of labor is limited, that is to say, by the number of possible purchasers of the goods produced, a high degree of specialization becoming profitable only where output levels can be high. One of the factors that most affects the extent of the market—though obviously not the only one—[7] is the size of the population. Is a continual increase in population therefore desirable?

It is useful here to recall that the nineteenth century, which is associated with the greatest population increase in history, was ushered in with a doctrine which expected from population growth only misery, want, and famine. This was the pessimistic theory of Robert Malthus (1766-1836). Since Malthus uttered his cry of alarm, more than a century has elapsed, and in this period many events have occurred which put his doctrine in an entirely different light. The populations of the industrial countries have multiplied many times over and yet the average standard of living in these countries has risen to an extraordinary degree. Simultaneously, the agricultural production of the world has increased in many countries to an extent where there is more concern about the problems of overproduction than of insufficiency. Concurrently, in one country after another techniques which permit the separation of sexuality and procreation have been ever more widely disseminated. Old mores have succumbed to new attitudes until the practice of birth control has become increasingly a simple matter of habit. The result has been a sharp decline in the birth rates of almost all the countries within the orbit of Western civilization.

At the same time, however, other occurrences caused populations in the civilized world to increase sharply in absolute terms. The gigantic strides in recent times of hygiene, medicine, and standards of living offset falling birth rates by declines in death rates. The decline in death rates occurred, first, among the youngest age groups. While in former centuries perhaps two of every ten children survived the hazards of infancy, it became possible in the nineteenth century to keep them all alive. Now if this development is not immediately redressed by an equally lower birthrate, there inevitably results a sharp vertical increase in population. This is precisely what happened in the civilized world of the nineteenth century and which is still happening in the young countries of the Western world and in the so-called underdeveloped countries. The extraordinary population growth of the nineteenth and twentieth centuries is thus the result not of a rise in the birth rate, but of a decline in the death rate in conjunction with a continuing high birth rate. Two historical developments overlapped each other: the newly discovered hygienic techniques caused a rapid decline in the death rate while the birth rate, influenced still by deeply rooted traditional mores, continued to hold to the old high levels. This is a thoroughly natural phenomenon, for though the death rate can be lowered by external and collective measures, a fall in the birth rate is a long term process, growing out of slow changes in people's attitudes. To express the point in more drastic terms: the chlorination of the communal water supply will result in an immediate and rapid decline in the death rate, but it will not reduce the birth rate.

Those countries which are now coming under the influence of Western civilization are experiencing just what the older nations experienced in the nineteenth century. The death rate declines at once and sharply, whereas the birth rate does not follow this decline until much later; as a result, population spurts up like a string bean after the rain. Sooner or later, there will occur a moment when the birth rate in such countries is "Westernized" and adjusts to the lowered death rate. The headlong increase in population in such case slows and may ultimately cease altogether. Most Western countries have come rather close to the final stages of this evolution of which they were the inaugurators. How very risky it is, however, to project a given trend dogmatically into the future, particularly where population movements are concerned, is shown by the example of the United States and France in which birth rates recently have risen to a remarkable degree. But there is little concern today over this phenomenon, in contrast to the fears of Malthus and his time. On the contrary, for contemporary Western statesmen, it is declines in birthrates which are the greatest source of worry.

The several reasons for this curious change in attitude can be examined here only briefly. The emphasis given to the national interest, for instance, is considerably greater today than in Malthus' time. We tend to be concerned lest the birth rate in our own country fall below that of other countries. In addition, we have learned to pay more heed than formerly to the unfavorable consequences of a falling birth rate. There are a variety of motives, of course, which underlie conscious restriction of family size and their moral content will be found to be decidedly uneven. There is no doubt that the small family is quite often the result of deliberate selfishness which, if widely practiced, can weaken the moral fiber of a whole people, not to speak of the religious objections thereto. Here we have the genesis of a tragic situation wherein the modern rationalist spirit, under whose aegis the startling decline in the death rate took place, may overreach itself and in its fall drag down both the birth rate and the moral health of the nation. Clearly, the birth rate must be adapted to the exigencies of a diminished death rate if social and economic catastrophe is to be averted. But if free rein is given to the forces able to bring about an equilibrium of births and deaths, namely, to rationalist thought, the decline in the birth rate may get out of hand.

In the final analysis, of course, declines in the death rate will encounter natural limits set by the present state of medical knowledge in the advanced countries. The birth rate, on the other hand, can theoretically fall to zero. Hence, it is conceivable that an overlapping of population movements such as we have described above could again take place, but in an inverse sense this time (stable or slightly rising death rate plus rapidly falling birth rate), resulting in an absolute diminution of population.

A further circumstance which has caused the decline in the birth rate to be regarded in an unfavorable light is its *differential character*. The experiences of all countries show that birth rate declines begin at the apex of the social pyramid, with the well-to-do and educated classes having one child or no children, whereas the poorer members of society typically beget numerous offspring. Indeed, more often than not, it is the drunkards and the feeble-minded who have the most children. The unfortunate aspect of such a differential decline in the birth rate is that parents who would normally transmit to their children exceptional gifts of heredity and who have the material means of providing them with a good education are not reproducing themselves. Clearly, the qualitative and eugenic aspects of population movements must be taken into consideration as well as the merely quantitative aspects. But these matters, about which there is much discussion at present, require a breadth of treatment which our present inquiry does not permit.

The main reason why the present decline in the birth rate is regarded differently than it would have been in Malthus' time must be sought in the domain of economics. The fact is that the enormous population increases of the nineteenth century have not resulted in an impoverishment of the masses; the catastrophe foretold by Malthus has not taken place. On the contrary, the population explosion has been accompanied by striking increases in the average standard of living. It is to be observed, however, that the population increases of the nineteenth century took place under special conditions which are not likely to recur. The same historic forces which resulted in a lowering of the death rate and thus in an explosive increase in population—viz., the scientific spirit, the belief in "progress," the breaking of the fetters of tradition—all these led to industrialization, to world trade, to the colonization of new rich lands of vast extent. England and Germany, and the other countries for which Malthus predicted overpopulation, solved the problem of feeding their additional millions by superimposing on the agrarian foundation of the national economy an industrial second floor. Concurrently, huge surpluses of foodstuffs were being produced in the new overseas territories, in great part by people who had in the course of the nineteenth century emigrated from the Old World.

But these are unique developments which are not likely to be repeated. The globe in the interim has been fully preempted and mankind no longer has at its disposal a second valley of the Mississippi or a second Argentina. Consequently, those countries which are only now experiencing the vertical upsurge in population which the industrial nations of Europe experienced in the nineteenth century are finding the population problem ever more difficult to solve. This is true of countries such as Italy and Japan, whereas Russia is in the fortunate position, as a result of its enormous territorial acquisitions in the nineteenth century (not to speak of its more recent gains), of being assured of an almost inexhaustible supply of room for further population increases.

To return to Malthus: the population increases which he predicted would be fraught with the direst consequences for mankind have, in fact, taken place, and at a rate which would have been inconceivable in his day. But the catastrophe which he foretold has failed to materialize. Later, as the nineteenth century merged into the twentieth, Malthus' first prophecy was proved false: the rate of population increase fell sharply. Do any of Malthus' pessimistic theories still have validity?

To judge Malthusianism fairly, we should distinguish in it two parts: prophecy and analysis. Prophetic Malthusianism had argued that an ineluctable law of nature will cause population to increase unrestrainedly to the limits of the available food supply. Subsequent developments proved this prediction to be completely false. Population growth is not subject to any unyielding natural law; it is a phenomenon of the civilized world and hence an extremely complex phenomenon resulting from the combination of a wide variety of factors. The failure of these prophecies to come true does not, however, constitute a refutation of *analytic Malthusianism*. This is concerned simply with determining whether a given population increase should be judged as good or evil. It is this question alone which possesses interest for us today.[8]

But the question in this form is too vague to admit of an unambiguous reply. The answer depends on the aspect from which population growth is viewed. He who is concerned primarily with the size of the country's military establishment will answer differently than the pacifist; he who considers the emergence of cities with millions of inhabitants as evidence of the progress of civilization will answer differently than the lover of solitude who views the rise of the masses as a development inimical to civilization. A final answer to the question of whether population increases are good or bad is thus dependent on one's value judgments and is outside the competence of strictly scientific inquiry. The economist must content himself with the more restricted but still very important task of studying the effects of population increases on the *material* welfare of individuals. But even this limited inquiry is itself so difficult and so complex that space does not permit us to pursue it in any but the broadest outlines.

The invariable answer made to those who are skeptical of the supposed material benefits of population increases is that since each man is born not only with a mouth but with a pair of arms, population growth increases not only consumption but production. Each human being, so runs the argument, creates his own additional economic room and, indeed, enlarges it since population growth permits of a greater degree of division of labor. According to this optimistic theory, population growth will result not in a lessening but in an increase in the average standard of living. Is this widely held opinion solidly established in fact?

That population growth allows of the attainment of a greater degree of division of labor is a fact on which we agreed at the beginning of this chapter. But this is no proof of the truth of the optimist population theory and for three reasons. *First,* population growth is, as we have seen, not the only condition required for an enlargement of the market. *Secondly,* the division of labor cannot be extended indefinitely without encountering dangers and difficulties (which we shall presently specifiy) which set effective limits to the process. The division of labor, moreover, cannot exist on an extended scale in the absence of those extra-economic conditions of whose importance the present world situation has made us painfully aware. A fateful nexus of cause and effect brings it to pass that precisely those internal and external political tensions caused by population growth contribute to the undermining of the foundations upon which an intensive division of labor rests. As the historical experiences of the most heavily populated countries show, these tensions soon lead to radicalism in internal and external policy. *It is unfortunate but true that our mass civilization has served to enfeeble rather than strengthen the fundaments of order and security which an intensive division of labor requires.*

At the very least, it must be conceded, we have no guarantee that population growth of itself will assure the maintenance of the extra-economic conditions necessary to an intensive division of labor in as automatic a fashion as it assures the existence of the necessary economic factor, to wit, the extension of the market. It is an enviable brand of optimism which, in the face of these reflections and in the face of the difficulties the world is currently experiencing, can continue to view with unconcern further population increases. But such optimism becomes a veritable enigma after examination of a *third point.* The productivity-increasing effect yielded by an intensification of the division of labor, which in turn results from an increase in population, is in direct conflict with an opposite productivity-diminishing effect caused by the increasing scarcity of the factors of production (land, natural resources, capital) relative to the increasing population. The growing population intensifies competition for these factors, raises their costs, and thus diminishes their yield, relatively speaking. Which one of these conflicting tendencies will prevail cannot be determined in advance; but obviously, the answer will be decisive in judging whether a given population increase will increase or diminish economic welfare.

Let us once again review these complex and exceedingly important considerations. Let us note, first, that it is not the total production of a country with which we are here concerned; for then countries such as China or India with their fabulous resources and enormous national incomes would be the richest countries and not the poorest. What is decisive, rather, is the amount of production *per caput* of the population. If we call this amount the *social share* (total production divided by total population) , we may pose the following decisive question: what is the effect of population growth on the social share of production? Does it increase or diminish it? The answer to this question, however, depends upon whether the increase in production which follows population growth develops proportionately, over-proportionately, or under-proportionately to such population growth. In the first case (if we ignore certain incidental influences on production such as inventions, etc.) , the social share remains the same despite the increasing population; in the second case, it increases, and in the third, it diminishes. To put the matter in more familiar terms, the increase of population in the first case leaves the average standard of living unaffected; in the second case it raises it, and in the third case, it lowers the standard. It is obvious that it cannot be determined in advance which of the three cases will occur, all three being possible in principle.

If we disregard the—for our purposes—uninteresting case in which the increase in production is proportional to the increase in population, there remain the possibilities of an over-proportional or an under-proportional production increase. If population growth brings in its train an over-proportional increase in production, we have a case of *underpopulation* because a population increase would now be to the economic advantage of the nation. If, on the other hand, population growth is accompanied by an under-proportional production increase, we are faced with *overpopulation* because continued population growth is no longer economically desirable. At some point between the condition of underpopulation and the subsequent condition of overpopulation is found the *optimum population*. When a country has reached the point of optimum population, it is placed before the necessity of opting for either an *increase in the standard of living* or an *increase in population*. One excludes the other. As population continues to grow, this optimum point must be reached, sooner or later, in every country; and it must be considered as exceeded when the social share of production is smaller than it would have been with a smaller population, other things being equal.

The foregoing considerations should serve to correct a number of misconceptions, for example, the belief that technical progress and the bringing of new lands under cultivation will continue indefinitely to furnish the wherewithal for additional millions of human beings. No one denies, of course, that the possibilities of increasing production are still very great. But this is completely irrelevant to the problem we are here analyzing. The question of prime interest is whether mankind would not be better off if these increases in production were not always accompanied by population increases. Why is it necessary that every enlargement of economic room which is achieved by the labors and the ingenuity of the existing population be immediately filled by millions of new individuals instead of serving to increase the well-being of those now on earth?

The point of significance here is that it is not legitimate to regard an increase in the social share of production as proof of the absence of an overpopulation problem. For the increase in the social share might have been still greater if the population had not increased. Such would be the case where the increase in production, which caused the increase in the social share, were the result not of a population increase but of technological and organizational innovations. By itself, a rise in the average standard of living does not, therefore, exclude the possibility that a country may be suffering from overpopulation in the sense here defined. The rise in the living standards of many European countries during the past fifty years is no proof that these countries had not already passed the optimum population point. What follows will help to clarify this relationship.

The sudden rise in living standards during the past one hundred years ought not be allowed to conceal the fact that this rise has not been as great as we might have expected considering the extraordinary increase in the productivity of the economic system in this period. There is a certain disproportion here which demands explanation. This is the *disproportion between "progress and poverty,"* a phenomenon which has perennially engaged the attention of socialists of every shade of belief and which has prompted them to seek its cause in alleged basic defects of our economic system. An inveterate complaint of such persons is that under our economic system "economics" destroys what "technology" gains. It is not surprising to find that it is the technicians who tend to entertain this opinion and to regard economists with the same indignation and condescension that military men are wont to display towards diplomats. We have not the space to examine the multitude of misconceptions upon which this attitude of the socialists and the technicians is based. Did space permit, we could make a number of points calculated to enlighten the technicians, in particular, for example, that 100 per cent efficiency is no more to be expected from the economic system than from the most perfect motor. One thing, in any case, is certain: the lag of standards of living behind technological progress and increases in productivity cannot be explained by the fact that a part of what was properly owing to the people of the fruits of such progress has been withheld in favor of a few rich capitalists. This theory, abandoned today by almost all serious socialists, is refuted by a simple calculation which shows how little the average income of the population would increase if recourse were had to a rigorously equal distribution of the existing wealth, even under the much too favorable assumption that total production would not suffer from such action. How then can the apparent contradiction be explained? The only explanation which remains is that technological progress has served mainly to facilitate the existence on earth of a larger number of people instead of serving to increase the living standards of the existing population. It appears that the "disproportions" engendered by capitalism are in large part explained by the fact that this economic system had to spread its immense creative force for well-being in two directions at once: (1) to increase average standards of living and (2) simultaneously to give a foothold in life to huge numbers of newcomers. It is evident that the dilemma of having to choose between an "increase in population" and an "increase in the standard of living" is not a dilemma of yesteryear alone. It is one which at present confronts such countries as Japan, India, and Egypt in particularly acute form.

It would take us too far afield to expatiate here on the qualifications, and they are many, which must be brought to the *theory of optimum population*. To forestall misunderstanding, it must be emphasized that the theory is concerned only with the purely material and individual consequences of population growth.[9] Thus, even when a country has passed the economic optimum of population, an increase in population may still be deemed desirable for noneconomic reasons. But within this wide range of possibilities, it is useful to have a clear idea about the alternatives which exist and to weigh these against each other.

There are, in sum, three possibilities. The first is to brake the rate of population increase by *increasing the death rate*. This method, obviously, cannot be part of a conscious demographic policy, although there are those who believe that the modern paraphernalia of hygiene, inoculation, and medical care with which we are surrounded from the cradle to the grave have their disadvantages. For these techniques conflict with the selection of the fittest individuals and thus weaken our natural forces of resistance to, for example, epidemics still unknown. That such epidemics, conjoined with the atom bomb and bacillus warfare, might make short shrift of our modern mass civilization is a possibility. But no one seriously entertains the idea that we can consciously decide to increase the number of deaths. Thus, if we wish to restrain population increases, we shall have to reestablish an equilibrium between births and deaths, not by increasing the death rate, but by *lowering the birth rate*, a method which is already in wide use in many countries. That this is a method attended with considerable risks and disadvantages has already been noted. Among these disadvantages must be included the fact that a decline in the birth rate causes a shift in the age structure of the population in favor of the aged, a development which cannot be regarded as good in all circumstances. The full significance of these dangers and disadvantages becomes apparent when we recall the alternatives which are open to us.

A conscious increase in the death rate is, as we have seen, out of the question. There remain only the alternatives of braking population increases by lowering the birth rate, or of perpetuating the disequilibrium between births and deaths by allowing population to increase unrestrainedly. Let us reflect on exactly what this latter course would mean. It would mean that an increase in world population which issued from a special set of causes and may be considered, in virtue of its extraordinary tempo and extent, a phenomenon unique in history, would suddenly be regarded as the normal experience of the human race. Every thinking person must reject this view and admit that, sooner or later, it will become necessary to restrain such population increases as we have witnessed in recent times and to reestablish the rate of growth which is sanctioned by history. So why not sooner than later? A cogent argument for present action is the fact that we are compelled, under modern conditions, to pay a double price for continued population growth: in the form of a very probable decline in average standards of living, and in the form of a certain increase in the rigidity and instability of our economic system as the result of a division of labor which is becoming ever more extreme. It is this last effect of which we must now speak.

5. *The Dangers and the Limits of the Division of Labor*

It is well known that too intensive a division of labor can result in the atrophy of certain of our vital functions. There are several reasons for this. To begin with, the greatest part of our waking hours is spent on the job which yields us our daily bread. To be compelled to pass these hours in the performance of one narrowly confined operation is to cause the atrophy not only of certain muscles of the body, but of faculties of the mind and spirit as well. The highly specialized man is robbed of the chance to experience the fulness of his own personality; he becomes stunted. The country youth who comes from an unspecialized milieu will quickly adapt himself to city life. Indeed, it is a popular maxim that the "small town boy" makes good in the big city. On the other hand, the specialized industrial worker who goes to the country is, more often than not, a failure. Modern man does less and less by himself for himself. Canned foods replace those that were once prepared at home; ready-made clothes are substituted for those formerly made by mother or wife; the phonograph, the radio, and now television drive out the music once made around the family piano; football "fans" crowd gigantic stadia to experience on the vicarious level thrills that were once procured by genuine participation. And this vicarious way of life is extended even to letting others manufacture our thoughts and our opinions through the instruments of the press, the radio, and the movies. If credence be given to information emanating from certain cities that the demand for illegitimate children for adoption exceeds the supply, then we have reached the point where people even have their children made by others. Thus, as it encroaches on new fields of human activity, the division of labor leads increasingly to mechanization, to monotonous uniformity, to social and spiritual centralization, to the assembly-line production of human beings, to depersonalization, to collectivization—in a word, to complete meaninglessness which may one day generate a terrible revolt of the masses thus victimized. If there were not at this time evidence of encouraging countermovements, if the birth rate had not already begun to decline, thus freeing us from the principal mechanism of this development, we might easily imagine that we were moving full tilt towards the dreadful termite state of which Aldous Huxley has given us such a shocking glimpse in his *Brave New World*.

The dangers of an intensive division of labor lie not only in the fact that specialized work causes the impairment, through lack of use, of important human faculties, but also in the fact that it reduces the human content of the specialized work itself. Thus, we have the worker in a modern mass-production plant going through the same monotonous motions day after day to make some part of whose end use he may be only dimly or not at all aware, an object which in any case is being made for total strangers in whom he has not the slightest interest, nor they in him. This may kill the joy of work and the pride of craftsmanship. There is a tendency, moreover, for quality to worsen when it is performed for anonymous third parties, with advertising making up in aggressiveness what the goods lack in quality. But lest we exaggerate these evils, it is well to remember that we are speaking here only of dangers and tendencies. It is not true that specialized work is always more monotonous than nonspecialized work, particularly since the progress of technology (automation) has made it possible to turn over to the machine, in large part, precisely those motions which are most monotonous. We would be equally in error if we were to believe that genuine enjoyment of work, meaningful work content, professional pride, and quality performance are necessarily denied to the highly specialized worker. Much can be done to restore real meaning to the work of the specialist by the right kind of plant organization and by awakening in him the professional pride of the craftsman in work well done. The problems of excessive specialization are primarily problems of large industrial establishments, so that the forces opposing industrial concentration (and the strength of these has been too often underestimated) may be expected to mitigate the evils here described.[10]

But much more immediate and obvious than the moral-cultural dangers we have mentioned are those which arise from the mutual dependence of one individual upon another which the method of specialization requires. *The denser and the more complex the division of labor, the more difficult it will be to achieve harmonious coordination and the more widespread will be the reverberations of every disturbance of this complicated process.* A simple example will serve to illustrate what this means.

Let us assume that a collection has been taken up for the construction of military aircraft, and let us see what effects this action will have upon a country's economy. The action begins with the contribution of money by different people and it ends with the construction of planes of metal and wood for the use of the state for whom the collection was originally taken up. The question we must ask is: How are all those goods and services which the citizens, by virtue of their contributions, must forego, changed into aeroplanes? The case would be simple enough if all of the things which the donors renounce could be immediately used in the construction of aeroplanes; no change would then occur in the country's economy beyond the substitution of one group of buyers (the state) for another (the donors). But this is a marginal case which we may exclude from our inquiry. Ordinarily, the donors are required to forego the consumption of quite different things than wood and metal.

In Turkey, some years ago, just such a collection as we have been describing was taken up. The population was urged to forego during the Kurban-Bayram (the Mohammedan spring festival) the feasts of mutton traditional on this occasion for the benefit of the national subscription for the construction of military aircraft. But why give up mutton? The Turkish government could no more make airplanes out of sheep than governments in Christian countries could make them out of Christmas trees or Easter eggs.

We can, at this point, glimpse the complications which a collection taken up for the construction of airplanes will involve. Let us suppose that the amount of my subscription compels me to give up a bouquet of flowers, or a taxi ride, or an evening at the theatre. The result of my sacrifice is to upset in some degree the markets which counted on my purchases. The bouquet wilts in the flower shop, the taxi driver awaits me in vain, my seat in the theatre stays empty. Each of the enterprises concerned sees its profits decline as the result of my abstentions. And these losses entail still further losses since the florist, the taxi owner, and the proprietor of the theatre will have to forego certain planned expenditures of their own in view of their diminished receipts. In all these cases, acts of consumption are foregone without others appearing to take their place. Moreover, the sacrifice which I impose on myself is multiplied throughout the economy until at last, by series of devious detours, production is adapted to the change in the flow of purchasing power. Disturbances of this kind affect, in the first instance, goods and services which cannot be used in alternative ways. We speak of such goods and services as having a "specific" character. The effects of such disturbances may be more clearly visualized if we compare the entire process of production to the biological process which goes on in a tree. As the sap mounts in the tree and penetrates to the very ends of the leaves, so production, as it advances from raw material to finished manufacture, removes farther and farther from goods with numerous alternative uses to direct itself towards the creation of goods having a more and more specific character. The cut flowers offered for sale represent, literally and figuratively, the "leaves" for which there is no alternative use. These "leaves" must wilt, unconsumed, if there occurs a change in the flow of purchasing power such as we have described. A rearrangement of production which will be adapted to the change in patterns of demand will take place ultimately, but such rearrangement requires time and inevitably entails some economic loss.

The problem we have just analyzed can be called the *general problem of economic transfer,* of which the much discussed "transfer problem" of Germany in connection with its World War I reparations payments represents a special case. It arises wherever there are *changes in the flow of purchasing power* regardless of the causes of such changes. Changes in taste and fashion, in the tax and expenditure policies of the state, in the velocity of circulation of money, fluctuations in harvests or in savings and investments, migrations, the rise and fall of population, inflation and deflation, the vicissitudes of foreign trade, technological progress, wars and revolutions— each of these can be the source of progressive disturbances in the structure of the division of labor. The more suddenly these changes occur, the greater is the amplitude and the severity of the disturbances they provoke.

There are a number of such changes, however, which it would be counter to the *general interest* to resist. Thus, if the consumers decide to spend less for alcohol and more for sport, if the urban population turns from rye bread to white bread, or from bread in general to vegetables, fruit, eggs, meat and cheese, or from automobiles to boats, it would be hardly proper for us to oppose these changes in demand in the interest of the producers of alcohol, of rye, of wheat, and of automobiles who are affected by these changes. For this would be favoring private interests against the general interest in defiance of the elementary economic truth that we produce in order to consume, and not consume in order to produce. We would evidence a like disregard for the general interest if we opposed changes in the flow of purchasing power and in the structure of production resulting from the introduction of *cheaper methods* of obtaining one or another good or service. Such a cheapening of production can take place in two ways which are basically similar in principle and in effect: by progress in technology and organization and by foreign trade. To take deliberate measures to destroy that which lightens our eternal struggle against scarcity, to dismantle the machines which can produce more cheaply than the old methods, to bar imports—all of this would doubtless be in the interest of the producers directly affected. But then it would also be in the interest of doctors to make the manufacture of cheap and efficacious remedies illegal, and in the interest of living authors to ban the publication of cheap editions of their dead confrères and to agitate against the translation of foreign writers.

In the last-named cases, we mean to direct attention to the attempts made in the interest of certain producers to oppose the lessening of the scarcity of goods which the general interest demands. But we can go a step further and consider the efforts, camouflaged usually in pseudo-economic theories, to *increase the scarcity of commodities* in the selfish interest of the producers and to have it believed that such increases in scarcity are advantageous in terms of general economic welfare. The hoodlum who has broken all the windows in the block may not have been hired by the local glazier for this job, but that he has acted in the interest of this glazier is just as certain as that he has grossly injured the general interest. An amusing variation on this same theme is the case of the East Prussian farmer who, many years ago, recommended with a straight face that German vegetable production be transferred to the maximum extent possible to Eastern Prussia, first, because the harsh climate of this area would necessitate the building of greenhouses, thus encouraging the iron, glass, and coal industries and secondly, because the higher costs of transport to German centers of consumption would stimulate the railroad and, indirectly, the coal industries. On the same reasoning, it would be possible to draw up a much longer list of promising developments that would follow the transfer of the whole of world agriculture to the spacious ice fields in the vicinity of the North Pole. Needless to add, this Prussian farmer's proposal was accompanied by a demand for a drastic increase in the German tariff on vegetable imports.

The proposal of our Prussian farmer was not the gesture of a clown but simply a particularly flagrant example of the kind of thinking which is encountered daily under multiple guises and which is one of the most influential undercurrents in the economic policies of every modern state. For this reason, the author has been somewhat reluctant to tell, even in jest, such an anecdote as the preceding. The uninstructed might have taken the Prussian farmer at his word! The instances in which the efforts of private interests to maintain or increase scarcity have been applauded as acts beneficial to the general interest are certainly numerous enough to justify such concern.

Plainly, it is in the interest of the individual producer to maintain or even increase the scarcity of the goods or services he supplies. But since the whole purpose of a rational human economy is to lessen scarcity, we have here an irreconcilable antagonism between individual and general welfare, between the interest of the individual and the interest of the commonweal. This is a perversity which in a self-sufficient, exchangeless economy would appear completely absurd. It is something which is peculiar to an economy based on the division of labor; indeed, it is legitimate to describe such an economy as marred by a *latent and persistent disharmony between the private interests of the producers and the general welfare.* It is no exaggeration to say that this disharmony is one of the gravest defects from which our free society suffers.

But what is of still more concern than this disharmony is the growing ease with which the special interests of the producers customarily prevail over the general interest. The reasons for this are, in large part, psychological in origin. Thanks to the division of labor, each one of us in our role as producers is desirous of keeping our goods and services as rare, and therefore as expensive as possible in relation to other goods. By the same token, in our role of consumer, each of us is desirous of having abundance and cheapness prevail in all categories of goods other than those which we ourselves happen to produce. But since the consumer's interest is spread over innumerable goods, the judgment of each man in economic matters is determined more by his position as producer than by his position as consumer. The concentration of producer interests in a given case will normally permit these interests to enjoy easy victories over the divided consumer interests. Thus, though the interests of the consumers taken as a whole are greater and more encompassing than the opposed interests of the producers in question, the latter will be easily able to override the dispersed and hence ineffectual power of the consumers. The producers' task is made all the easier by the use of pseudo-economic theories which lull consumers into accepting their own impotence as a normal and beneficial state of affairs.

There is another important fact, closely connected with that just mentioned, which explains the ability of producers to exploit consumers. In our economic system, the general interest is secured by the mechanism of competition. In recent decades, however, increasing success has attended efforts to discredit competition as something egoistic and inimical to an integrated society. The result has been a substantial weakening of the psychological supports of competition. And the attackers of competition have been all the more successful to the extent that they have managed to identify it as "liberal" (in the European sense) , thereby stamping it as an object meriting general contempt. Such attacks conveniently ignore the fact that it is the liberal economic philosophy* which recognizes the latent disharmony between consumer and producer and which sees in competition the means of mitigating this disharmony and thus of safeguarding the consumers' interests. Piquantly enough, the enemies of competition answer this argument by saying that it was liberalism, after all, which developed the doctrine of the *harmony* of economic interests. Thus we find the real advocates of disharmony engaging with high glee in the task of obstructing those who seek to mitigate the evil by ridiculing them as the naive adherents of outworn doctrines of "harmony." *But our economic system can remain viable only if this disharmony is redressed by effective and continuous competition.* Of course, we cannot overlook the fact that competition

---

*The contemporary use (or abuse) of the term "liberal" in the United States to designate a philosophy which advocates increasing government interference into private life should not be confused with the meaning which Europeans attach to it. By Europeans, liberalism is still understood in its pristine sense of *freedom from* governmental regimentation; this is the sense in which Röpke employs the term throughout. Implicit in Röpke's use of "liberalism," at the same time, is an important distinction between old-style liberalism ("paleo"-liberalism), which is identified with economic laissez-faire, and neo-liberalism in which the positive role of the state in establishing the juridical, competitive, and monetary framework necessary to a viable market economy is recognized and supported.— *Translator's note.*

occasionally entails costly shifts in the structure of production which must be weighed against its long run benefits to the whole community. These considerations must, at all events, underlie any constructive economic policy, i.e., one which aims at minimizing the losses and inconveniences caused by such shifts in production and at mitigating the personal hardships involved without hindering the adjustment itself.

The extreme sensitivity of a society founded on a highly developed division of labor means that a disturbance in one sector of the economy (as illustrated by our innocuous miniature example of the collection for aeroplanes) will be transmitted, avalanche-style, through the whole of the system. A proper awareness of this sensitivity helps us understand more fully those disquieting phenomena known as "boom" and "bust," or the cyclical alternation of prosperity and depression. A study of cyclical movements must properly begin with the recognition that in a mechanism as complicated and differentiated as that of the modern economic system a degree of friction among the moving parts cannot be avoided. It is inevitable that the different parts of this most complex machine will mesh with each other sometimes better, sometimes worse. We can understand now—and when we have become familiar with the sources of monetary disturbances and the especial complications connected with the production of capital goods we shall understand even better—how the friction among the moving parts of the economic machine may become so great as to result in the total breakdown known as a depression. Remembering our miniature Turkish example, we can also understand why "overproduction" may be found, paradoxically, side by side with increasing poverty and why a depression can lead to unemployment and "excess capacity." Where the structure of production and the flow of purchasing power significantly diverge, the economy suffers from a glut of cut flowers, passengerless taxis, unoccupied theatre seats, and of other and even more important kinds of "unused capacity": superabundance in the midst of poverty.

The paradoxical character of a Western depression becomes even more apparent when we consider the effects of a depression on the undifferentiated economy of a country like China. For the Chinese peasant of the pre-Communist era, content with the subsistence that could can be eked out on the land, "hard times" occurred when the pressure of rising population caused the average peasant holding to shrink. The obvious remedy, in such case, was to work the available land harder and longer. The Chinese peasant would have been unable to comprehend the Western phenomenon of unemployment. He would have taken it as a joke in rather bad taste to be told that there are countries where at times a job may become an envied privilege, begged for like bread, where those who hold two jobs are hatefully labeled "moonlighters." Such things he would have held to be grotesque and irrational and we must admit that he is not far wrong. These periodic absurdities are nevertheless the price we must pay for the extraordinary productivity of a highly refined division of labor. The greater the refinement of the division of labor, the less is the economic system able to resist internal and external disturbances but conversely, the greater is its productivity. To ensure a state of equilibrium that would be proof against all disturbance, we would have to return to the primitive and impoverished conditions of a Robinson Crusoe-type economy. If this alternative repels, then we must accept the present economic system with its sensitivity and its instability.

This is the dilemma on which we are driven. But as a matter of fact we are no longer free to choose. The die is cast. For the growth of productivity which accompanied the extensive and intensive development of the division of labor is now claimed as a birthright by the new millions of individuals who owe their very existence to it. We cannot go back, we cannot cause a contraction in the division of labor without putting in peril the lives of numberless millions of human beings and thereby the very existence of our social order. This is the fact, as brutal as it is prosaic, which explodes the fond reveries of economic romanticists and autarkists. It is a fact, moreover, which should lead us to view with anxiety the continuation of the present rate of population growth and to hail its diminishment with a feeling of relief. The contemporary instability of the economies of all advanced countries indicates that our industrial civilization with its ever more extreme division of labor may be approaching some sort of limit in this respect. Moreover, when the political consequences of mass civilization are taken into account, it is patent that the psycho-moral fundaments of our society have become increasingly inadequate in respect to the existing degree of division of labor.

In the space of one unique century, mankind has simply attempted too much at once. Too much emphasis cannot be placed on the fact that the chief cause of our present difficulties must be sought not in the kind of economic system we have, but in a division of labor which has been carried to an unhealthy extreme. A socialist economy, compelled as it would be to preserve the present degree of division of labor, would change nothing in this respect. We shall have occasion later in a special section (Chapter VIII) to study these matters in detail.

NOTES

1. (p. 42) *The Location of Production*

The factors which determine the optimum location for each kind of production constitute the object of a special *theory of location*. See O. Englander, "Standort" in *Handwörterbuch der Staatswissenschaften* (4th ed.); Th. Brinkmann, *Economics of the Farm Business* (Berkeley, Calif., 1935); Alfred Weber, *Theory of the Location of Industries* (Chicago, 1928); E.A.G. Robinson, *The Structure of Competitive Industry* (London, 1935); T. Palander, *Beiträge zur Standortstheorie* (Stockholm, 1935); Edgar M. Hoover, *The Location of Economic Activity* (New York, 1948); A. Lösch, *The Economics of Location,* tr. by William H. Woglom and Wolfgang Stolper (New Haven, Conn., 1954); Melvin L. Greenhut, *Plant Location in Theory and in Practice: The Economics of Space* (Chapel Hill, N.C., 1956); W. Isard, *Location and Space-Economy* (London, 1957).

The several factors determining the location of a given industry combine in a complicated way either to reinforce or to offset each other. They include climate, quality of the soil, proximity of the sources of raw materials, proximity of markets, availability of qualified and inexpensive labor, proximity of complementary industries, transport facilities, the political climate, tax advantages, etc. According to the importance of the one or the other factor, the best location will be near the sources of raw materials (the canning industry, for example), or in the vicinity of large sales outlets (the milling industry), or in an area where there is a reservoir of skilled workers (the garment industry in large cities), etc. If the sources of needed raw materials are in widely separated places (the iron ore and the coke which are used in the production of iron, for example), the choice of location will depend on the comparative importance of the raw materials in question. It is of fundamental importance to determine, in the particular case, whether it is more advantageous to locate production near a given factor or to have this factor transported to some previously selected location. Just as Mohammed was compelled to go to the mountain, so mining operations must, perforce, be undertaken on the spot where the ores are located, and agriculture where the terrain and climate are favorable to the particular crop being raised. But should mining or agricultural operations be undertaken wherever these minimum conditions are realized? That will depend on the advantages to be derived from mining or tilling the soil on the one hand and the costs of transporting the goods to market on the other. If the latter are too high, the land may not be worth cultivating, regardless of the quality of the soil, nor the mine worth operating, regardless of the grade of ore.

If we confine our attention to agriculture for the moment we can see that the optimum location of agriculture will be determined by such fixed natural data as the quality of the soil and climate as well as the costs of shipment to market. The close proximity of the market has the same effect as an improvement of the soil, which is why vegetable farms, among other types of production, are established around large cities. But while the natural factors of agricultural production are immobile and for all practical purposes unchangeable, the transport factor is subject to relatively rapid change: transport costs may decline or the old markets may disappear and new ones arise. The result is likely to be a significant change in the optimum locations for the different branches of agriculture. A good example of this is the case of German agriculture. The industrialization of Germany and the sharp drop in overseas shipping costs in the 19th and early

20th centuries conjointly exercised their influence to remove the optimum location for grain production farther and farther away from Germany, while the optimum location for the production of higher types of goods such as meat, dairy products, and vegetables moved perceptibly closer to Germany. For generations, the efforts of German commercial policy were nevertheless directed to circumventing, at great sacrifice to the people, the effects of this shifting of the optimum location.

2. (p. 45) *The Economic System and the Law*

We have already made reference in the text to the fact that our economic system founded on the social division of labor presupposes the existence of a corresponding juridical order which, as the expression "civil code" indicates, is also a civic order. The essentially liberal principles of our juridical order—sanctity of the person, the right of private property, inheritance rights, freedom of contract, freedom to choose one's job or profession, constitutional guarantees against the arbitrary use of state power—constitute the indispensable legal framework of our economic system. See George Ripert, *Aspects Juridiques du Capitalisme Moderne* (Paris, 1946); F. Böhm, *Wettbewerb und Monopolkampf* (1933); W. Eucken, *The Foundations of Economics* (London, 1950); W. Lippmann, *The Good Society* (Boston, 1937); M. Watkins, "Business and the Law," *Journal of Political Economy* (April, 1934); A. Egger, *Ueber die Rechtsethik des schweizerischen Zivilgesetzbuches* (1939); Cooke, "Legal Rule and Economic Function", *Economic Journal* (March, 1936). The problems connected with the legal framework of the economic system have been the subject of special study in the annual volumes of *ORDO, Jahrbuch für die Ordnung von Wirtschaft und Gesellschaft,* ed. Walter Eucken and Franz Böhm (Düsseldorf, 1948 ff.).

3. (p. 47) *Multilateral and Bilateral Trade Movements*

The comparison of the multilateral structure of domestic trade and international trade is illustrative of the essential features of both. The flow of multilateral international trade takes place as follows: Austria exports knitted goods to England, England exports yarn to Germany, Germany exports chemical products to the United States, the United States exports wheat to Brazil, Brazil exports coffee to Turkey, and Turkey exports tobacco to Austria. Since coffee does not grow in Austria, Turkey uses the exchange she has acquired from her export of tobacco to Austria to pay for the coffee she must import from Brazil. The consequence is for the balance of trade of Austria to be favorable vis-à-vis one country, England, and unfavorable vis-à-vis another, Turkey. Formerly, a large share of international trade was actually carried on in this roundabout way. As a result of this complicated crosswiring of the international trade mechanism, there would be no necessity of Country A buying the industrial products of Country B simply because it was supplying Country B with raw materials. In this ingenious international network, it was a thoroughly normal occurrence for the trade balance of a country to be persistently favorable vis-à-vis one country and persistently unfavorable vis-à-vis another. It is no exaggeration to say that the growth of the world economy to its present dimensions would have been impossible without multilateral trade. Thanks to multilateralism, industrial nations could obtain essential raw materials without the least difficulty by a chain of exports running through three, four, or more countries. For the nations linked together by this network there existed no economic need for colonies.

Indeed, in the liberal era, colonies did not have very much economic importance. Thanks to multilateralism, moreover, the raw materials-supplying countries could sell their goods on a homogeneous world market, pay their foreign debts, and maintain the value of their currencies without chronic difficulties.

It is only by considering the operation of the world economy in the liberal era that we can measure the ravages caused in recent decades by the destruction of multilateral trade. Foremost among the instruments of destruction have been the preferential clauses of reciprocal trade agreements, the progressive disappearance of the most-favored-nation principle from such agreements, and most pernicious of all, the increasing resort to exchange control and to clearing agreements of the kind described in the text of this chapter. The ultimate effect of the use of these devices was a *short-circuiting of the world economy* with the following predictable results: a decline in world trade, the breakup of the world economy into separate blocs, the politicalization of international economics, uneconomical alterations in the composition and direction of imports and exports, price rises in the bilateral blocs (termed with involuntary irony "Grossraum economies") with a consequent diminishment of the competitiveness of these blocs in the still free sector of the world economy, chronic "dollar shortages" and recurring balance of payments crises. The great progress made in the restoration of health to the world economy in recent years is a reflection of the extent to which destructive bilateralism has been overcome by multilateralism. See *The Network of World Trade* (Geneva: League of Nations, 1942); M. S. Gordon, *Barriers to World Trade* (New York, 1941); W. Röpke, *International Economic Disintegration* (London, 1942); W. Röpke, *International Order and Economic Integration* (Dordrecht, Holland, 1959). See also the following note.

4. (p. 51) *International Economy and International Law*

The points discussed in the text show how absurd it would be to see in the disintegration of the world economy, which still has not been completely halted, the beginning of a new kind of world economy constructed on the principles of the planned economy. Even if we ignore for the moment the catastrophic effects on present living standards which a deliberate reduction of multilateral to bilateral trade—the "short-circuiting" of the world economy noted above—would entail, we are driven on the unpleasant truth that the disintegration of the foundations of a *liberal* world economy will prove even more fatal to any future *planned* world economy. This hypothetical planned world economy, required as it will be to regulate international economic relations in the smallest detail, will be in even greater degree than the liberal world economy dependent upon a functioning world monetary system and upon a secure international juridical system. The very least that planned economy implies is centralized control of all economic life. Planned economy is statism in its fulness. A world state is the *sine qua non* of a planned world economy, but no such world state exists. It is absurd to speak of the possibilities and the chances of a planned world economy precisely at the moment when the equivalent of the world state which the liberal era had created (an international legal, monetary, and moral framework) has disappeared. It is little short of ridiculous for the advocates of the planned world economy to continue to hold to an ideology which must cause the downfall of any world economy, regardless of the label it bears. Or to put it differently, we cannot destroy the philosophical and political foundations of the liberal world economy and hope thereby to build an antiliberal world economy; for lacking these foundations, such an economy will be even less capable of functioning than the liberal world economy. We do not have far to seek to discover what the real character of a "planned" world economy would be, minus the gold standard and minus a sound moral and juridical system, for this *is* the world economy we now have and whose deficiencies we are still struggling painfully to make good. See W. Röpke, *International Economic Disintegration* (London, 1942); W. Röpke, *International Order and Economic Integration* (Dordrecht, Holland, 1959); W. Röpke, *Economic Order and International Law* (Academy of International Law, Leyden, 1955).

5. (p. 51) *The Problem of the "Underdeveloped" Countries*

See my article "Die unentwickelten Länder als wirtschaftliches, soziales, und gesellschaftliches Problem" in the anthology *Entwicklungsländer—Wahn und Wirklichkeit* (Zurich, 1961).

6. (p. 52) *International Economic Integration*

See W. Röpke, *International Order and Economic Integration* (Dordrecht, Holland, 1959); W. Röpke, "Gemeinsamer Markt und Freihandelszone" in *ORDO*, Vol X (Düsseldorf, 1958); W. Röpke, "Zwischenbilanz der europäischen Wirtschaftsintegration," in *ORDO*, Vol. XI (Düsseldorf, 1959) .

7. (p. 53) *The Law of the Extent of the Market*

Adam Smith's formulation of the law of the extent of the market can easily lead to serious misunderstanding. This law is concerned not so much with the extent of the market in space nor with the number of people participating in market transactions, but rather with total purchasing power as it manifested on the market. We must not, therefore, confuse people and square miles with francs, shillings, or dollars. It is francs, shillings, and dollars which are the determining factors. *Because purchasing power is possessed individually, it must not be concluded that total purchasing power is equal to the sum of the purchasing power in the hands of individuals.* This is the fallacy committed by all who imagine that the possibilities of disposing of goods are limited by the size of the population. There are, doubtless, certain demands of low elasticity whose total amounts are determined by the number of demanding individuals. This is especially true of the demand for grains. But excepting these inelastic needs, an equal amount of goods may be demanded by many poor men or by a few rich men. The number of Christmas trees demanded in any one year will obviously be determined by the number of families in the market for Christmas trees, but the number and the value of the gifts placed under the Christmas trees will vary from one family to another, according to the income in each case. We may conclude from this that an intensification of the division of labor can be effected as much by increasing the purchasing power of the existing population as by increasing the population itself. See W. Röpke, "Die säkulare Bedeutung der Weltkrisis," *Weltwirtschaftliches Archiv*, Vol. 37 (1933); Allyn A. Young, "Increasing Returns and Economic Progress," *Economic Journal*, Vol. 38 (1928); W. Röpke, *Crises and Cycles* (London, 1936), pp. 4 ff.

8. (p. 57) *Quantitative Aspects of the Population Problem*

The inquiry into the economic significance of the size of population (quantitative population problem) is still in a very unsatisfactory state for the relationship in question is one which eludes exact measurement. This increases the likelihood, unfortunately, that the population problem will be debated in subjective and emotional contexts of one kind or another. Partisan discussion of this sort has contributed greatly to confusing the economic issues involved. The following references are suggested: H. Wright, *Population* (London, 1933); W. Rappard, "De l'optimum de population," *Zeitschrift für schweizerische Statistik und Volkswirtschaft* (63rd year, 1927); L. Robbins, "The Optimum Theory of Population," in *London Essays in Economics in Honour of Edwin Cannan* (London 1927); H. Dalton, "The Theory of Population," *Economica* (March, 1928); J. J. Spengler, "Population Theory" in *A Survey of Contemporary Economics,* Vol. II (1952); S. S. Cohn, *Die Theorie des Bevölkerungsoptimums* (1934 [a dissertation for the University of Marburg under the direction of the author and containing extensive bibliography]); E. F. Penrose, *Population Theories and Their Application* (Stanford University, 1934); D. Villey, *Leçons de démographie* (Paris, 1957).

9. (p. 61) *The Economic Consequences of a Decline in the Rate of Population Growth*

The prevailing pessimism with which the possible slowing up of the rate of population growth is viewed is certainly the result, in large part, of failure to think through the relationships involved. It is to be noted, however, that the deceleration of population growth may result in an alteration of the structure of the economy which can mean financial loss and painful readjustment for individual sectors. In particular, those for whose output demand is inelastic will be unable to count on new extensions of the market. Chief among the branches of production that will be affected in this way is grain production, whereas the production of higher types of agricultural goods such as meat, dairy products, etc. will probably tend to profit from structural shifts of the kind in question.

10. (p. 64) *The Problems of the Giant Enterprise*

The giant industrial firm with its army of proletarians, its workers' quarters, its impersonality, its unfreedom, is surely one of the most disturbing phenomena of our economic system. It is important, therefore, that the following points be kept in mind: (1) the giant firm is not always and under all circumstances a higher type of industrial mechanism just as a skyscraper is not under all circumstances a superior form of architecture. See W. Röpke, *Mass und Mitte* (Zurich, 1950), pp. 176-200; S. R. Dennison, "The Problem of Bigness," *The Cambridge Journal* (November, 1947); (2) the problems associated with mass production would not disappear with the advent of socialism. On the contrary, they would become even more vexatious, for then the last remnants of self-reliance, spontaneity, and of a way of life suited to the nature of man would be obliterated by the mammoth economic machine of the state. Indeed, it is highly probable that the socialist worker, having only one choice of employers, viz., the state, would become even more dependent and unfree than at present; (3) the hope that the giant enterprise can be "humanized" is not a vain one. Much can be done to restore to the worker the opportunity of expressing himself creatively in his work and to enable him to see that what he is doing has meaning and value for himself and for the community. See W. Hellpach, *Gruppenfabrikation* (1922); E. Rosenstock, *Werkstattaussiedlung* (1922); O. Veit, *Die Tragik des technischen Zeitalters* (1935); W. Röpke, "Zur Renaissance des Berufsgedankens," *Soziale*

Praxis (31st year, 1922); G. Briefs, *The Proletariat* (New York, 1937); W. Röpke, *The Social Crisis of Our Time* (Chicago, 1950); W. Röpke, *Civitas Humana* (London, 1948); L. Hacker, B. Selekman, *et. al., The New Industrial Relations* (Ithaca, N.Y., 1948). In this connection, it is interesting to note that Japanese industry—thanks to the electric motor and the combustion engine which have considerably reduced the advantages of the big mass-production plant—has exhibited a marked tendency to develop as a congeries of small independent enterprises (K. Akamatsu and Y. Koide, *Industrial and Labour Conditions in Japan* [Nagoya, 1934]).

CHAPTER IV

MONEY AND CREDIT

"The sole fact that credit is today the normal and proper expression of value and of exchange has introduced an element of extreme instability into all contemporary economic systems. Modern economic systems appear to be balanced on a knife's edge as it were; the tiniest excess or deficiency of national credit can tip the balance in one direction or the other. This system is minutely adjusted, so to speak, to reflect the smallest increment in weight which it can just support, and that is why it is so extremely sensitive."

KARL LAMPRECHT

1. *What Is Money?*

We have already established that money is a device which is indispensable to an economic system founded on exchange and on an intensive division of labor. Consequently, any investigation of the modern economic process remains incomplete without a special chapter on money. It is, moreover, certain that we shall be unable to understand the operation of our economic system so long as we do not have a clear apprehension of the peculiar qualities of money. It is in the deepening of our knowledge of these qualities that economics has made its most notable advances in recent years.[1] We can go even further and say that the history of peoples and of civilizations cannot be fully understood if attention is not given to the important role which money has played in history, and in the development of the way of life of different epochs.[2]

79

We do not know when money first appeared in human history. Very probably, it was not invented in the same manner as the electric light bulb or the typewriter. What most likely happened is that one day, many thousands of years ago, people suddenly became conscious of the fact that money existed. Only one thing we can say with certainty: to be really money, money must have had to fulfill, thousands of years ago as today, the essential condition of being generally exchangeable and acceptable as a means of payment. We can understand, therefore, why the earliest form which money took was some particularly desirable commodity which could, if need be, serve for *real* satisfaction. Early money was constituted at times of bars of iron, at times of strips of cloth or of leather, and most often of cattle, proof of which we find in the fossil remains of language, in the Latin word "pecunia" and in the English "fee" which corresponds to the German "Vieh" (= cattle). Eventually, the precious metals, for many and obvious reasons, attained preeminence as money. Thence begins the history, open to our investigation, of money and currency.

We are already familiar with the economic revolution which followed the introduction of exchange based on money. Exchange was henceforth separated into two acts: the act of "selling" one's own commodity against the receipt of a sum of money, and the act of "buying" another's commodity by surrendering a sum of money. We can see that each of these two acts is an act of exchange: exchange of commodity against money, and exchange of money against commodity. In place of the original exchange of commodity against commodity, we now have the concatenation: commodity—money—commodity. Simultaneously, money made possible the participation of more than two persons in the act of exchange. The end result of the process of exchange in a money economy is, of course, an exchange of commodities against commodities, but in contrast to the economy of exchange in kind, this result is obtained in an indirect way by a detour passing through several individuals who make use of a general medium of exchange.

If we term a "good" every object or service to which we attach value, then money too is a "good." Nevertheless, it is a good of a very special kind. We value an ordinary good because it is capable, in some way, of ultimately satisfying a want. In the act of satisfying a want, it renders up its economic soul, so to speak; it achieves the purpose of its existence. In a word, every other good but money serves for "real" satisfaction. From the raw material to the packaged product, chocolate goes through numerous stages and passes through many hands, but its final inglorious destiny is to be eaten. It is not so with money. If commodities providing real satisfaction are by essence and destination mortal, money is essentially immortal because it is not used for real satisfaction but for "circulatory" satisfaction. In other words, we do not derive satisfaction from money by eating it, but by spending it and by making it circulate, intact, from hand to hand. This does not mean that money, insofar as it is constituted of some material substance, may not also furnish real satisfaction. People can collect coins, melt them, or hang them on a watch chain. A man can paper his walls with bank notes, if he is willing to allow himself this extravagance. But money in these cases at once ceases to be money. It becomes a simple commodity, just one more addition to the strongly mixed company of chocolate bars, sugar buns, and phonograph records. It is essential to the concept of money that it circulate, and in a direction opposite to the (finite) circulation of ordinary goods. Whereas chocolate bars, phonograph records, etc. are always leaving the stream of goods in order to be consumed, it is the essential characteristic of money that it remain in circulation as money.

Money accomplishes its mission by enabling us to widthdraw from the huge store of the economy's goods those which we desire. Ordinarily, we obtain this right by contributing, on our side, to this same store of goods. Money has thus been compared to an admission ticket providing access to the "social product," that is, to the current stock of goods and services. Money may be compared, if we wish, to a "promissory note" on the social product. Such comparisons are permissible on the condition that we do not forget that money implies neither a qualitative nor a quantitative determination of a right to the commodities, nor any juridical claim on the store of commodities. The determination of the if, the what, and the how much is always subordinated to the market and to the formation of prices, in such a way that the "right" to something is narrowed to a simple possibility. From the purely juridical point of view, money should be defined only as "a final means of liquidating debts," providing that it has been imbued by law with the quality of being "legal tender for all debts, public and private." Such money confers on him who is obliged to pay (the debtor), vis-à-vis him who is entitled to receive payment (the creditor), the right to an acceptance which frees him from his debt.[3]

But if we employ—with this reservation—the comparison of money to a promissory note, we can see at once that it is possible to imagine a money which is incapable of furnishing any real satisfaction and which is thus without material value. But this lack will not negate the functions of money as a general medium of exchange provided that it retains the essential quality of "general acceptability" (F. von Wieser). The lack of a material content offering the possibility of real satisfaction does not exclude the possibility of a circulatory satisfaction, and if we value money according to what we can buy with the monetary unit, money without material value of its own possesses "value" just as well as money with material value. The value of money in the former case reflects the value of the goods which we can buy with the monetary unit; it does not flow from the value of the money material, but arises from the function of money which is to circulate and to be exchanged against commodities. Money in this context has a *functional* value and not a material value. The belief that it is the very essence of money to be incarnated in a piece of precious metal (metallism) is therewith refuted. The question of *what* will circulate as money is ultimately determined by the confidence of the people in the possibility of returning money to circulation. This confidence can be strengthened in two ways: either by endowing money with its own material value (coin), or by making it legal tender (nonredeemable paper money of fixed par value). As a general rule, it is necessary to educate the population to accept paper money which is nonredeemable and without material value. In the eastern provinces of Turkey, for example, it was still recently almost impossible to compel the peasants to accept the government's (then stable) paper money. A Turkish official related to the author that while on an inspection trip, he had succeeded in getting a village wagoner to accept paper money rather than gold only by using his fists (admittedly, a somewhat crude illustration of the concept of fixed par value!). In our case, fisticuffs have been replaced by war which has so accustomed us to the use of paper money that we can scarcely recall a time when paper money was redeemable in gold. Indeed, we find it hard to imagine that our fathers could take their bank notes to the banks and obtain pieces of gold as naturally and as easily as postage stamps. Plainly, then, the connection of money with a precious material is not essential, though this does not exclude the fact that such connection may be very desirable. Normally, there is no need of making theatre tickets out of candy, unless it is feared that the management will sell more tickets than there are places, in which case we can console ourselves a little with the tickets made of candy.

In the case of inconvertible paper money, we see with special clarity the nature of money as a simple but indispensable auxiliary to economic activity, a kind of poker chip as it were. From the point of view of economics, money is a way-station, an item in the national ledger which disappears in the final accounting and which does not itself constitute an integral part of a nation's wealth. A nation does not become richer or poorer because its supply of money increases or diminishes, but only when the supply of goods of which it disposes grows greater or smaller. If the supply of money in a country increases or diminishes while the supply goods remains the same, it follows that the supply of goods which can be purchased by the monetary unit will become smaller in the first case (inflation) and greater in the second (deflation). If the bank notes of a private individual are destroyed in a fire, his loss, which may be very great, does not necessarily represent a loss for the national economy, apart from the negligible value of the paper and the costs of printing. Indeed, the sum of which this unlucky individual is deprived actually benefits the rest of the population, for the purchasing power of all the other bank notes increases by the fraction corresponding to the amount of the burned bank notes. What has taken place is a sort of miniature deflation.

Pursuing this notion still farther, we see that however we use our money, our conduct will exercise an influence on the whole of the national economy. If we spend it, the way in which we spend it affects, in the fraction corresponding to the amount spent, the way in which goods are produced. If we do not spend it, we can either put it in a bank and thereby give to others the possibility of buying raw materials and machines, or we can pile it up in the cupboard at home. In the latter case, the purchasing power of the money becomes inactive to the profit of all the other members of the payment community who can now buy more cheaply. Whatever we do, we can never escape the responsibility which is imposed on us by the possession of money.

Money is one of those objects whose essence can be explained only in terms of their *functions*. Thus, the essence of money resides in its function of being a *general medium of exchange*. Of critical importance, in this connection, is how the broad masses of the citizens will react in a period, say, of hyper-inflation when once they become fully aware that money is no longer "functioning" as it should. Money is so indispensable to the modern economy that where the state-issued currency is rendered worthless, the country's ongoing trade and business activities, even where they are at a low level, will of themselves bring into existence a substitute means of calculation. Such *ersatz* money may take the form of stable foreign monies as in the inflationary period following World War I when the dollar, the guilder, etc., supplanted the worthless local currencies in many countries. Or it may take the more unusual form of some scarce commodity such as the cigarettes which did yeoman service in those European countries which were devastated by World War II.

Only money makes possible the satisfaction of the complex pattern of consumer desires by causing the highly differentiated structure of production to shift continuously in response to such consumer desires. Only money makes possible rational economic calculation in that it provides a device for comparing production and consumption, profits and costs, and, as we have already seen, reduces all economic quantities to a common denominator. "Money alone is the absolute good: not merely because it satisfies a want *in concreto* but because it satisfies want as such, *in abstracto*" (Schopenhauer). It is, as Dostoievsky once expressed it, "coined freedom." Finally, money has supplied the foundations for our modern credit system, without which the contemporary economy would be unthinkable. But it can furnish these manifold services only so long as it remains a general medium of exchange and meets the requirements of a "healthy" money.

When we consider somewhat more closely those services which money renders in virtue of its quality of being a general medium of exchange, our attention is drawn especially to the aforementioned attribute of money which enables us to compare all the objects of exchange with one another in such a way that we can express their value as a multiple of the common monetary unit. This is what is meant when we say that one of money's functions is to be a *general measure of value*. However, we cannot regard this function of money as being equally important and equally necessary as its function of being a general medium of exchange. It is more accurate to say that because money in its concrete form is a general medium of exchange, the exchange value of marketable goods will inevitably be expressed in units of money. Money as a general medium of exchange consists of the concrete dollar notes or checks which I use to buy goods. Money as a measure of value, on the other hand, is the dollar as an abstract unit of account.

Closely connected with the exchange function of money is another of its functions, that of being a *general means of payment*. Every money payment need not involve an exchange transaction; payment of taxes, of penalties, of damages, gifts of money and many other examples show that money can also function as a means of unilateral value transfer. But this again is possible only because it is a general medium of exchange.

A further consequence of the exchange function of money is its ability to be an intermediary in capital transactions, i.e., its quality of making possible the emergence of debtor-creditor relationships and the transfer of the ownership of capital from person to person or group to group.

Finally, money's function as a medium of exchange renders it an appropriate means of *capital saving* and *capital movement*. Or to express this idea somewhat differently, money becomes a vehicle of value through time and space (von Mises). Actually, money nowadays—except in periods of distress—no longer serves in any significant degree as a means of capital saving, since the average person is apt to put what is not mere working capital or simple cash reserves into investments which will yield a profit, or he turns over his savings to a bank to administer. It is as a vehicle of capital *movement* that money has retained a larger measure of significance.

In general, all monetary functions are exercised in a given country at a given time by one and the same monetary system. Indeed, its capacity for assuming all of its functions may be regarded as one of the criteria of a healthy money. It may happen, however, that the different functions are accomplished by different kinds of money. Such a process of *division of functions* was very well illustrated during the German inflation following World War I. The more worthless the mark became, the more of its functions it had to abandon. The first of its functions which the mark was to surrender was that of being a means of capital saving and capital movement; subsequently, it had to forego its function as go-between in capital transactions. Only an uncommon lack of economic insight could have induced anyone in the year 1923, at the height of the German inflation, to hoard mark bank notes or to buy mark securities. Next to go overboard was its function as a measure of value as more and more people turned to calculation in gold or used the "index" and the multiplier. The government itself was compelled in the end to collect its taxes in "gold marks." Thus was the mark increasingly restricted to being merely a means of exchange and of payment. It was just about to lose even these last functions when the successful stabilization of the mark was accomplished in November 1923.

2. *From Cattle to Bank Notes*

If we contemplate a collection of old coins, we can readily perceive some of those important features of a sound money about which we have been speaking. What first strikes us is the great variety of coins and of coin systems which appear to have existed in former times side by side within the frontiers of a single country. What a muddle of doubloons, continentals, florins, threepenny pieces, marks, ducats, and gold louis! We may rightly conclude that our ancestors' patience must often have been tried with the continual counting and recounting made necessary by such a multiplicity of systems. Plainly, the elimination of such confusion by the establishment of a homogeneous monetary system must be numbered among the primary aims of monetary policy so soon as business activity has expanded beyond the rudimentary stage. Homogeneity of the monetary system is thus one of the principal requirements of a sound money: all monetary units within the same economic system should be exchangeable against one another at as stable and firm a ratio as possible. In spite of the antiquity which attaches to the discovery of the coin system, thousands of years of experimentation were required to develop the homogeneous monetary systems which, to our generation at any rate, seem so self-evident, and to put an end to the confusion in computation and, what was even more disagreeable, in prices. Actually, the homogeneity of national monetary systems is an accomplishment only of recent times. The close of the 19th and the beginning of the 20th centuries witnessed, moreover, the successful creation of *international* monetary homogeneity paralleling that existing on the national level, thanks to the gold standard which united all countries within the framework of one monetary system. The abandonment of the gold standard in our times means then, with regard to the postulate of monetary homogeneity, an unfortunate step backwards, for so far there has been discovered no other international monetary system. A special and thoroughly unhappy phase of the age-long struggle for national monetary homogeneity is represented in the attempts to combine the use of both gold and silver, in a fixed ratio, in one monetary system (bimetallism).[4]

The collection of coins we are contemplating tells us something else which is perhaps of even greater importance. Many of the silver coins will be seen to give off a suspicious reddish glint, indicating the presence of a strong alloy of copper. No great powers of imagination are needed to conjure up the coin debasements of past centuries (and the monetary depreciations which accompanied them); they are, in fact, the historical prototypes of the inflations of our own times. These experiences of the past make clear the importance of that other requirement of a sound money, *stability of value,* and the strenuous and repeated efforts required in the course of history to establish it. In this instance, too, the introduction of the gold standard in the nineteenth century was the factor most responsible for the establishment of money upon a solid base. Again, too, it is our own destructive age of wars and revolutions which is responsible for the sabotaging of this accomplishment. Once more, the maintenance of monetary stability has become an economic problem of the first magnitude.

There is one fact, however, which an examination of our coin collection does not reveal to us, but with which we have become intimately familiar as the result of our own painful experience. Though the people in whose pockets our collection of coins once jingled were plagued by a confusion of monetary systems and of coin debasements with a resulting lack of monetary homogeneity and stability, one thing was self-evident: their *freedom* to exchange their money against goods or against other kinds of money. Of course, there were instances in these earlier periods of where an unscrupulous ruler of the modern stamp such as King Philip the Fair of France would proclaim, as he did at the end of the thirteenth century during his struggle with the Papacy, an embargo on the export of money and letters of credit, thereby introducing what we term at the present time exchange control. But we have no record of Erasmus, Luther, or Goethe encountering any difficulties in exchanging their money on their respective journeys to Italy. Restrictions on freedom to exchange domestic money against foreign money are in fact an invention of our own time, and we have little reason to be proud of having made *exchange control* a normal procedure and therewith deprived money of that freedom which in the eyes of our forbears pertained to its very essence. Moreover, we find that in some countries even the freedom to exchange money against goods has been so restricted by rationing regulations that for the purchase of certain categories of goods money is worthless unless accompanied by a special permission to purchase. Out of such restrictions collectivist Russia has made a permanent system, a proof that in the collectivist economy money completely changes its role and in any case can no longer be equivalent to "coined freedom."

If we keep in mind that the three most important postulates of a sound money are homogeneity, stability of value, and circulatory freedom, then we may regard the history of money as a history of the tribulations which it has endured: a history of debasements, of risky experiments, of repeated violations of these postulates. At the very least, valuable insights can be gained by reviewing the history of money from this angle. Another vantage point for the study of monetary evolution is found in the interesting fact that from earliest times to the present day, money has become progressively more abstract, more "aenemic."

The cattle in which Homer counted out the value of Achilles' shield was evidently a very concrete kind of money. Even in the age when men began to use specific weights of the precious metals as money, the purely material aspect of money was still of prime consideration. This primitive method of payment which consisted of weighing out amounts of the precious metals ("weight payment" according to G. F. Knapp) is memorialized in the fact that many contemporary words for money were originally nothing more than designations of weight, as in the obvious cases of the English "pound" and the Italian "lira," but also in the cases of the German "mark" and the Yugoslav "dinar" (from the Latin "denarius"), among others. Nor did the evolution towards an even more complete dissociation of money from its purely material content end here. Those of us who have ever had to buy a railroad ticket at the last minute will appreciate the difficulties attendant upon the method of "payment by weight," difficulties which disappeared after the tremendous forward step taken in antiquity—probably for the first time in Crete in the second millenary B.C., then later in Asia Minor—when unitary weights of the precious metals were introduced, embossed with an official stamp guaranteeing their weight and purity.

With the stamp of guarantee, there came into being a money which made it possible to make payments not by weighing, but simply by counting. The exchange value of this fully-valued money (currency) was still identical with its material value. But the next stage of development saw the issue of token money or subsidiary coin, that is, of under-valued monies whose material value represented only a fraction of their exchange value. This marks the further progress in the direction of monetary aenemia; and in fact in most civilized countries today, people know no other coins than these. These aenemic coins, however, are used only in transactions involving small sums; by far the greater part of payment transactions in all civilized countries is effected by means of money still more ephemeral in nature, viz., stamped pieces of paper.

In the beginning, paper money still had a certain material aspect, in the sense that it was a receipt for a deposited amount of precious metal. This early paper money, moreover, had a 100 per cent coverage and could always be converted into precious metal. It was, therefore, originally a circulating claim against the "bank" which had assumed the safekeeping of a quantity of the precious metals and issued in exchange therefor a receipt (bank note). The banks soon noticed the influence of the "law of great numbers" on their increasing volume of business: their deposits and withdrawals largely offset each other. And they noted the even more important fact that the bank notes began to circulate as money, supported by the confidence that people had in the possibility of redeeming them. Consequently, it did not appear necessary to cover the notes to the extent of 100 per cent. Even where full convertibility of the paper notes was maintained, a given ratio of reserves to liabilities was sufficient to enable the bank to meet the demands for redemption which could be expected in the ordinary course of business, a ratio which was later legally fixed in most countries, in one form or another. This meant, of course, that the bank of issue could put into circulation many more notes than the equivalent of its reserve in precious metal and could thus issue more promises of payment than it would have been able to meet if they had all been presented at once. Such additional bank notes got into circulation when the bank of issue used them to accord commercial credits, primarily in the form of purchases of promissory notes from which the interest was deducted in advance (discounting). By using these additional bank notes to furnish credit, the bank had succeeded in a bit of legerdemain which to this day many people fail to understand: it had furnished credits which did not arise from previous savings but from the issuance of additional bank notes (creation of credit).[5]

The bank notes thus put into circulation were born of a credit operation and hence represented a combination of the monetary system and the credit system. So long as the notes remained redeemable (full gold standard, gold circulation standard),[6] they preserved a certain indirect connection with the concrete matter of money. But this connection became increasingly attenuated when redeemability was restricted to certain categories of payments (such as payments to foreign countries) and when the domestic circulation of gold coins was prohibited (gold bullion standard).[7] The divorcement of bank notes from a precious metal was made complete with the abolition of redeemability in any form (paper standard). Before World War I, the full gold standard prevailed in the economically developed countries; subsequently, it was the gold bullion or gold exchange standard which became the dominant type. And today we find the paper standard, under various forms, almost everywhere in operation.

3. *Money and the Banking System*

But even paper money, abstract and ephemeral though it be, cannot be considered as the final stage of that "aenemia" which has characterized the development of money. Paper money is, after all, "cash"; it is a visible concrete currency. Now it is commonly known that most business transactions in the economically most developed countries are consummated not by the use of actual cash but by the transfer of bank deposits. The participants in such transactions maintain bank accounts against which they write checks. In disposing of their bank deposits in this way, they make use of a variety of money which is designated as *credit money* (bank money, check money, or demand deposits). In this, the dominant medium of exchange today, money has found its most abstract expression. Even the simple counter, as it were, has disappeared from the gaming tables of finance—people simply "keep track of the score." If, under the general heading of "the banking system" we include both banks of issue and banks which handle demand deposits (commercial banks), it is evident that in the economically advanced countries the monetary system is intimately connected with the banking system. Thenceforth, money and credit constitute an inseparable entity.

We find, too, that the same sequence of credit expansion which is associated with the issuance of bank notes occurred in the case of demand deposits. Thus, to the extent to which demand deposits circulated as money, the banks felt themselves freed of the obligation of maintaining a 100 per cent cash reserve behind these deposits, despite the fact that they are debts of the bank subject to payment on demand (hence the name "demand deposit"). To provide the necessary minimum liquidity (the ability to meet expected demands for cash) it was deemed sufficient to maintain a supply of ready money equal to, let us say, 10 per cent of the total demand deposits oustanding. The banks could loan out the remaining 90 per cent and earn enough in the process to administer the deposits without charge or even to pay a small amount of interest on them. Henceforth, the whole art of bank management consisted in effecting a daily compromise between the two opposed principles of liquidity and profitability, with the over-all goal being the maintenance of minimum liquidity and maximum profitability. Small errors of calculation could be corrected by recourse to the so-called "money market." Thus, the whole system is truly "minutely adjusted to reflect the smallest increment in weight which it can just support." We can now observe what an important bearing banking has on the entire monetary system. Prior to the development described above, only cash money circulated. Thenceforth, demand deposits circulated simultaneously with the greater part of the cash which gave rise to these same deposits. The circulation of demand deposits or check money was equivalent in short to the "creation" of an additional supply of money.

There is yet another angle from which we can observe how the modern banking system affects the supply of money. A businessman, for instance, may establish a demand deposit (checking account) not only by depositing hard cash in the bank, but by getting the bank to extend him a loan for this purpose. Thus, by adhering to a proportion of 1 : 10 between cash reserves and outstanding demand deposits, with 90 per cent of the actual currency paid in being loaned out, the bank can, by granting cerdits, create new checking accounts (demand deposits) to an amount nine times greater than that which has been paid into it. It is clear in this case that the bank, following the same procedure as a bank of issue, grants credits not out of preceding savings, but from additional resources obtained by the creation of credit. To what extent is a bank capable of creating credit? This depends upon the bank's liquidity requirements, that is, upon the amount of the reserve which the bank must maintain to meet the demands for the conversion of check money into actual cash. This preoccupation with the maintenance of liquidity, which no bank can safely ignore, more or less effectively limits the bank's power to create credit. The liquidity requirements of banks fluctuate with the degree of confidence placed in banks, with the amount of the payments made to those who are outside the circle of the bank's regular clients (payrolls, small payments to retail merchants, farmers, etc.), and with the turnover of individual bank accounts. But more significantly, the fluctuations to which bank liquidity is subject—and *pro tanto* the fluctuations to which the total supply of credit is subject—coincide to a very large extent with the *cyclical fluctuations of prosperity and depression.* In a period of expansion the economy's supply of credit increases, while the banks' liquidity is proportionately lowered (credit expansion); in a period of depression the banks seek greater liquidity and are forced, in the process, to contract credit (deflation).

It is of great importance that we thoroughly understand the above relationships, for without such understanding we cannot adequately comprehend the perils and the problems which currently beset our economic system. Hence, no effort should be spared in getting to the bottom of these relationships.[8] One way of doing this is to imagine an economy where all payments are effected without the use of actual currency. Evidently, in such case, there would no longer be any limit to the power of the banks to create credit. The more widely extended is the system of transactions effected without cash, the greater becomes the power of the banks to "manufacture" credit. Yet again, we may compare a bank with the cloakroom of a theatre. In both cases we deposit something: in the bank, currency and in the cloakroom, our hats; in both cases in exchange for a receipt which authorizes us to reclaim what we have deposited. But while the cloakroom employees cannot count on the theatre-goer's *not* presenting his receipt because he regards it as just as good as his headgear, the bank may safely assume that its clients will in fact consider their receipts (i.e., their right to claim their deposits) to be equally as good as their deposits. A bank is in consequence an institution which, finding it possible to hold less cash than it promises to pay and living on the difference, regularly promises more than it could actually pay should the worse come to the worst.

Indeed, it is one of the essential features of a modern bank that alone it is unable to meet a simultaneous presentation for payment of all the debts owed by it ("run on the bank").

When the whole banking system of a country is subject to a run, as in the United States in 1933, it is an event of very grave import. For then the whole ingenious system of immaterial money, founded on convention and on trust, suddenly crashes down and the desire of the public for solid cash erupts with elemental force. What then takes place is a sudden panic collapse of the credit edifice to some anterior stage of monetary evolution. In this headlong retrogression money may fall back past even the paper bank-note stage to full-value coins or, in more drastic cases, to unstamped pieces of the precious metals. In the '30's, a number of countries underwent such monetary crises and their effects are still being felt.

The so-called "creation of credit" by commercial banks is possible only because the circulation of short-term credit is equivalent to a circulation of money. To create credit, then, is to create money. This mysterious and seemingly sinister phenomenon may be better understood by once again comparing checks (or demand deposits) with bank notes and by recalling the historic discussion of the problems of bank note issuance. Two important facts emerge from such reflection: (1) bank notes can be printed *ad hoc,* as the occasion demands; (2) the commercial bank, with its power of creating credit, differs in this respect only in degree and not in kind from the note-issuing bank. No one, certainly, will gainsay the first point. For the truth of our second observation, we have only to recall that the transfer of a demand deposit from one person to another by means of a check, coupled with the confidence of the parties to such a transaction in the solvency of the bank, causes this deposit to circulate exactly as money.

Checking accounts may be regarded as money held on the bank's books and awaiting withdrawal; checks and drafts drawn on these accounts are, therefore, simply means by which such book money is put into circulation. In the extent to which, in accordance with the law of great numbers, deposits and withdrawals offset each other, and to the extent, furthermore, that the circulation of demand deposits is confined to the banking system's circle of customers, it is not required to maintain a 100 per cent reserve behind such deposits. On the contrary, a bank can, as we have seen, loan out a part of its deposited funds, even though such funds are callable by the bank's depositors at any time. Bank notes and demand deposits are thus very similar to each other. Both have this in common, that they are circulating claims which the banks write against themselves and which they can create to an extent equal to some multiple of their cash reserves. The only difference between them is that the acceptability of demand deposits for purposes of general circulation is more limited than that of bank notes, but this is a difference of degree and not of kind.

Few will contest the fact that since bank notes are actual money and can be issued theoretically in unlimited amounts, there should be some kind of legal control over the note-issuing power. This is all the more necessary since in practically all countries bank notes are full legal tender even though they are no longer redeemable in specie. But it is interesting to recall that the power of banks to issue notes at will and thus to increase the supply of money was once just as controversial as is today the corresponding, if more limited power of the commercial banks to create credit.

To be sure, the issuance of bank notes has always been regarded as an undertaking fraught with risk to the community. The history of the note-issuing banks is a long and anguished one, dotted with ruined banks and—what is even more depressing—strewn with the memorials of wrecked monetary systems. "Never," said the English economist Ricardo 150 years ago, "has a bank which had unlimited power to issue paper money not abused that power." Thus the conviction grew that the issuing of bank notes should be subject to definite limitation. But where ought the limits to be placed? On this point there was a very heated argument one hundred years ago between two schools—the Currency School and the Banking School. Their differences, even after the lapse of a century, have lost none of their significance.

The opinion of the Banking School with respect to the phenomenon of credit creation may be summarized as follows: bank notes and demand deposits are similar inasmuch as both are phenomena pertaining to banking—hence the name "Banking School"—but neither exert any active influence on the monetary system. In the rigid view of this School, the monetary system will remain shipshape so long as bank notes enter circulation through banking operations alone, that is, through short-term credit transactions. In these circumstances, every legal barrier to the issuance of bank notes would be harmful while, conversely, unrestricted powers of issuance would

be absolutely indispensable to maintaining elasticity of the supply
of currency, and to adjusting this supply to the fluctuating needs
of business. This adjustment would ensue automatically because
demands for credit on the note-issuing banks would rise or fall as
general economic activity rose or fell. Thus, the position of the
note-issuing banks with respect to the increase or decrease of the
volume of bank notes would be a completely passive one, since the
volume of bank notes would depend on the money and credit needs
of the business community and not on the volition of the note-issuing banks. A change in the volume of currency would be not the
cause but only the effect of events occurring in the sphere of production, or of changes in the price level, or of cyclical changes, or of
variations in the rates of foreign exchange, etc. Every attempt of the
banks to alter the volume of currency above or below the requirements of business would fail; if too many notes were issued, the
excess would flow back to the banks, while if not enough were
issued, business would resort to other circulating instruments.

The Currency School, in contradistinction to the Banking School,
considered bank notes to be a money phenomenon and not a credit
phenomenon. It reasoned, therefore, that the issuance of bank notes
should be just as jealously supervised as the issuance of any other
kind of money. In opposition to the Banking School, it argued
logically that the sum total of bank credits is not unaffected by the
policy of the note-issuing bank which fixes the conditions of credit,
particularly the rate of interest. The issuance of bank notes is to
be considered like any other creation of money and there is nothing
in the nature of the operation of the note-issuing bank which could
prevent either an excessive creation of credit (credit inflation) or
an insufficiency of credit (credit deflation). Hence, the issuance of
bank notes requires strict legal supervision. But this much established, the Currency School forgot that demand deposits can be just
as much a source of credit inflation or of credit deflation as bank
notes. As a result, the adherents of this school suffered considerable
disillusionment when the severe restrictions on the issuance of
bank notes embodied in the famous English Bank Act of 1844 failed
to solve the problems incident on credit creation; indeed, these
restrictions on bank-note issues served to stimulate the growth of
the demand deposit (check) system. The more rapid the increase in
the last hundred years of the importance of demand deposits in
business transactions, the clearer it has become that regulation of

the note-issuing banks alone will not suffice to cope with the exceedingly difficult problems attendant on credit creation. Control of the note-issuing banks must be supplemented by regulation of the demand-deposit system.

Though academic economists are now unanimously of the opinion that commercial banks can and do create credit, there is many a practical man of affairs who is inclined to view such "theories" with skepticism. There are still people in the banking world who hold that their own experience invalidates the creation of credit theory *in toto*. Such skepticism may be traced, in part, to exaggerated or incomplete descriptions of the process of credit creation. We must guard against overstating our case, for there are, of course, the limits to this process which were noted in an earlier part of this chapter. We also must take into account the optical illusion which causes the individual banker to view the aforementioned process in a radically different way than the economist who surveys the banking system as a whole. Thus the individual bank cannot continue indefinitely to make loans, for the cash reserve it must maintain clearly sets a limit to its loanable funds. If Bank A considers a reserve of 10 per cent adequate, then it can only loan out 90 per cent of its deposited cash. But the process of credit expansion is not therewith concluded because this 90 per cent will ordinarily become a *primary* deposit in Bank B which again loans out 90 per cent, etc. When the process is continued throughout the entire banking system it will be found that eventually nine times the original amount of cash deposited in the system will have been extended in loans ($9/10 + 9/10 \cdot 9/10 + 9/10 \cdot 9/10 \cdot 9/10 \ldots$ $\ldots 9/10^n$). We see that the "enigma of the banking system" (Philipps) consists in a given amount of cash becoming the basis for a towering edifice of credits and deposits, though this is clearly not the case with respect to the individual bank. Hence, by the very nature of the complicated process to which we have just alluded, it becomes impossible to distinguish between genuinely primary cash deposits and those derivative deposits that come into being through the creation of credit. Consequently, we can readily see why an individual banker will so vehemently deny the process of credit creation, a process that to us appears so self-evident. Such denial absolves the individual bank of the "guilt" (or at any rate of the responsibility) of creating additional credit. Now when we said that a bank must pay heed to its cash reserves, we said nothing more than that it must stay *liquid*. The degree of liquidity desired or required fixes the outer limits to a bank's powers of credit creation, provided, of course, that actual currency is not completely displaced by demand deposits (check money) centralized in a single bank.

Two conclusions may be drawn from the foregoing analysis. First, that the global sum of a country's demand deposits does not represent pure saving, but is in large part a consequence of the creation of bank credit. This is something which must never be lost sight of in considering any economic problem. The second conclusion is that money and credit constitute an entity, the complexities of which place a number of formidable difficulties in the path towards economic and monetary stability. A bank is no ordinary commercial enterprise. It is not just a cloakroom where we deposit our monetary property for safekeeping, or a kind of shop where one rents costumes for a masquerade, but an enterprise which exercises a profound influence on the circulation of money and thus on the entire economic process. Consequently, the thought never occurs even to the most intransigent European liberal to abandon the control of such an enterprise to itself. And so we repeat: he who does not understand the role of the banking system is incapable of understanding the operation of the modern economic system.

4. *Inflation and Deflation*

The foregoing description of credit creation and of the problems generated by this process has shown us how important it is that the economic system be assured of monetary stability. We also learned how difficult it is to prevent those monetary diseases (inflation and deflation) which destroy this stability. Let us begin by setting forth the nature of the problem as realistically as we can. Let us suppose that, in the year 1913, a dentist made a wager with his patient that the price of the gold filling he was about to insert would follow the general rise in prices which was then getting under way. The dentist, of course, would have lost his wager; a quick glance at his files on his previous gold purchases could have told him as much. For the simple and ingenious coupling mechanism of the gold standard, by defining the monetary unit as a fixed weight of gold, tied gold to money in such wise that the price of gold remained stable though all other prices fluctuated.

A contrasting and yet equally illuminating experience is one which was recounted to the author by a lady of his acquaintance. She showed him a magnificent belt of wrought silver which she acquired in India on a visit there with her husband towards the end of the last century. She explained proudly that she had got a wonderful bargain inasmuch as the native jeweler had demanded for his silver belt neither more or less than its weight in silver rupees. Had she not thereby gotten the exquisite handiwork for nothing? In truth, the lady's satisfaction in her bargaining ability was premature for at the time of her visit the pure silver standard in India had been replaced by a blocked silver standard. When the Indian government discontinued the free coinage of silver, silver became scarcer in minted form than in unminted form; the bonds linking money to a precious metal, corresponding to those of the gold standard, had been broken, causing the mint value of the silver rupee to exceed considerably the value of silver itself. The rupee became a kind of metal bank note whose scarcity was determined not by the production of silver but by the decision of the issuing government. To underscore the moral of this story, we have only to visualize a transaction wherein a purchaser of visiting cards is required to pay a quantity of paper money equal to the weight of the cards.

And now a third illustration which takes us from the gold standard and the blocked silver standard to *paper money*. More than a quarter of a century ago, an astonishing and ingenious crime was committed which resulted in the institution of a most interesting civil suit. A band of international swindlers succeeded in convincing the well-known London firm of Waterlow & Sons, engravers of postage stamps and bank notes, that they were the representatives of the Central Bank of Portugal come to place an order for the printing of a large quantity of Portuguese bank notes. The order was duly filled and the bank notes delivered to the swindlers. When the fraud was finally discovered, the Bank of Portugal caused all of its extant notes (of whose genuineness there was, naturally, no question) to be withdrawn from circulation and replaced with a new issue. Since it proved impossible to catch the criminals, the Bank of Portugal sued Waterlow & Sons, demanding that the engraving firm make good the losses resulting from the issue of the fraudulent notes. The English courts presently discovered that the case involved issues of unusual subtlety and complexity, adjudication of which necessitated the admission of testimony by leading monetary theorists. The question before the courts was: how great were the actual losses incurred by the Bank of Portugal? If it had been post-age stamps instead of bank notes in which the swindlers had traf-ficked, it is perfectly clear that the loss of the Portuguese government would have equaled the total value of the stamps. With respect to the bank notes, however, no such simple calculation could be made. Among the many questions which troubled the experts the follow-ing stand out as particularly relevant to our study: would the Bank of Portugal have issued the same amount of notes even if the swin-dlers had not done so? If not, was the increase in the supply of money resulting from the introduction of the fraudulent notes good or bad for Portugal? The answer to this question would depend on whether the circulation of the fraudulent notes disrupted the orderly processes of the Portuguese economy looking to the regula-tion of the volume of money; it would depend, in other words, on whether the additional notes served to avert an otherwise imminent deflation, or whether they resulted in an inflation. If the first supposition were true, then the swindlers would have unintention-ally done a favor to Portugal. These and other considerations did, in fact, influence the highest English court to award the Bank of Portugal only a fraction of the damages it had claimed.*

What lessons are contained in these three illustrations? They point to the truth of at least these three principles: (1) the value of money is determined by its relative scarcity; (2) monetary policy has no more important task than to regulate this scarcity in such wise that the value of money remains as stable as possible; (3) this task can be accomplished in different ways. Under a gold standard (or a silver standard with free coinage of fully-valued coins), the scarcity of money is automatically fixed by the scarcity of the standard metal. This, in turn, is affected primarily by the quantity of the metal which is produced in a given period. Such relationships are char-acteristic of so-called *tied monetary standards* under which money is linked securely to a precious metal with the regulation of the quan-tity of money being a function and a reflection of variations in the quantity of the precious metal. Under the "blocked" silver stand-ard and, *a fortiori*, under the paper standard, the quantity of money is independent of the quantity of the precious metal and is regu-lated by the arbitrary decree of the government *(free or manipu-*

*See C. H. Kisch, *The Portuguese Bank Note Case* (London, 1932).

lated standard). The determination of whether the control of the quantity of money should be submitted to the automatic forces of gold and silver production or to the conscious decree of the government is one of the cardinal problems confronting those entrusted with the making of monetary policy and upon the answer to which depends the choice of the particular monetary system in each case. A liberal—one [in Europe] who puts his trust in economic laws rather than in the whims of government—will generally opt for the tied or automatic standard. A collectivist—one who is willing to trust the caprice of the government over natural economic forces —will prefer the untied or manipulated standard. Since, however, the linking of money to a precious metal implies a much stricter control over the quantity of money than can be expected from arbitrary government regulation, we find that, paradoxically, it is the [European] liberal who, in money matters at least, demands a discipline far stricter than the collectivist.

It is, indeed, not surprising that the liberal should attach such importance to the maintenance of effective and positive control over the quantity of money and that he should desire in this case at least, that nothing should be left to chance. It was an English liberal of the early nineteenth century and one of the leading adherents of the Currency School, Lord Overstone, who drew the clear and emphatic distinction between money and goods. There is no sense, he observed, in applying to the manufacture of money the principle of cheap and abundant production which, with regard to the manufacture of goods, the liberal expects to find operating in a competitive economy. What is essential in the case of money, on the contrary, is strict control of its quantity. While the liberal holds private initiative and free competition to be desirable in the realm of goods production, he knows that judicious regulation of the quantity of money cannot be expected to emanate from those sources. What is needed instead is a carefully thought-out system of monetary control instituted and supervised by government. *If in the production of goods the most important pedal is the accelerator, in the production of money it is the brake.* To insure that this brake works automatically and independently of the whims of government and the pressure of parties and groups seeking "easy money" has been one of the main functions of the gold standard. That the liberal should prefer the automatic brake of gold to the whims of government in its role of trustee of a managed currency is understandable.

This distrust of the manipulated monetary standard is not alone a consequence of the liberal philosophy. Almost the whole course of monetary history vindicates this distrust. For as money has become increasingly etherealized—attaining the pinnacle of incorporeality and insubstantiality in the form of credit money—the danger of arbitrariness and caprice in the regulation of the quantity of money has become correspondingly greater. It is, of course, true that even the standard metals have been at times subject to considerable fluctuations in value. But these have been negligible compared with the monetary fluctuations which have occurred since manipulated standards have been adopted, and the laws of nature and of economics exchanged for the unpredictable caprices of politicians and governments. It was the paper standard which first taught us the meaning of the word "inflation." Indeed, it would be difficult to cite a single paper standard which has not sooner or later succumbed to depreciation because the government concerned was unable or perhaps even unwilling to keep the quantity of money within limits.

It should by now be clear that the quantity of money in circulation decisively affects the *purchasing power of money,* an increase in the supply of money lowering its purchasing power (inflation), a decrease raising it (deflation). In the long run, the first mentioned danger of an inflationary increase in the money supply has always been decidedly greater than that of a deflationary reduction in the supply of money. The temptation to engage in inflation is omnipresent for its immediate consequences are usually very popular. Recent history knows no case of the murder of a statesman responsible for inflation. On the other hand, there have been at least several instances in which statesmen thought to be responsible for deflation have been done in (e.g., in Czechoslovakia and Japan). This one example may suffice to show that arbitrariness in the matter of issuing money tends more in the direction of the "too much" than in the direction of the "too little." And indeed every money of which we have record has at some time in its history been prey to the disease of inflation which, if it has not proved fatal, has left the permanent scar of depreciation. If we lay side by side a modern bank note and the gold coin which is its equivalent, we could lay heavy odds on the certainty that in a hundred years' time the bank note—even the "hardest" and most respectable—will have suffered the ignominy of depreciation while the piece of gold will still enjoy the same valuation and the same esteem as the gold pieces of King Croesus of Lydia enjoyed 2,500 years ago. The most finely-spun theories on the stupidity of the gold standard, all the clever satires on mankind's frenetic digging for the yellow metal, and all the ingenious schemes for creating a gold-less money will never change the truly remarkable fact that for thousands of years men have continued to regard gold as the commodity of highest and surest worth and as the most secure anchor of wealth. One may protest this as often as one likes—the fact remains. It is this stubborn fact that continues to make the gold standard the best and most eminently useful of all monetary systems.

Our researches thus far have perhaps yielded sufficient proof of the theory that the value or the purchasing power of money is determined primarily by the proportion of the quantity of money to the volume of goods *(quantity or scarcity theory of money)*. Hence, those abrupt changes in the purchasing power of money which are the characteristic symptoms of the monetary diseases of inflation and deflation will be found to have originated in a marked increase or decrease in the quantity of money (including credit money). The most important prerequisite of an orderly monetary system is therefore the regulation of the quantity of money in such wise that the monetary system is immunized against the ever-present contagion of inflation.

These considerations need to be emphasized at a time like the present marked as it is by a rash of risky monetary schemes aimed at banishing the dominant bogey of our time—deflation.[9] In the long run, we repeat, it is inflation, and nowadays especially the insidious inflation of credit money, which constitutes the greatest and most imminent danger. Indeed, the effectiveness (or lack of it) in keeping money scarce may well serve as a criterion by which we may judge and understand, in its minutest operations, the performance of any monetary system whatsoever. The linking of money to a precious metal, the establishment of reserve requirements by central banks, the strenuous efforts to control the operations of the note-issuing banks—all these measures serve the same ultimate aim of keeping money scarce. And now for decades the world has been wrestling with the ever more acute problem of finding the most efficacious methods of braking the credit-creating powers of the modern banking system. In the long run, moreover, it is the greater or smaller degree of scarcity of money in an economy which determines the exchange relationships between domestic and foreign money (the exchange rate).[10]

Our generation, which recalls the despair caused by the inflations in the post World War I era and which was required to undergo the self-same catastrophes following World War II, needs no instruction concerning the fact that the worst disease with which a monetary system can be afflicted is that kind of inflation which is caused by a deficit of the government budget. The German inflation of the years 1920-23 will always remain as a horrible example of what happens when a government attempts to cover its budget deficits by resorting to the deceitful and irresponsible expedient of the printing press. What in Germany began as "deficit financing" ended in a series of catastrophic price rises which caused the shameless enrichment of some at the cost of the hopeless impoverishment of others, and in a serious undermining of the whole economic and social structure. But the inflationary creation of money caused by the budget deficits of government need not necessarily lead to the economic and social disorders attendant on an *open inflation* of the kind that followed World War I. Beginning in 1933, National Socialist Germany demonstrated that a determined government can change an open into a *repressed inflation* by placing the country in the economic strait jacket of a command economy. Rationing, the imposition of stringent controls on wages, consumption, capital investment, rates of interest, and similar measures aimed at restricting the free use of the increasing amount of purchasing power may succeed in containing for an indefinite period the mounting inflationary pressure on prices, wages, exchange rates, stock prices, etc.

Since Hitler has shown how far and how long a government can neutralize an inflation by means of the command economy, we may well ask ourselves whether from now on there will be any government which will not follow the same road when it disposes of a functioning coercive apparatus. The greater the inflationary pressure the stronger will be the counterpressure of the command economy needed to repress it. By the same token, the command economy must resort to ever more comprehensive and ruthless controls if it is to effectively contain the mounting forces of inflation. This leads logically to the question of whether such a command economy is possible without totalitarian slavery (of which the Third Reich was such a repellent example).

The experience of Germany demands that we consider a little more closely this peculiar phenomenon of *repressed inflation*. As we have seen, it consists, fundamentally, in the fact that a government first promotes inflation but then seeks to interdict its influence on prices and rates of exchange by imposing the now familiar wartime devices of rationing and fixed prices, together with the requisite enforcement measures. As inflationary pressures force up prices, costs, and exchange rates, the ever more comprehensive and elaborate apparatus of the command economy seeks to repress this upward movement with the countermeasures of the police state. The repressed inflation can be conceived of, then, as the deliberate maintenance of a system of coercive and fictitious values in which, economically speaking, there is neither rhyme nor reason. Such a system is an inevitable feature of a collectivist economic regime and is to be encountered wherever socialism has gained control of influence (Soviet Union, National Socialist Germany, Austria, Great Britain, Sweden, and some other European countries). Where this repressed inflation leads was shown with tragic incisiveness in the complete disintegration of the German economy, a process which was arrested only by the comprehensive economic and monetary reform which restored a free price system in which actual rather than fictitious supply-demand relationships were reflected (Summer, 1948). The prolongation of a policy of repressed inflation means that all economic values become increasingly fictitious, and this in a twofold sense: (1) stated values correspond less and less to actual scarcity relationships and (2) fewer and fewer transactions are completed on the basis of such values. The distortion of all value relationships which accompany the division of the economy into "official" and "black" markets, and the struggle between the directives of the market and those of the administrative authorities finally lead to chaos, to a situation in which any kind of order, whether of the collectivist or the market economy type, is lacking.

We see, then, that a repressed inflation is *worse* than an open one because, in the end, money loses not only its function as a medium of exchange and as a measure of value (as happens in the last stages of an open inflation), but also its even more important function as a stimulus to the production and distribution of maximum quantities of goods. Repressed inflation is a road which ends inevitably in chaos and paralysis. The more values are raised by inflation, the more will the authorities feel compelled to use their machinery of compulsion. But the more fictitious the system of compulsory values, the greater will be the economic chaos and the public discontent and the more threadbare either the authority of the government or its claim to be democratic. If the repressed inflation is not stopped in time it will, drawing strength from its own momentum, lead to the dissolution of economic activity and perhaps even of the state itself. This modern economic disease is one of the most serious of all; it is doubly pernicious since it tends to be recognized only when it is in an advanced stage.[11]

Today in 1962, inflation, in the particularly pernicious form of repressed inflation it took in the immediate postwar period, has been overcome in a majority of the developed industrial countries of the free world, if not in a large number of underdeveloped countries and in the Communist states of whose economic systems it constitutes an integral part. This does not mean, of course, that inflation may be considered as banished. Instead of the clearly distinguishable forms it has hitherto assumed, inflation has taken on a *creeping* character, the analysis of which is not an easy task. Two particularly noticeable types of this "creeping inflation" are the so-called "wage inflation" and the so-called "imported inflation."[12]

By wage inflation is meant the inflationary impulses originating in the labor market, and which take the form of wage increases which —in those labor markets dominated by powerful labor unions—are so rapid and of such large amount that the ratio between goods and money is upset. The result is on the one hand an inflationary overpressure of demand and, on the other, an increase in costs which may bring an increase in prices in its train, though in both cases inflation is possible only to the extent that the monetary and fiscal authorities permit the creation of a corresponding addition to the supply of money. Were such additions to the supply of money not permitted, the wage and/or price increases would have the effect of making some portion of domestic output unsaleable and thus cause unemployment. But when the government and the central bank of a country believe themselves obliged to maintain full employment despite wage increases, the choice they then face of accepting some unemployment or some inflation will often be decided in favor of inflation. The decision may also be, as has been the case for some time in the United States, to effect a compromise between these two alternatives. In such case, unemployment and economic stagnation are joined to continuous, if mild price increases. In the United States, labor union power of a degree unknown in Europe has caused a wage inflation of such a severe and chronic type that the government and the central bank (the Federal Reserve System) have been obliged—in the interest of avoiding unfavorable effects on the balance of payments—to go further in the direction of tight money than they would otherwise dare to go, given the risks implicit in such policies of unemployment and economic stagnation.

We may speak of *imported inflation* where a country such as West Germany achieves a continuous surplus in its balance of payments (i.e., an excess of payments from abroad over payments to abroad, irrespective of the transactions giving rise to such payments). Since the surplus takes the form of a net receipt of foreign monies or gold which the central bank (the Deutsche Bundesbank) is obliged to convert into domestic currency, its end effect is to expand the domestic money supply. Because the increase in the quantity of money is not offset by an increase in the quantity of goods—the surplus itself being due to the exportation of a portion of domestic output without any corresponding importation of goods—such "monetization of the balance of payments surplus" becomes the agent in an inflationary increase of prices, wages, investments, consumer demand, and in the emergence of an acute shortage of labor (over-employment). The inflation in such case is not the "fault" of the domestic monetary authorities, but is brought in from outside, is "imported." The origin of the balance of payments surpluses which cause such imported inflation lies, paradoxically, in the fact that in the affected country (Germany in our example) efforts to control creeping inflation by means of stricter monetary and fiscal discipline are more successful than elsewhere. In the specific case of West Germany, moreover, part of the reason for the surplus was the fact that the competitiveness of the German economy was continually increased as the result of advances in production and distribution techniques and the reestablishment of contact with foreign markets in the years following war and occupation. The result was that Germany was a country which, until the revaluation of the Deutschemark in March 1961, remained "cheap" in relation to other countries. The only effective remedy for this particularly virulent form of inflation was the surgical operation of changing the rate of exchange: the international purchasing power of the Deutschemark was increased in order that its internal purchasing power be prevented from falling.[13]

5. *The Purchasing Power of Money and Its Measurement*

Implicit in the preceding section are a number of exceptionally complex problems which we must seek to make explicit, at least. Even the concept of the purchasing power of money—called also the "value of money"—is a problematical one. In contrast to ordinary goods, money, the good in terms of which the prices of the "ordinary" goods are expressed, has itself no price, at least within the area in which it circulates as money. Outside of this area, it cannot logically be used as money, so that the price at which it sells on currency markets in terms of the monetary units of other payment areas (exchange rate) represents not the price of money considered as money but of money considered as merchandise. As an indicator of the "value" of money, the exchange rate is consequently of no use to us, no more than the fact that for one dollar we can obtain one hundred cents. For help in this problem, we must turn to another concept, viz., that the purchasing power of money is a function of the height of the price level; or in other words that it is a reflection of the average rate at which goods and money exchange for one another. If prices rise, the purchasing power of money falls; if prices fall, the purchasing power of money rises. However, every rise in an individual price is not equivalent to a fall in the purchasing power of money. A genuine fall in the purchasing power of money will take place only if there is an average rise in prices all along the line, a rise in the "general price level." Otherwise, we have to do simply with a rise in the prices of some goods, not with a depreciation of money. The purchasing power of money can be measured, therefore, only by the average "bundle" of goods and services that can be bought for a monetary unit.

But such a definition does not advance us much, as the following illustration will show. As it happens, our forbears in antiquity have left us the interesting piece of information that the construction of the Propylaea on the Acropolis in Athens cost a little more than 2,000 gold talents. Was this dear or cheap? Naturally, the talent is not negotiable on the exchanges of our day, but on the basis of its gold content we can establish that a sum of 2,000 talents would be equivalent to about 4,000,000 gold dollars. But was the purchasing power of the 2,000 talents equal to that of 4,000,000 gold dollars? We must admit that we are completely in the dark about this. It is possible that in ancient Athens, bread and eggs were much cheaper than they are today in New York or London; on the other hand, some things were probably more expensive than they are today, some, indeed, infinitely more expensive—things which all the gold in antiquity could not buy for the simple reason that they did not exist. Such were the radio, the telephone, electricity, and other goods upon which we moderns place such great value. Since the composition of demand has completely changed, we lack the means of comparing the purchasing power of money of those times with that of our own. Moreover, comparisons of purchasing power cannot be made unless we know the relative importance of each item in that average or typical "bundle" of goods of which we have spoken, and this relative importance of the different items varies in the course of the years. Hence, *historical comparisons* of purchasing power are always matters of conjecture, more or less. Furthermore, since the relative importance of each commodity varies not only from century to century but also from country to country, comparisons of the value of money are exceedingly difficult to make not only in time but also in space. True, we hear talk of expensive countries and cheap countries, and there is no denying that with an equal sum of money a traveler may be better off in one country than in another. But it is only with serious qualifications that we can accept the flat assertion that four German marks have the same purchasing power as one United States dollar.* Many who have spent longer periods of time in the one and in the other country, and whose scales of preferences differ, may rightly question the validity of such parities, proving once again how questionable are all such calculations of average purchasing power.

The extremely problematical character of such average estimates may be seen in an analogous kind of measurement. Every skier knows that meteorological data describing the snow as being of a depth of so and so many inches will often be unreliable; violent winds or a hot sun may have left his favorite slopes bare of snow. The practice of announcing the average fall of snow is not, for all that, devoid of utility. But if we would really like to establish what the average fall is, we should eventually have to measure the depth of the snow in all locations and to reduce to an average these numerous particular data. But even then we would have omitted to consider a fact of

*The official rate of exchange as of 1962 was 4 Deutschemarks to 1 dollar.

especial interest to skiers, namely, that though some slopes may be superbly covered, there will be others completely denuded of snow. Measurement of the snowfall in all places is patently impossible, but another possibility remains. We can content ourselves with measuring the fall of snow in fifty places, and with these partial measurements estimate the average fall, taking into account the area covered at a given height by the snowfall. In other words, we use a practicable number of particular measurements and then "weigh" the results according to their importance. This is exactly the way in which we attempt to estimate the average level of prices (and the variations from it): we ascertain this level by means of so-called *index numbers*. We are now aware, however, that there is a certain arbitrariness which enters into all such calculations.[14] This arbitrariness, we may add, is limited in its effects, being of less importance the greater is the change in the value of money. For example, during the German inflation, the crudest index numbers still served their purpose. Vice versa, a change in the value of money can be unambiguously determined only when the change is one of large degree.

If the concept of the purchasing power of money is problematical, the supposed connection between the purchasing power of money and the quantity of money, of which we have already made mention, is equally so. It does not detract from the fundamental truth of the quantity theory of money to add that there are features of this theory which are, to say the least, highly problematical.[15] As it is hardly possible to give here even a brief description of the more doubtful aspects of the quantity theory, we shall content ourselves with two important observations. We should note, *in the first place,* that the quantity of money is not the sole determinant of its purchasing power. It is clear that if the quantity of money remains the same while the quantity of goods offered for sale varies, the purchasing power of money will vary correspondingly. *Secondly,* it is clear that it is not simply the quantity of money which determines purchasing power but only that fraction of it which is actually spent in a given period. If the *rate* at which money is expended (velocity of circulation) increases, the effects on the purchasing power of money will be the same as those caused by an increase in the quantity of money, velocity remaining *unchanged.*[16] *Thirdly,* particular attention should be directed to the fact that the connection between the quantity of money and its purchasing power is less and less problematical the greater is the change in purchasing power. The greater the degree of monetary depreciation, the simpler becomes the analysis of its causes. In the macroscopic proportions of the great German inflation (1920-23), even the crudest form of the quantity theory which attributed the depreciation of the mark only to the gigantic increase in the money supply fitted the facts immeasurably better than those explanations which sought to ascribe the blame to other factors, in particular to Germany's then "passive" (unfavorable) balance of payments.

NOTES

1. (p. 79) *The Recent Evolution of Monetary Theory*

This evolution is marked by a growing tendency to end the isolation of the theory of money from the main body of economic thought. Increasingly, monetary theory has been merged into the theories of credit, of capital, of wages, of interest, of foreign trade, and especially of cyclical theory. There is also increasing recognition of the fact that money is indissolubly linked to all economic phenomena, so that it is no longer sufficient in rigorous analysis to "abstract" from money in order to apprehend more precisely the "real" nature of economic processes. Representative contributions to this—for beginners, rather rarefied—area of inquiry are: J. M. Keynes, *A Treatise on Money* (London, 1930); J. M. Keynes, *The General Theory of Employment, Interest, and Money* (London, 1936); F. A. von Hayek (ed.), *Beiträge zur Geldtheorie* (Vienna, 1933); F. A. von Hayek, *Prices and Production* (2nd ed.; London, 1935); L. v. Mises, *The Theory of Money and Credit* (New Haven, 1953); D. H. Robertson, *Banking Policy and the Price Level* (3rd ed.; London, 1932); R. G. Hawtrey, *Currency and Credit* (3rd ed.; London, 1931); D. H. Robertson, *Essays in Monetary Theory* (London, 1940); Ch. Rist, *Histoire des doctrines relatives au crédit et à la monnaie* (Paris, 1938); G. N. Halm, *Monetary Theory* (2nd ed.; Philadelphia, 1946); G. N. Halm, *Economics of Money and Banking* (Homewood, Ill., 1956); L. Baudin, *La monnaie et la formation des prix* (2nd ed.; Paris, 1947). The following works are suitable as introductions to the theory of money: D. H. Robertson, *Money* (6th ed.; London, 1948); F. Lutz, *Das Grundproblem der Geldverfassung* (Stuttgart, 1936); Luigi Federici, *La moneta e l'oro* (2nd ed.; Milan, 1943); Otto Veit, *Der Wert unseres Geldes* (Frankfurt am Main, 1958).

2. (p. 79) *The Influence of Money on History*

The theory which considers that changes in monetary systems have exerted an active influence on world history may be designated as the monetary interpretation of history. This theory is by no means to be summarily rejected. Cf. J. M. Keynes, *A Treatise on Money, op. cit.,* Chapter 30; M. Herzfeld, "Die Geschichte als Funktion der Geldbewegung," *Archiv für Sozialwissenschaft,* Vol. 56, 1926, pp. 654 ff.

3. (p. 81) *The Legal Character of Money*

Money acquires a strictly legal character when the state confers upon its possessor certain legal rights. Most notable of these are:

1. The right to convert money into other kinds of money. A money endowed with this right is known as "provisional" money (for example, the bank notes which circulated in the gold-standard countries before World War I as contrasted with inconvertible definitive money).

2. The right of the possessor to have his money accepted in payment of debts. Money endowed with this right (legal tender) must be accepted by creditors in settlement of all debts. This right is found in the following three forms:

(a) in the form of an unqualified right of the debtor to have his money accepted in payment of "all debts, public and private" (full legal tender, currency);

(b) in the form of a right to acceptance by creditors up to a certain maximum sum (limited legal tender, subsidiary coin such as silver coins and "minor coins" [nickels and pennies]);

(c) in the form of a right to acceptance only by the state treasury, for example, the gold certificates issued by the United States Treasury and now held only by Federal Reserve banks, or the Rentenmark in Germany after the stabilization of the mark in 1923.

The endowment of the different kinds of money with one of these rights or with a combination of several of these rights represents the principal means of which the state disposes for the regulation and stabilization of the monetary system. But it is an exaggeration to say that this legal character of money constitutes its origin and essence as was maintained by G. F. Knapp in his celebrated *State Theory of Money* (London, 1924). This view is refuted by the simple fact that in every age, including our own, we find monies which manage to function successfully without the sanction of the authorities (optional money or trade money; for example, the dollar notes used in Germany during the great inflation, or the silver Maria Theresa thalers struck in Vienna and used for decades in Abyssinia). The best criticism of Knapp's theory is found in H. S. Ellis, *German Monetary Theory*, 1905-1933 (Cambridge [Mass.], 1934). See also A. Nussbaum, *Money in the Law* (2nd ed.; Brooklyn, N. Y., 1950).

4. (p. 87) *Bimetallism*

When both gold and silver are standard money, the maintenance of the homogeneity of the monetary standard and of monetary stability becomes a knotty problem since, as we know from the experience of the last hundred years, the value relationships of the two metals to one another are subject to wide fluctuation. Two cases must be distinguished: (a) The *parallel standard*. This type of standard exists where gold and silver coins of full value circulate simultaneously without a legal ratio being fixed between them. In this case, the homogeneity of the monetary system is destroyed; there are now two monetary standards within one country between which emerges an exchange relationship (intra-monetary exchange rate) which fluctuates with market conditions exactly as the exchange rate between the currencies of different countries. Even the establishment of an official ratio between the two metals will not eliminate the inconveniences of this system, unless there is a real effort to enforce the ratio. The parallel standard was in general use throughout the world until the beginning of the nineteenth century. Eventually, the growth of business activity led to proposals for a reform of this split standard. (b) The *double standard* (alternative standard). In this case, gold and silver are made standard metals with an exchange ratio between them legally fixed and maintained, at 1: 15½, for example. If there is a change in this value relationship in the metals market, money minted from the metal which has become dearer disappears from circulation (*Gresham's law:* "bad money drives out good"). Under the double standard, coins minted from the metal which has become cheaper will become the dominant medium of exchange. This is so because the public stands to profit by bringing to the mint the lower-priced metal (which was silver at the close of the nineteenth century) and exchanging it for silver coin, since the nominal value of the "under-valued" silver coins is the same as that of the "over-valued" gold coins. If the price of silver should drop sharply, the standard is automatically established on silver as silver alone will be brought to the mint. This result may be forestalled by abolishing the free coinage of silver and by restricting its use to the minting of subsidiary coin. Gold will then be reestablished as the standard money. This, in fact, marks the last stage in the nineteenth-century evolution of monetary standards.

5. (p. 90) *The Function of the Note-issuing Bank*

The problem of the early note-issuing bank—and later of the deposit bank—lay in the fact that it was at once a bank and an institution for issuing money, and that in it were combined the manufacture of both credit and currency. The history of more than a hundred years of banking shows that the dangerous situations thus produced were the prime concern of those entrusted with the making of banking policy. Out of this historical experience have crystallized the following principles:

1. A central bank of issue should be a state enterprise, or at least be placed under rigorous state control (principle of government monopoly).

2. Limitations should be placed upon the issuance of bank notes by the several methods available for this purpose (fixing of reserve requirements, establishing maximum quantities in which bank notes may be issued, taxing of bank notes, etc.).

3. The issuing of bank notes should be closely regulated and the nature of the credit operations involved strictly defined.

The practical result of the application of this last principle has been to limit the granting of credit by banks of issue to short-term working credits for business and industry, and to a particular species of these operations (discounting operations). A study of these limitations, which have been the subject of considerable debate, would take us deep into the domain of credit theory. Cf. L. von Mises, *The Theory of Money and Credit, op. cit.;* Argentarius, *Die Notenbank,* (1922); F. Somary, *Bankpolitik* (3rd ed., 1934); R. G. Hawtrey, *The Art of Central Banking* (London, 1932); J. M. Keynes, *op. cit.;* Victor Morgan, *The Theory and Practice of Central Banking, 1797-1913* (Cambridge, 1943); Otto Veit, *Der Wert unseres Geldes, op. cit.*

6. (p. 90) *The Gold Standard*

Under the gold standard as it existed in most countries prior to 1914, a variety of arrangements caused money and gold to be so closely coupled that the material value and the nominal value of money were identical and all types of money were freely convertible into gold. This coupling mechanism was such that at all times money could be converted into gold, and gold into money at an unchanging and practically identical price. It was the maintenance of this kind of convertibility which was the objective of the prescriptions concerning free coinage of gold, the obligation of the monetary authorities to buy and sell gold at a fixed price, and the freedom to export and import gold. Under such a system, the prices of all goods can change while the price of gold remains the same; gold becomes the "pole star of the monetary universe." The inestimable advantage of the gold standard is that it stabilizes the value of money and protects it from the caprices of governments. Despite the hopeful promises of monetary reformers, not even an approximate equivalent for it has as yet been discovered. Therewith is connected a further advantage of the gold standard, viz., that it united all the countries employing it into an essentially homogeneous monetary system supplied with a *de facto* world money. Cf. W. Röpke, *International Order and Economic Integration* (Dordrecht, Holland, 1959).

7. (p. 90) *The Gold Bullion Standard*

The gold bullion standard, as distinguished from the pure gold standard (gold circulation system), is a system under which the free coinage of gold is abolished and gold coins cease to be legal tender. The coupling mechanism is restricted to the maintenance of a stable ratio between money and a *central fund of gold*. From this fund, gold is sold as before at a fixed price, but only for a limited number of specific purposes, and not in the form of gold coin. Nevertheless, the state treasury must continue to buy gold at a fixed price as it is offered. A variant of the bullion system is the gold exchange standard in which the central fund may consist of foreign exchange instead of, or in addition to gold. This, however, is an extremely questionable substitute which, as experiences with this system up to 1931 demonstrated, can easily lead to international inflation. The gold bullion standard may be properly describe as a "gold" standard since, as a result of its retention of the coupling mechanism, it assures a fixed price for gold, avoids arbitrary fixing of the money supply, and automatically stabilizes rates of exchange. Compared with the true gold standard, it offers the advantage of economizing gold, but it is an advantage which is secured at the cost of certain serious inconveniences. Above all, the automatism of the system is seriously weakened, bringing us one step closer to a paper standard. Cf. F. Machlup, *Die Goldkernwährung*, (1924); W. A. Brown, Jr., *The International Gold Standard Reinterpreted, 1914-1934* (New York, 1940); X. Zolotas, *L'étalon-or en théorie et en pratique* (Paris, 1933); T. E. Gregory, *Gold, Unemployment, and Capitalism* (London, 1933); W. Röpke, *International Order and Economic Integration, op. cit.;* Luigi Federici, *La moneta e l'oro, op. cit.*

8. (p. 92) *The Origin of Credit Money*

The most important sources of further information on this subject are: L. A. Hahn, *Volkswirtchaftliche Theorie des Bankkredits* (3rd ed., 1930) ; L. A. Hahn, *Geld und Kredit* (Frankfurt am Main, 1960); F. A. von Hayek, *Geldtheorie und Konjunkturtheorie* (Vienna, 1929); J. M. Keynes, *A Treatise on Money, op. cit.;* Hans Neisser, *Der Tauschwert des Geldes* (1928); C. A. Philipps, *Bank Credit* (New York, 1920); W. F. Crick, "The Genesis of Bank Deposits," *Economica,* June 1927; Hans Gestrich, *Kredit und Sparen* (2nd ed.; Godesberg, 1948). On the problems connected with the manufacture of credit see F. Lutz, *Das Grundproblem der Geldverfassung, op. cit.*

9. (p. 102) *Projects for Reform of Monetary Standards*

It is undoubtedly correct that a reform of our economic system may be effected, to a large extent, by a reform of the monetary system. But we must proceed with great prudence in order to prevent such an undertaking from ending in disaster. It is unfortunate that the most imprudent of such reform projects are the ones which have the most enthusiastic backing; they attract by their radicalism and by the almost religious zeal which informs their promises to save the world economically and socially by revolutionizing its monetary system. All these theories of "monetary redemption," of which Silvio Gesell's *theory of stamp money* is perhaps the best known, tend with monotonous regularity to end in inflation. Cf. F. Haber, "Geld (Geldreformer)", *Handwörterbuch der Staatswissenschaften,* (4th ed.), Vol. IV; H.T.N. Gaitskell, "Four Monetary Heretics" in *What Everybody Wants to Know about Money* (Cole ed.; London, 1933); L. Federici, *op. cit.,* Chapter III.

10. (p. 103) *The Theory of Exchange Rates*

To explain adequately the theory of exchange rates would require a book, a fact which gives some idea of the complex interrelationships involved. It should never be forgotten that one of the most important determinants of foreign estimate of the value of money is the domestic purchasing power of that money as compared with the domestic purchasing power of foreign money (*theory of purchasing power parities*). Here too, the more macroscopic the relationships involved, that is, the greater the changes in the purchasing power ratios, the more will this factor outweigh others in the final determination of the exchange rate. During the German inflation even the crudest form of the purchasing power parity theory was infinitely more correct than the attempts to explain the fall in the exchange rate of the mark by the "balance of payments deficit." In other words: the principal cause of the fall of the mark exchange rate was an excessive use of the Reichsbank printing press, resulting in a rapid depreciation of the mark within Germany. In comparison with this principal cause, other factors were reduced to insignificance. Under the microscopic conditions of normal times, the interrelationships in question are far more complicated. Cf. G. Haberler, *The Theory of International Trade* (London, 1936); B. Whale, *International Trade* (2nd ed.; London, 1934; a small book which makes an excellent introduction to the subject); F. Machlup, "The Theory of Foreign Exchanges," *Economica*, November 1934; H. v. Stackleberg, "Die Theorie des Wechselkurses bei vollständiger Konkurrenz," *Jahrbücher für Nationalökonomie u. Statistik*, Vol. 161.

11. (p. 105) *Currency Diseases and Their Cure*

From the extensive literature on this subject may be mentioned: C. Bresciani-Turroni, *The Economics of Inflation: a Study of Currency Depreciation in Post-War Germany* (New York, 1940); Frank D. Graham, *Exchange, Prices, and Production in Hyper-Inflation: Germany, 1920-1923* (Princeton, 1930); E. L. Hargreaves, *Restoring Currency Standards* (London, 1926); E. W. Kemmerer, *Modern Currency Reforms* (London, 1928); J. Rueff, *L'ordre social* (Paris, 1947). On "repressed inflation": W. Röpke, "Offene und zurückgestaute Inflation," *Kyklos*, Vol. I, no. 1, 1947; W. Röpke, "Repressed Inflation," *Kyklos*, Vol. I, no. 3, 1947; F. A. Lutz, "The German Currency Reform and the Revival of the German Economy," *Economica*, May 1949.

12. (p. 105) *The "Creeping Inflation" of Today*

For more extensive treatment of this phenomenon, see my book *A Humane Economy* (Chicago, 1960), Chapter IV. Excellent treatments of the subject are G. Haberler, *Inflation, Its Causes and Cures* (Washington, D.C., 1960); Henry Hazlitt, *What You Should Know About Inflation* (New York, 1960).

13. (p. 106) *Imported Inflation*

The phenomenon was described first in my essay of 1956, "Das Dilemma der importierten Inflation" (reprinted in my book *Gegen die Brandung* [2nd ed.; Zurich, 1959]) in which this terminology was also suggested. See also the special section on inflation in my previously mentioned book *A Humane Economy*, pp. 199 ff.

14. (p. 109) *The Measurement of Purchasing Power*

An index number is constructed by selecting the prices of fifty or more representative commodities and multiplying these prices by a coefficient which corresponds to their economic importance (weighted index number). The amounts thus obtained are added together. The average of prices for the year which is selected as a "base", say 1913, is equated with 100; subsequent changes in prices are then expressed as a percentage of the base average (100). For comment on the problematical aspects of such calculations see G. Haberler, *Der Sinn der Indexzahlen* (1927).

15. (p. 109) *The Quantity Theory of Money*

Our observations on the theory of exchange rates apply equally to the quantity theory of money. Considered in detail, it has many problematical aspects, but its basic truth is indisputable; and it is the more apt, the greater is the fluctuation in the value of money. For extended discussion of this theory see the bibliography listed under Note 1.

16. (p. 109) *The Velocity of Circulation of Money*

This concept is based on the fact that within a certain period of time the same piece of money may be used over and over again to purchase different goods. Here again, we may observe the essential difference between money and goods: a loaf of bread can be eaten only once, but a piece of money can be repeatedly used as a medium of exchange so long as it remains in circulation. The faster money is passed from hand to hand or, what amounts to the same thing, the briefer are its rest periods in our pockets, the more it can buy within a given period of time. This speed of circulation of money (or its reciprocal, the average rest period) is affected by various factors, such as the average intervals between income payments, the mode of payment, the degree of differentiation in the economy, the proportion of durable goods to total production, bookkeeping customs, and other factors. Velocity of circulation is an especially sensitive barometer of the public's confidence in the stability of money. Hence, in times of inflation there will be sudden and marked changes in this velocity. The effects on the value of money of an increase in the quantity of money will be aggravated by a rise in the velocity of circulation or, vice versa, a fall in velocity may offset the effects of an increase in quantity. It was particularly easy to follow the working of this monetary law during the great German inflation which followed World War I. It was observed that in the first phase of this inflation, the depreciation of money was less than proportional to the increase in the quantity of money. The reason was to be found in the fact that the public, in the expectation of a future appreciation of the mark, was less disposed to spend money; for this and other reasons (tax evasion and general political uneasiness), the public increased its cash holdings; it "hoarded" money. At the peak of the inflation, however, the depreciation of money was much more than proportional to the increase in the quantity of money. The reason for this was the tremendously accelerated rate of bank-note circulation which followed the complete collapse of public confidence in the mark, the general flight into "real values," and the shortening of all payment intervals necessitated by the galloping currency inflation. The velocity of circulation increased enormously and thereby multiplied many times over the inflationary effects of the increased supply of money. It is interesting, also, to note that while the value of the paper marks in circulation reached an astronomical figure, the gold value of the money supply based on the dollar rate of exchange continued to fall, finally amounting to only a few millions, a clear indication that the depreciation of money was proceeding at a faster rate than the increase in its quantity. On the difficult problems connected with the velocity of circulation of money see M. W. Holtrop, *De Omloopssnelheid van het geld,* (Amsterdam, 1928); F. A. Lutz, "Velocity Analysis and the Theory of the Creation of Deposits," *Economica,* May 1939; H. S. Ellis, "Some Fundamentals in the Theory of Velocity," *Quarterly Journal of Economics,* May 1938; L. Federici, *op. cit.,* Chapter V.

CHAPTER V

THE WORLD OF GOODS AND THE FLOW
OF PRODUCTION

"The world is like a shop stocked full of goods. They
are on sale for work—toil may buy them."*
FRIEDRICH VON LOGAU (1604-1655)

1. *The Social Product and the National Income*

Now that we have studied the structure of the division of labor and discovered in money the indispensable auxiliary of that division of labor, let us go a step further and examine more closely the process which unfolds on these bases, namely, how goods are supplied and distributed.

Let us emphasize at once that the concept "economic good" must be understood in a very broad sense; i.e., it includes all those things which serve as means for satisfying wants. In our economic system these are things for which, as a rule, a price must be paid. Hence, this concept embraces not only material goods as such, but also a wide variety of services (a lawyer's counsel, a physician's examination, a scholar's lecture, a singer's concert) and a final category that may be grouped under the loose designation of "rights and relationships" (right to use a dwelling, patents and copyrights, a physician's practice, the "goodwill" of a firm, etc.). The criterion of price does not always suffice to characterize an economic good. This is especially

---

*The original German verse runs as follows:
"Die Welt ist wie ein Kram, hat Waren ganze Haufen,
Um Arbeit stehen sie feil und sind durch Fleiss zu kaufen."

true in respect to those collective goods which, as in the case of measures taken to ensure internal and external security (e.g., protection against epidemics), satisfy a collective need. These goods the state "produces" and distributes according to the system of collective economy. Thus the work done by a civil servant is an economic good albeit there is no "market" for it. Indeed, it is because of this very circumstance, as we have shown previously (Chapter II, Note 5), that we cannot always be sure that such a "good" answers to a general need.

A procedure which proves useful on several counts is to consider, in concrete terms, the total output of goods and services produced by the nation in a given period of time, say a year. This total yearly output we may term the *social product* (or gross national product), a helpful abstraction of which we shall make use frequently henceforth. It should be remarked that the total of available goods is not identical with the total of consumable goods. A large part of the gross national product is composed not of consumption goods, but of producer goods (capital) which serve for the maintenance of the apparatus of production (renovation, replacement) and also for the extension of that apparatus (expansion, net investment, accumulation of capital). To determine the net national output (i.e., the supply of commodities and services which constitute a real addition to the national economy and which are over and above those required to maintain the productive apparatus intact), we must subtract from the total output (gross product) those goods and services needed for replacement purposes. This subtraction we may designate as "the costs of doing business." Anyone who has ever figured out an income tax will know what this means. An economy in which reserves are not built up to the necessary extent would "eat" its capital; it would "feed on its own substance." Its productive apparatus would fall, bit by bit, into a state of disrepair and, as a consequence, national output would become smaller and smaller in the future. This, in fact, is what occurred in many countries during and after both World Wars.

Just as we designate as personal income what remains at our disposal after subtracting our costs of doing business, so too may we regard *national income*. If this national income is represented in terms of goods and not of money, it is identical with the net national output. Hence, national income may be determined from a study of gross output statistics. In practice, however, it is customary to calculate the national income in another way, viz., by adding together personal incomes, a fact which gives rise to several instructive considerations. For example, do the monthly allowances given to students by their parents figure in the national income? Obviously not, since what may be included under national income are only those incomes arising from the actual production of goods, services, and utilities of whatever kind. Such incomes are a kind of monetary reflection of a corresponding addition to the total of real goods (original income). Clearly, we may not include in the total income those incomes which represent merely transfers of original income (derived income). Otherwise, we would be making the mistake of counting the same thing twice. On the same reasoning, we would not be counting the same thing twice were we to include in the national income the incomes of the household domestic and the government clerk since these incomes result from the "production" of immaterial goods, proof of the demand for which is the fact that they have been paid for.[1] These reflections underscore the broad interpretation which must be given to such concepts as "good" and "productive" if we wish to grasp the essence of economics.

2. The Essence of Production

Of the many heads under which we can classify goods, there is one which takes precedence over all others. The essential note of an economic good is its scarcity in the sense with which we have now become familiar. For certain goods, this scarcity is immediately given, viz., for those goods which cannot be increased by production. Such are the paintings of the old masters or rare vintage wines. The true significance of this category of *scarce goods* will become clear to us when we consider that it includes such important and irreplaceable goods as land (though pedants might insist that land can be increased in quantity by building dikes to wrest it from the sea). And then there is the most important and productive good of all—human labor power. Certainly, it cannot be "produced" in the ordinary sense of the word. In contradistinction to these goods whose scarcity is immediately and unalterably given, there is the great mass of goods which can be increased by production, a circumstance which, as we have seen, does not preclude their possessing the quality of scarceness, but is of sufficient importance to merit our close study.

If the concept "good" must be understood in a very broad sense, so also must the concept *production*. This point must be particularly insisted upon since the layman is always quick to classify as unproductive every activity which does not immediately serve for the production of material goods, especially trade and transportation. To make this point unambiguously clear, let us consider the following: production is never a new creation of matter, but only the creation of a "good," just as consumption is never the annihilation of matter but only the annihilation of a "good." Production cannot add a single atom to the existing quantity of matter but only transforms matter in such wise that it is capable of satisfying a given want. Hence, all production is really only the transformation, the refinement, and the combining of matter, and this applies not only to so-called primary production (agriculture, fishing, forestry, mining, etc.) but also to commercial-industrial production. What is after all the purpose of mining if not to transport to a suitable place material found in an unsuitable place—in other words, to change its location? Hence production is, broadly interpreted, the process of making economic goods available; its quiddity is economic, not technical. The railroad "produces" as does also the merchant, the hotel-keeper, the clerk, the actor. Even a speculator is a producer insofar as he fulfills an economically useful function, and is not to be confused with the unproductive individual who merely exploits the available opportunities for reaping unearned profit.[2]

These considerations are illustrated in the following example. We have seen that the production of coal is nothing else, at bottom, than a change in its location. Coal is of no use to the inhabitants of West Virginia so long as it has not been brought to the surface. Nor is West Virginian coal which has been brought to the surface of any use to the inhabitants of Pittsburgh until it has been transported to that city. What mysterious difference is there between the vertical and the horizontal movement of coal? To satisfy a want, a good must not only exist as such, but it must be in the place where it is demanded. Moreover, it must be in that place at the *time* when it is demanded. And there are a number of other requirements which we as consumers ordinarily expect "goods" to meet: we prefer goods to be available in a wide range of choices; we expect not to have to become connoisseurs in order to be able to rely on the quality of the goods we buy; and we attached increasing value to customer conveniences, to elegant shops, courteous service, attractive packaging, home deliveries, and many other things. All these things, of course, the manufacturer can undertake to do and, in fact, often does (shoe shops run by shoe manufacturers). Nevertheless, in these instances as elsewhere, the principle of the division of labor has proved its worth: most such accessory operations are better performed by enterprises specialized for the purpose. Trade, transportation, and speculation fulfill these intermediate "service" functions. Their apparently autonomous character should not be permitted to obscure the fact that they are really "producing" utilities and services without which the material goods would have for us little or no value. Such enterprises are, indeed, no less "productive" than those concerned with producing material goods. To wax indignant over the difference between the factory price and the retail price ("retail markup") is no more rational than to complain of a "manufacturing markup," i.e., of the increase in the value of the product added within the factory. This does not exclude the possibility that in both cases avoidable costs and wasteful practices will be present, but these are defects which can be most effectively eliminated by competition of greater or lesser degree. If, in recent years, the retail markup has noticeably increased in many sectors of the economy, this merely expresses the fact that we attach increasing value to such ancillary activities.

Much confusion is generated on the above point by continually contrasting the distribution function of trade with production *per se*. The distinction is certainly not fallacious but it must not be forgotten that the distribution of goods appertains equally to production, since it represents a function which is distinct and separate from others and is compensated as such. Unfortunately, the word distribution is also used in quite another sense, namely, in the sense of a distribution of *income,* i.e., the distribution of individual claims on the social product by way of the formation of income. The distribution of goods by trade is a part of production, but, in consequence of the income which he acquires thanks to his distribution function, the merchant, as all other producers, participates in the process of income formation and income distribution. Since we are here dealing with two entirely different things, it would seem preferable to employ different expressions for them and to find some other word for the less abstract concept of goods distribution.[3]

3. *The Economic Process as a Whole*

We have now managed to marshal practically all the data which we need to acquire understanding of the individual parts of the *economic process*. By making a number of simplifying assumptions, in particular, that the social division of labor and the price system are the dominant features of the economic system and that we are concerned with a "closed economy" (one, i.e., without foreign trade), we may picture the operation of the economy in global terms as follows. There is, first, production in the broad sense of that activity which makes available the largest quantities and most numerous kinds of goods possible. Following our previous assumption, this total output is then exchanged on the several markets and its value determined by means of price formation (circulation of goods). The formation of prices, in turn, determines by way of the formation of income that share of the total output which accrues to each individual (distribution). Finally, these shares are used or consumed by the individual economic units. What we have done thus far is to list the several parts of the economic process in their logical order, a procedure which does not imply their successive occurrence in time. We do not suggest, for example, that during a given period of time goods are produced, are later apportioned to the recipients by circulation and distribution, and are finally consumed. In reality, all of these operations take place simultaneously. The economic process is thus a simultaneous process and one in which all the parts are intimately connected to each other and conditioned by each other. This network—which represents a major difficulty in the understanding of theoretical economics—will become even more apparent in the course of the subsequent analysis.

To simplify our inquiry, we have thus far admitted a number of hypotheses, the first of these being that the total output (gross national product) of the economy equals the total supply of the economy in a given time period. This follows naturally from our admission that the whole of production enters the market. But since the producers buy each other's products, the gross national product (i.e., total supply) must, in a state of equilibrium, also equal total demand. If in any considerable degree this is not the case, we are then faced with that total disturbance of the economy known as a *crisis*. It is a truism, moreover, that the gross national product is always equal to the gross income of the economy during the period in question. The latter we may define, initially, as the sum of the various money incomes, incomes which are converted into real goods only by the exchange of "vouchers" acceptable in the "general store" of the national economy; in other words, incomes are converted into goods by market demand. We must, therefore, distinguish between the formation of income and the use of income. But here again we must reckon with the possibility of a twofold disturbance. In the first place, the expenditure (use) of income may be retarded because income earners may hesitate a long time before spending their money (deceleration of the speed of circulation of money, hoarding, deflation). Secondly, the expenditure of income may not correspond to the actual composition of output. In such case, the producers have produced at cross purposes. In this connection, it is necessary to direct attention to the three ways in which income may be used: (1) to obtain goods for immediate use (consumption); (2) to obtain producer goods for the maintenance of the productive apparatus (replacement); (3) to obtain producer goods for the purpose of expanding the productive apparatus (accumulation of capital). This division of the different kinds of income use must correspond, in a state of equilibrium, to the composition of the national output. Otherwise, we shall again have to reckon with the emergence of a state of disequilibrium (crisis). But this is a discussion we have reserved for a special chapter.

One of the most fruitful results of the above analysis will have been to put us on our guard against regarding any one part of the economic process as autonomous and given. All the components of this process are joined together, all are interdependent: supply and demand, producers and consumers, production and purchasing power, the formation and the use of income. For the beginner, nothing is more difficult than to visualize this total process in concrete terms; nothing is more difficult than the job of making it clear to him and, by the same token, nothing is more important than the understanding of this process.[4]

The analysis of the total economic process by manipulation of the gross magnitudes of the economy—macroeconomics as it is now termed in contrast to microeconomic theory which will concern us in the following chapter on "Markets and Prices"—is as old as economics itself. Heavy emphasis on macroeconomics is a characteristic mark of the economic thought of recent decades, a result primarily of the experience of the Great Depression (1929-1933). The ever greater refinement of macroeconomic concepts and the rise of a self-contained national income theory has been accompanied, as well, by an increasingly successful use of statistics to measure the actual global movements of the economy in the course of a year. The usefulness of such calculations is undeniable. But there are also unmistakable dangers connected with the use of the new techniques. They can be avoided only where there is awareness of the limitations of this kind of analysis.[5]

In our analysis of the economic process thus far, we have assumed a "closed economy"; that is to say we have deliberately ignored the actual connection of the domestic economy with the rest of the world. If we now relax this assumption, we find that the domestic economy is joined to the world economy by a multitude of transactions and activities involving the exchange of goods and services, and of a corresponding number of payments made to foreign countries and received from them. This connection may be clearly seen and statistically measured by grouping the various foreign transactions and payments of a nation under several principal headings, somewhat in the manner of a firm's balance sheet. The *balance of payments* of a country is so constructed as to show payments (in domestic currency) received from abroad on the plus or credit side of the balance, and payments to foreign countries on the debit or minus side of the balance. The principal categories of such a balance of payments are: (I) the savings account which shows the net total yield (+ or −) of (1) the merchandise account (the "balance of [visible] trade"), (2) the services account (tourism, transportation, insurance, banking services, copyright payments, etc.), (3) the investment income account (dividends and interest received from abroad or paid to abroad), (4) unilateral transfers (receipts or payments); (II) the investment account which shows the total of capital investments by foreigners in the domestic economy and total investments by domestic residents in other countries; (III) the cash account which shows the increase or decrease in a country's holdings of foreign exchange and/or gold. This yields the following scheme in which the plus or minus sign in each case indicates whether the transaction in question is to be assigned to the credit or debit (active or passive) side of the balance of payments.

I. The Savings Account

1. The balance of trade (visible)
   (a) merchandise exports (+)
   (b) merchandise imports (−)
2. The services account
   (a) services of residents to foreigners, also called "invisible exports" (+)
   (b) services of foreigners to residents, also called "invisible imports" (−)
3. The investment income account
   (a) dividends and interest received from abroad (+)
   (b) dividends and interest paid abroad (−)
4. Unilateral transfers (aid and gifts)

II. The Investment Account

1. Capital imports (+)
2. Capital exports (−)

III. The Cash Account

1. Increase of monetary reserves (−)
2. Decrease of monetary reserves (+)

It is clear that a net surplus yielded by the algebraic sum of the items in any of the above categories may be offset by a net deficit in another category (or categories). Thus in the balance of payments of Switzerland for the year 1959, the large net deficit in the (visible) trade balance was offset by a still larger net surplus yielded by the other items in the Savings Account so that this account as a whole showed a substantial surplus (+ 758 million Swiss francs). This surplus in turn was offset partly by a net debit in the investment account (excess of capital exports over capital imports) and partly in an increase of Swiss monetary reserves. Different was the situation yielded by the West German balance of payments for 1960 in which both the Savings Account and the Investment Account closed with large net credits. The Savings Account was "active" because of the extremely large (favorable) balance of (visible) trade which more than offset the large deficit on services account. The Investment Account yielded a net surplus because of the substantial excess of capital imports over capital exports. The net surplus resulting from the sum of the Savings Account and the Investment Account was offset in turn by a debit on cash account, that is, by a correspondingly large *increase* in Germany's monetary reserves (of almost DM 8 billion [about $2 billion]). In this growth of German monetary reserves was reflected the aforementioned (p. 106) "imported inflation."

It is evident that in the evaluation of the balance of payments position, the greatest caution is indicated. The "activity" or "passivity" of the individual items in the several accounts signify relatively little, as we have seen; what is significant is the *net* position yielded by the sum of all the accounts. But here too circumspection in passing judgment is required.[6] Even to speak of an "active (favorable) or passive (unfavorable or adverse) balance of payments makes for difficulty since such a balance, like a firm's balance sheet, always balances in the sense that the algebraic sum of the credits and debits necessarily equals zero (for every credit there *must* be an offsetting debit, and *vice versa*).

To qualify the balance of payments as active or passive has meaning only to the extent that we abstract from the balance of payments as an accounting device and omit certain accounts (the offsetting ones) in order to focus attention on the disposition of others. Customarily, the cash account is neglected in determining whether the balance of payments is active or passive; it is said to be active (or in surplus) when the algebraic sum of all the accounts except the cash account yields a net surplus, and passive (or in deficit) in the converse case in which the sum of all the accounts except the cash account yields a net deficit. Alternately, one may focus attention solely on the cash account, qualifying the balance of payments as active when monetary reserves increase and passive when they decline. But even here it is not necessarily true that an active balance of payments is something good and a passive balance something bad. Indeed, an active balance of payments can represent a danger for the economy as shown in the example of the imported inflation in West Germany and in other European countries at the present writing (1962). Conversely, a passive balance of payments of a certain duration and amount can serve to restore a disturbed equilibrium of international payments.

It is under no circumstances permissible, however, to see in an active balance of payments the proof of the riches and capital wealth of a country nor in a passive or deficitary balance of payments proof of the poverty and capital insufficiency of an economy. The activity or passivity of the balance of payments involves merely the external equilibrium of an economy (which is, in turn, primarily dependent on monetary factors), not the quantity of commodities and real capital of which it disposes. For years West Germany achieved balance of payments surpluses because it was a comparatively cheap country, but West Germany was made not one penny richer on that account. The United States has suffered for years from a balance of payments deficit, thanks chiefly to the wage policies of American labor unions, and has become a comparatively expensive country. But the United States is today far richer than it was when the world still suffered from a "dollar shortage." France, too, was not poor and insolvent because it suffered from a passive balance of payments thanks to the financial mis-economy of the Fourth Republic. And France did not become rich and solvent overnight merely because the De Gaulle government changed the international value of the franc, put an end to inflation, and thereby converted the balance of payments deficit into a surplus.

4. *The Factors of Production*

Our admonition to regard the economic process as a whole made up of many parts is the more justified in view of the close relationship between the act of production and the act of exchange (circulation). In this connection, the Silesian poet Logau, in the candid aphorism which we have selected as motto for this chapter, happened 300 years ago upon an economic truth which it was left to modern theory to elucidate: *production is, at bottom, nothing else than a perpetual exchange transaction with Nature* by which we seek to exchange on the most advantageous terms our efforts against the produced commodities. It is a transaction in which the concept of marginal utility finds just as pertinent application as in exchange in the narrower and more usual sense.[7] Conversely, it may be said that *exchange is nothing else than production*, i.e., the procuring of goods through the making of corresponding sacrifices. Production and exchange are similar in that both require certain expenditures to obtain a good: indeed, the whole meaning of the social division of labor resides in this, that it permits each of us to choose the most economical way of procuring needed goods. That is the whole secret of the division of labor, especially of the international division of labor, which many find it so hard to understand.

Of what then do the expenditures made in production consist? If we push our inquiry still farther back, we find that all these expenditures may be traced finally to three categories of production elements (*factors of production*) which in turn are not further divisible: labor, land, and capital.

Of these three factors of production, *labor* requires the least explanation. There is no need to define it for it is clear to everyone that labor is the really active and directing element in production. So preeminently important is this factor that it is easy to understand the constantly repeated efforts to make it the sole factor of production and of costs. At all events, we must keep ever in mind that the concept "labor" is to be taken in a sense sufficiently large to encompass all human activity, intellectual as well as physical, directive as well as directed. Thus, the activity of an entrepreneur must be there included. It follows further that the labor factor of production will fall into numerous sub-classes, each of these possessing its own market, its own wage scale, its own special features. Moreover, these individual labor markets will not necessarily stand in close relationship to one another.[8]

Similarly, little difficulty is experienced in comprehending the significance of *land* (or Nature in general) as a factor of production. Its role in production is characterized by the fact that it serves simultaneously as a location (*cf.* Chapter III, Note 1) and as a reservoir of the raw materials and the energy which lie dormant in the land. The latent energy and the raw materials of the earth, to the exploitation of which primary organic production (agriculture, forestry, fishing) and primary inorganic production (mining) are devoted, comprise the final and most basic sources of mankind's supply of goods. In common with the labor factor of production, land exhibits the special characteristic of not forming a homogeneous mass but of falling (according to its location or to its varying content of raw materials) into innumerable sub-classes. The location of the land is of especial importance because, in contrast to the other factors of production, land is immovable: Mohammed must, in truth, always go to the mountain.

Labor and land are things easily grasped, their importance is self-evident and their role in production is clear. Everyone knows that they are indispensable, that they represent ultimate elements of production which are not reducible to any further common denominator. But what about the factor of production we call *capital*? Here begin the difficulties.

Let us start with a fairly simple situation in which capital will figure—the production of grain. When we say that for this purpose we require capital in addition to land and labor, what do we mean? Concretely, we visualize the following requirements: tools, draft animals, seed, fertilizer, farm buildings, machines, and lastly, a supply of foodstuffs (subsistence fund) to be consumed during the time which elapses between sowing and harvesting. This is a roundabout way of expressing the fact that man cultivates the land not only with the bare strength of his arms but with all sorts of auxiliary means as well. But what is the justification for regarding these auxiliary means as a third independent factor of production? Cannot all such items be subsumed under labor and land? For example, a plough contains wood and iron and its manufacture requires the expenditure of a certain amount of labor. The truth is, however, that the plough contains still a third component whose presence, though not immediately visible, can be ascertained by a process of deduction. Let us assume that the farmer makes the plough himself and that in consequence he will have to employ a part of his time in the production of a plough instead of in the production of food. For the farmer, this entails a diminishment of his current supply of consumption goods. As long as he is engaged in making the plough, either he will eat less or he will live from a supply of foodstuffs which he has previously stored up. Should he choose the latter alternative, he will still have had, during some former period, to reduce his consumption in an amount corresponding to his present stock of such foodstuffs. This restriction of consumption pays for itself in the future, however, for a plough, compared with primitive forms of cultivation, will result in an enormous increase in yield. Thus we see that the production of a plough requires not only the combined services of land and labor but a further essential condition—the restriction, in one form or another, of consumption. It is only after this current sacrifice is compensated in the future by the larger yield obtained thanks to the plough that the balance, so to speak, is struck. Until then, the farmer is obliged to wait for the rewards due to his work and to his restriction of consumption. We arrive at the same result if we come somewhat closer to reality and assume that the farmer does not make the plough himself but orders it made by the smith. The smith is then paid in money which the farmer could otherwise have used to buy consumption goods.

By this renunciation of complete enjoyment at the present moment in favor of the future, i.e., by "waiting," capital acquires the character of an independent factor of production, a factor which cannot be subsumed under either land or labor. Since present supplies can be diminished in favor of the future only within fixed limits, the capital factor of production is always scarce. This is a point of the greatest importance and one which has to be borne constantly in mind. Were it not for this fact, it would be difficult to understand why all the scythes in the world have not long since been replaced by mechanical reapers, all the sewing needles by sewing machines, all bicycles by automobiles, and all streetcars by subways. Hence it is that we are obliged to pay a price for this scarce "something" just as we do for butter or for string, and this price is nothing other than interest.

"Waiting," the essential ingredient of the capital factor of production, may take different forms. The form it takes in the case of the (purchased) plough is clear. The money which has been "put" into the plough has been withheld from current consumption uses and the farmer must wait until the extra yield obtained with the plough offsets the amount of his investment. The same principle is involved in building a house where the landlord must wait until the sum of his rents equals the costs of constructing the house. In either case we have to do with that kind of "waiting" which is associated with the *investment of capital* (fixed capital). The purpose of this capital investment is to provide means of production which are to be used over several production periods. But the farmer must take into account still another kind of waiting. Between the plowing and the seeding of the soil and the sale of the harvest stretches a period of several months: in autumn, there are expenditures for labor, seed, and fertilizer which are recovered only after the sale of crops in the summer of the following year. In the meantime, the farmer and his family must live; he must, therefore, have either a supply of consumption goods in reserve or a sum of money for the purchase of such consumption goods. Here again, a period of waiting is involved, but waiting of a different character than that which we observed in the first instance. The farmer must await repayment (for the duration of the period of production) not only for the labor, raw materials, and auxiliary equipment used in the process of production but also for the consumption goods required during this process (subsistence fund). Waiting of this type involves the use of what is termed *working capital* (circulating capital). The relation of fixed capital to working capital is the same as that of a meat-grinding machine to the meat which is put through it.

Naturally, it is not required that the producer himself do the "waiting." By obtaining a loan he can, in effect, shift the burden of waiting onto the shoulders of some other person, the latter receiving his indemnification in the form of interest. Depending upon the kind of "waiting" involved, the credit thus obtained is either an investment credit or an operating credit. The possibility of obtaining such a credit obviously changes nothing with respect to the fact that for the capital thus supplied someone must undergo a period of "waiting," of adjournment of his consumption irrespective of whether this occurs in some sector of the national economy or—as in the case of an international transfer of capital—of the world economy.

We can now see from the very fulness of explanation which it requires that capital is set off from the other two factors of production by a number of peculiarities. It is these peculiarities which make the analysis of capital one of the most difficult problems of economics.[9] Part of the difficulty derives from the circumstance that capital, differently from land and labor, is subject to quantitative changes effected by human decisions and economic considerations. The quantity is increased in a process known as the *formation of capital* and is diminished by the *consumption of capital*.[10] Here it should be observed that a certain fixed amount of capital is available to the economy at any given moment; this amount can be increased within a given period of time, but only within certain limits. There is a way, of course, of stretching these limits and of forcibly increasing the quantity of capital, viz., through credit expansion. But an increase of capital which is effected by such a radical method is ordinarily purchased at the cost of a subsequent crisis.[11]

Finally, we must touch briefly on that aspect of capital which renders it so repugnant to the adversaries of our capitalist system, *the socialists*, and one to which we too cannot remain indifferent. This is the circumstance that capital is not only an elementary factor of production but, in its current context, also a source of private income for which apparently no services are rendered in return. Both notions must be kept rigorously distinct, however. Saying that capital is an indispensable factor of production does not imply that we are taking a position on the question of who should own this factor of production. The first point is uncontested whereas perennial controversy rages around the question of the *ownership of capital*. Naturally, even a socialist state cannot do without capital as a factor of production since in a socialist state, as in any other, it will be necessary to economize so that worn-out machines can be replaced and new ones built. The Russian Five Year Plan is nothing if not such a socialist method of creating capital on a colossal scale. It is not the use of capital which distinguishes the socialist from the capitalist economy, but only the fact that this capital, under socialism, belongs to the state. But we must not imagine that we have refuted socialism simply because we can show that capital is necessary even in a socialist state. No serious socialist questions the necessity of capital; what he demands is that it belong to the "community." Whether this demand is reasonable or not is a question we have reserved for discussion in another place.

5. *The Combination of the Factors of Production*

Under present conditions, it is usual to find the three factors of production combined with one another in every type of production. What is of especial significance in this connection is the fact that it is possible, in considerable degree, to substitute one factor of production for another (*substitution of the factors of production*). Agriculture, for example, can be carried on by combining a given area of land with little labor and capital (extensive agriculture) or with much labor and capital (intensive agriculture). Labor and capital, in turn, may be substituted for one another; there are many tasks which we may choose to entrust either to manual labor or to the machine. Every housewife who buys a washing machine substitutes capital for labor. Careful reflection on her part is required before deciding whether she should or should not make such a purchase. Two motives can influence her decision, one of which has already engaged our attention. We found that the purchase of a machine is warranted only insofar as there exist sufficient opportunities for its use. In calculating whether her laundry is regularly of a sufficient quantity to require the full use of a washing machine, the housewife is unconsciously employing a general principle of great significance designated commonly as the *law of mass produc-*

tion. Using our household laundry as example we may explain this law as follows. The costs of using a washing machine fall into two large groups: the costs which increase or diminish with the amount of laundry (electricity, water, attention required, soap) and those which are given once for all as a fixed amount (interest and amortization on the washing machine). The more clothes there are to wash (the mass or amount of production) the smaller will be the costs of laundering per piece of laundry since the fixed costs are distributed over a greater number of production units.[12] The last piece of laundry is thus the cheapest to do as the last passenger to board a train is, from the point of view of the railroad, the cheapest to transport. Hence the dominant consideration in purchasing a washing machine is that the household regularly furnish a sufficient amount of soiled laundry. To artificially soil the laundry for this purpose, as a kind of harmless family sport, would hardly be the ideal of good housekeeping. It would be well if this point could be driven home to those numerous individuals who strive by equally artificial means to extend the system of mass production throughout the economy.

In deciding whether to buy a washing machine, our housewife will be guided by still another consideration—the relation between the prices of the two factors of production. Where labor is less costly as compared to capital (i.e., where wages are low and interest rates high), the washing machine would prove uneconomical. Where these conditions are reversed, it will pay to use such a machine. This explains why in America many more machines are used—in the home as well as in industry and everywhere else—than in Europe, and why in Europe more machines are used than in Asia. It is for the same reason that in American agriculture, labor is much more sparingly used in relation to land and capital than is the case in Europe. In most Asian countries, labor is the cheapest of the factors while land and capital are the dearest; in the United States, labor is the dearest of the factors and land and capital the cheapest. In China, human labor is so cheap that it figures as an important source of motive power in the public transportation system (ricksha coolies). No further explanation is needed to show that in all these cases the price relationships existing among the several factors of production reflect the supply relationships of these factors in the national economy: that factor of production which is at a given moment the "scarcest" is also the dearest, and since it is the dearest it is used, perforce, sparingly. A socialist economy must be guided by similar considerations if it wishes to dispose economically of the several factors of production. A principle of primordial importance is herewith revealed, one which not only enables us to understand how the prices of the factors of production are formed (the wages of labor, the rent of land, and interest) but which also shows that the optimum combination of the factors in a given country is determined by the individual economic structure of that country. Once again we observe that what may be technically impressive is by no means always what is best economically.

It is now clear that one of the chief tasks of the organizer of production—the one who in industry is called the *entrepreneur*—consists in a continual search for the most advantageous *combination of the factors of production*. Since all producers tend to aim at this objective, they all collaborate in the formation of the prices of the factors of production. The optimum combination at any given moment is decisively influenced by the fact that the quantity of one of the factors cannot be continually increased without ultimately causing a fall in the yield due to such increase. It is this process which is meant when in agriculture we speak of a "law of diminishing returns." This means that if to a given area of land we apply ever greater amounts of labor and capital, there occurs a fall in the rate of yield following an initially over-proportionate increase of yield. Here is a truth which everyone can verify experimentally by subjecting some hapless tomato plant to ever heavier doses of artificial fertilizer. This law applies generally to the whole of production in the sense just illustrated, viz., that the continual addition of new increments of one of the factors of production to fixed quantities of the others produces an increased yield which is at first over-proportional and then under-proportional. This is such a commonplace and undisputed principle that cooks make use of it daily. The first dose of salt that is put into a given quantity of potatoes greatly enhances their taste while the utility of succeeding doses becomes increasingly doubtful. The cook knows that there is an optimum combination of potatoes and salt. Thus we arrive at the momentous principle that for every type of production the factors must stand in a harmonious relationship to one another, since otherwise the yield of the one will develop disproportionately to the yields of the others. The average office can certainly benefit by the employment of at least one stenographer, but if the manager of that office hires a second he soon becomes aware that she is by no means as indispensable as the first, that a third stenographer would be even less valuable, etc. Their productivity declines and it is clear that the productivity of the last stenographer hired—the "marginal productivity" of this species of productive factor called labor—can hardly be higher but also hardly lower than her wage.

NOTES

1. (p. 120) *National Income and National Wealth*

Calculation of the national income is an uncertain procedure at best; even greater uncertainty enters into the calculation of national wealth. It must be emphasized, to begin with, that we lack any really accurate means of evaluating those items of the national wealth for which there are no markets. At what figure should the streets and canals be assessed? To evaluate them on the basis of their costs of construction would be incorrect inasmuch as their final value to the community may have no relation to these original costs. But there is a further fundamental difficulty here and a highly instructive one. If, as the result of some natural disaster, a country's supply of water is suddenly and drastically diminished, water would figure as an item in the national wealth even though in real terms the country would have suffered an impoverishment. These few observations may serve to show the minimal value of calculations respecting the national wealth. *Cf.* Colin Clark, *National Income and Outlay* (London, 1937); Colin Clark, *The Conditions of Economic Progress* (2nd ed.; London, 1950); J. R. Hicks, *The Social Framework* (2nd ed.; Oxford, 1952); see also the literature listed under Note 5.

2. (p. 121) *Speculation*

The word speculation has such unpleasant connotations that most people have great difficulty in associating it with any useful function. To properly evaluate the role of speculation, however, we have only to reflect on the fact that, given the uncertainty of the future, there is a speculative element in every economic act. Every undertaking involves the assumption of risks and an element of gambling and a businessman is, at bottom, only a specialist in the weighing of probabilities. The fact that certain individuals make a profession of computing future risks manifests merely the usefulness of the division of labor. Just as the merchant relieves the manufacturer of the specific functions of merchanting, so the speculator relieves him of the risks of speculation. In this connection see: W. Röpke, article "Spekulation," *Handwörterbuch der Staatswissenschaften* (4th ed.); F. H. Knight, *Risk, Uncertainty, and Profit* (Boston, New York, 1921). The above literature also examines the circumstances in which speculation is unproductive and even harmful (as is popularly held to be the case, in an unjustified generalization, with respect to all speculative activity). Speculation may be effectively controlled by ensuring that speculators are provided with as few opportunities as possible of engaging in parasitic business practices. Thus, the evils of the black market, which are common to all command-type economies, could be far more effectively combated by reestablishing a free economy than by police interventions. A particularly serious view must be taken of speculation in urban real estate. Speculation of this type may be curbed by purposeful city planning, by a forward-looking land policy, by taxation, and by the adoption of certain legal measures. Here we encounter the special characteristics of land rent which we have reserved for discussion in another place (pp. 195 ff.). *Cf.* H. Sieber, "Die Bodenspekulation und ihre Bekämpfungsmöglichkeiten," *Wirtschaft und Recht*, No. 2, 1957. On stock exchange speculation see: A Hunold, *Die schweizerischen Effektenbörsen* (Zurich, 1949); F. W. Hirst, *The Stock Exchange* (London, 1949).

3. (p. 122) *Production and Distribution*

A proposal that merits consideration is one made by Franz Oppenheimer (for the first time in his *Theorie der reinen und politischen Oekonomie* (Berlin, 1910) to employ the expressions "production" and "distribution" in the technical senses illustrated in our text. The term "production" would then be equally applicable not only to the production of material goods (primary production, manufacturing) but to trade, transportation, and other activities as well.

4. (p. 124) *The Economic Process*

For further clarification of the economic interrelationships discussed in the text, consult the diagram shown below. *Cf.* C. Bresciani-Turroni, *Economic Policy for the Thinking Man* (London, 1952), Chapter II. See also J. R. Hicks, *The Social Framework, op. cit.,* and the literature listed under Note 5.

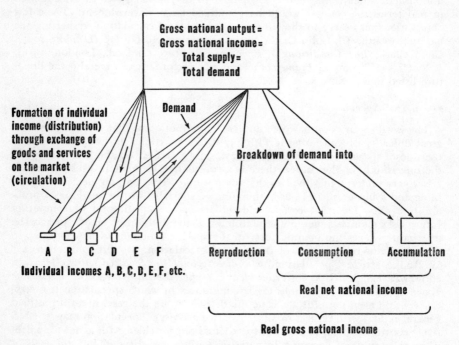

Figure 1.

5. (p. 125) *Macroeconomics*

From the voluminous literature in this field may be mentioned: Wilhelm Krelle, *Volkswirtschaftliche Gesamtrechnung* (no date); Erich Schneider, *Einführung in die Wirtschaftstheorie, I. Teil, Theorie des Wirtschaftskreislaufs* (8th ed., 1960); Werner Hofmann, *Die volkswirtschaftliche Gesamtrechnung* (1954); H. C. Edey-A. T. Peacock, *National Income and Social Accounting* (London, 1954). A special type of macroeconomics is the "input-output" analysis developed by the American economist Wassily Leontief (*The Structure of the American Economy* [New York, 1953]) which seeks to measure the flows of commodities entering and leaving the process of production.

For the limits and problems of the macroeconomic approach, see: W. Röpke, *A Humane Economy, op. cit.*, p. 252 ff.; F. Machlup, *Der Wettstreit zwischen Mikro- und Makrotheorien in der Nationalökonomie* (1960); S. Schoeffler, *The Failures of Economics: A Diagnostic Study* (Cambridge [Mass.], 1955).

6. (p. 127) *The Balance of Payments*

For further discussion and literature see my book *International Order and Economic Integration, op. cit.*, pp. 194 ff. See also my article "Zahlungsbilanz und Nationalreichtum" in W. Röpke, *Gegen die Brandung* (2nd ed.; Zurich, 1959), pp. 306 ff.

7. (p. 128) *The World—"this shop"*

One of the most important of latter-day theorists has written: "La nature n'est autre chose qu'un grand bazar à prix fixes ou bien une série de machines automatiques. Voulez-vous du charbon, du fer, des fruits, de la viande? Vous pouvez avoir tout ce que vous voulez; vous n'avez qu'à passer à la caisse, c'est-à-dire, vous n'avez qu'à vous soumettre aux conditions, aux prix fixes qu'elle réclame" (M. Pantaleoni, *Du caractère logique des différences d'opinions qui séparent les économistes* [Geneva, 1897], p. 34)

8. (p. 129) *The Heterogeneous Character of the Labor Market*

It is well known that a shortage of one type of labor (or of professionally trained individuals) can persist simultaneously with an oversupply of another type. The transition from one category (of labor) to another is extraordinarily difficult, as much for one who has already been trained for a certain occupation as for his children. The several categories of labor thus form groups among whom competition is more or less frustrated ("noncompeting groups" in the terminology of J. E. Cairnes, *Some Leading Principles of Political Economy* [London, 1874]).

9. (p. 132) *The Theory of Capital*

We have to do here with a problem which was the leading concern of the economists of the last century and which is once again the center of a lively controversy. Among the most recent books on this subject the following deserve to be noted: F. A. von Hayek, *Prices and Production* (2nd ed.; London, 1949); W. Eucken, *Kapitaltheoretische Untersuchungen* (1934); R. v. Strigl, *Kapital und Produktion* (Vienna, 1934); J. R. Hicks, *Value and Capital* (London, 1939).

10. (p. 132) *Capital Formation and Capital Consumption*

The formation of capital can follow several modes as suggested by the following scheme (W. Röpke, *Die Theorie der Kapitalbildung* [1929]):

I. *Capital formation in a natural economy,* termed also the direct formation of capital. Here capital is formed without resort to the detour of money. Example: the farmer who makes his own plough. Similarly illustrative of the formation of capital in a natural economy is the farmer who refrains from selling his young animals and instead raises them to maturity in order to increase the number of his own livestock. Thus, even in the contemporary money economy, this method continues to play an important role in the domain of agriculture. For the rest, however, capital formation at the present time takes place indirectly, i.e., by the detour of money.

II. *Capital formation in a money economy:*

(1) Formation of capital through saving, i.e., some portions of income are voluntarily set aside and put at the disposal of the capital market. This is and remains the principal method of capital formation in the free world.

(2) Formation of capital by the entrepreneur which occurs when profits accruing from operations within the firm are used for the purchase of new equipment ("self-financing", corporate saving).

(3) Formation of capital through fiscal policy, e.g., the state may divert taxes to the construction of factories, the building of railroads, etc. In contrast to the preceding, there is an element of compulsion involved in this mode of capital formation ("fiscal forced saving").

(4) Bank formation of capital which is a consequence of the banks' power to create credit. The process involved is the following: when the banking system grants additional credits to businessmen for the construction of factories, the general demand for goods is increased, but without a corresponding increase in supply. The result is a more or less perceptible rise in prices (boom). This compels consumers to restrict their consumption. As before, the restriction of consumption necessary to the formation of capital has occurred, but with this difference, that it takes place "from behind" as it were, and compulsorily ("monetary forced saving"). With the development of the modern banking system, this type of capital formation has become extremely important.

11. (p. 132) *Credit Expansion as a Cause of Crisis*

That the expansion of credit is an act of violence to the economy which, after the initial boom, is avenged in the crisis and depression which follow, is a fundamental part of all theories of the business cycle. Thus, the last world crisis (1929-32) was preceded by a gigantic expansion of credit in the economically advanced countries. Further discussion of this subject will be found in the special chapter reserved for it (Chapter VIII).

12. (p. 134) *The Law of Mass Production*

The relationships involved in this law may be roughly set forth: if we let k stand for the cost of production per unit of output, p for the quantity of output, g for fixed (general) costs, and s for variable (special) costs, the following equation holds:

$$k = s + \frac{g}{p}$$

But since the variable costs (s) per unit of output remain the same regardless of the quantity of output, the costs per unit (k) must constantly diminish as the quantity of output (p) increases, since in this case the quotient $\frac{g}{p}$ will become constantly smaller. Hence, unit costs approach, asymptotically, variable costs. In reality, the relationships involved are considerably more complex than this. Thus, the assumption that the variable costs (per unit of output) remain constant will rarely be realized; more often, in fact, variable costs will be found to have a slightly degressive character. We must be especially on guard against accepting the law of mass production as one of limitless application. There are several circumstances which put effective limits to its use, sooner or later. In the case of the washing machine, for example, it is clear that if the volume of laundry is continually increased, the original washing machine will no longer suffice, so that a new and larger machine must be procured. But there are obviously limits to the dimensions which such a machine can assume in the ordinary household. In this case, too, then, there exists an optimum. Where this optimum lies for each of several different sizes of machine can be determined only by technical investigation. Probably, it lies at a lower level, on the average, than most people think. Also, with the increasing size of operations, other difficulties appear which raise costs. Chief among these are the increasing cumbersomeness of the coordinating and supervising functions of management and the increasing need for ever greater uniformity of operations. On these matters, see E. A. G. Robinson, *The Structure of Competitive Industry* (London, 1935); Colin Clark, *The Conditions of Economic Progress, op. cit.*

For the rest, we must be careful not to confuse the law of mass production with the law of diminishing returns. The widely held opinion that industry falls under the law of increasing returns and agriculture under that of decreasing returns ignores the fact that we are here contrasting two wholly different things. The extremely complex interrelationships involved in these phenomena hold a large place in recent (cost) theory. The reader who desires a thorough understanding of these matters should consult P. H. Wicksteed, *The Common Sense of Political Economy*, Vol. 2 (London, 1933); pp. 527 ff. See also: F. X. Weiss, article "Abnehmender Ertrag," *Handwörterbuch der Staatswissenschaften* (4th ed.); O. Morgenstern, "Offene Probleme der Kosten- und Ertragstheorie," *Zeitschrift für Nationökonomie*, March 1931; J. M. Clark, *Studies in the Economics of Overhead Costs* (Chicago, 1923); E. Schneider, *Theorie der Produktion* (Vienna, 1934); H. v. Stackelberg, *Grundlagen einer reinen Kostentheorie* (Vienna, 1932).

CHAPTER VI

MARKETS AND PRICES

"The member of Parliament who supports every proposal for strengthening this monopoly is sure to acquire not only the reputation of understanding trade, but great popularity and influence with an order of men whose numbers and wealth render them of great importance. If he opposes them, neither the most acknowledged probity nor the highest rank, nor the greatest public services, can protect him from the most infamous abuse and detraction, from personal insults, nor sometimes from real danger, arising from the insolent outrage of furious and disappointed monopolists."

ADAM SMITH

1. *Free Prices Clear the Market*

In the preceding chapters we have carried our analysis of the mechanism of our nonsocialist economic system to the point where we can now understand why the formation of prices on the different commodity markets is the process which directs and regulates the whole, a process to which every economic problem must be inevitably referred. It is now our task, proceeding from the simple to the complex, to concentrate our inquiry into this process.

The best procedure will be to take as our starting point the popular axiom which states that market price at a given moment is determined by supply and demand. In so doing we shall be making our first near approach to the problem. The axiom states that increasing supply and decreasing demand cause prices to fall, and that decreasing supply and increasing demand cause them to rise. We may express this simple and familiar relationship by saying that prices vary directly with demand and inversely with supply. Therewith we have by no means exhausted all the interconnections of supply, demand and price, however. It is important to note that not only does price depend upon supply and demand but that, conversely, supply and demand depend upon price. This dependence, too, is one with which we are all familiar. We may express it, axiomatically, by saying that supply varies directly and demand inversely with price.

These two observations lead us to a third, namely that demand, supply and price are mutually interdependent. The mechanism of price formation based on these interrelationships functions in its simplest form as follows: when there is a disparity between supply and demand, the price rises or falls until, under the counterinfluence of price, supply and demand are brought into equilibrium. The price which results is the *equilibrium price* which will not vary so long as the market situation does not change. This price is characterized by the fact that no seller or buyer prepared to accept it will leave the market unsatisfied. Until the price has found this level, it will continue to fluctuate. *The equilibrium price is that price which clears the market.* This is one of the most important and elementary of the whole body of economic principles; it should be fixed firmly and indelibly in our minds.[1]

A natural consequence of this elementary axiom is that the expressions "supply" and "demand" must always be used in a relative sense. A good is not simply offered or demanded, but offered or demanded in relationship to a certain price. If the price changes, supply and demand change with it. This does not mean, however, that supply and demand depend only upon price. It goes without saying that even if the price remains the same, more of a given commodity will be supplied if a technical improvement (for example) results in a lowering of its costs of production; likewise, the demand for a commodity will increase (its price remaining constant) as it grows in favor with the buying public. It remains true that supply increases with rising prices and that demand increases with falling prices, but the level at which this occurs will meanwhile have changed. It is customary to describe such movements as shifts of the supply and demand schedules (or of the curves of supply and demand). Consequently, an increase in supply may result equally from a rise in prices (the supply curve remaining unchanged), or from a shift in the supply curve (prices remaining unchanged), or from both at once; inversely, a fall in prices, or a shift in the supply curve, or a combination of both can bring about a decrease in supply. The same holds true for an increase or decrease of demand. Hence, all these expressions have a double meaning which should not be lost sight of. Our first elementary axiom applies only in the case where the curves of supply and demand are given. Should these change, a displacement of the equilibrium price takes place. If we were to seek the causes of this displacement we would be led to analyze on the one hand, every circumstance which figures in the buying public's valuation of a good, and on the other, the manifold conditions governing supply. This would lead us into complications which, at this juncture, can only be hinted at.

The elementary relationships thus far exposed are exemplified in striking fashion in every attempt of government to establish, by decree, a price other than the equilibrium price. An example of this with which we are by now familiar is the "ceiling price" policy which, during both World Wars, attempted to prescribe a price lower than the equilibrium price. The prices of the basic subsistence goods rose in wartime as a result of inflation but also and quite naturally because supply diminished while demand increased. In this situation, the understandable but nevertheless superficial view prevailed that consumers were being arbitrarily exploited and that to put an end to this abuse it was required simply that a system of maximum prices be imposed by government fiat. The result was that the regulatory function of the free formation of prices was arrested, provoking the now familiar chain reaction in which the unsatisfied segments of demand produced first the queue and finally rationing. Simultaneously, disturbances developed on the supply side, remedies for which were sought in forcible interventions in production (compulsory deliveries of goods, compulsory crop-planting, etc.). The lesson for the future yielded by these experiments is that the mechanism of price formation is such a vital cog in the greater mechanism of our economic system that it cannot be tampered with without forcing us to enter upon a path which ends in socialism pure and simple.

The experiences with the system of maximum prices had their parallel in the results observed with the opposite system of minimum prices which was in effect following World War I. Just as the scarcity of goods during the war led to efforts to protect *consumers* by setting maximum prices, so too the surpluses existing in many categories of goods during the Great Depression resulted in efforts to insure *producers* against further sharp price declines by establishing and

enforcing minimum prices. The artificially high prices which
ensued prevented the clearing of the market through the lowering
of supply and the augmenting of demand. The surpluses which
resulted from the imposition of these artificial prices could not be
disposed of other than by having the state purchase them and store
them at great expense (valorization, parity price policy). And thereby
hangs a tale—of woe. As was demonstrated in every instance, e.g.,
the valorization of Brazilian coffee, the maintenance of high prices
not only prevented the adaptation of production to the market situation but, under the incentive of the prices offered by the state, actually
caused an extension of production. The more the warehouses bulged,
the higher rose the costs and the more the market groaned under the
pressure of this latent supply. Thus it was that the valorization of
Brazilian coffee, to take this one example, ended in a lamentable
debâcle, leaving to the state huge debts and mountains of unsold
coffee, a part of which was ultimately dumped into the sea. It would
be well if those who continually reproach "capitalism" for its destruction of coffee would keep in mind that it was precisely a planned-
economy correction of "capitalism" which provoked this chain reaction whose end result appears, and rightly so, as so senseless.

It could perhaps be objected that an economy of minimum prices
might succeed if the spade were pushed deeper and the control over
supply extended to the entire apparatus of production. The objection is doubtless valid but serves only to illustrate once again the
principle that interferences with the price mechanism lead to ever
more drastic and extensive interferences culminating in the completely planned economy of socialism. We have also to notice that
the application of the planned economy to production as, for instance, in the various species of crop control, in the rationing of
output and similar measures, leads in turn to still other and greater
problems. If, for example, one country restricts the production of a
given commodity in order to keep its export price high, the result
will be that other countries will simply increase their production of
that commodity. This explains why restrictions placed on rubber
cultivation in the English colonies after World War I ended in a
fiasco and why, at a later date, similar consequences were observed
to flow from the cotton policy of the United States.

Still other problems are generated by market interventions. Thus
in agricultural production, where the above difficulties have been
most in evidence, truly effective control of production is very difficult

to realize so long as the whole of agriculture has not been collectivized according to the somewhat unattractive Russian model. But it is to just such a result that this whole policy can lead if the state is compelled to apply its planned-economy interferences on an ever wider scale. One circumstance, in particular, tends to accelerate this tendency, namely, that when a restriction is placed upon the production of one agricultural commodity, farmers will tend to increase the production of another by as much. In fine, disorder breeds disorder, requiring in the end an ever more comprehensive control of production according to planned-economy methods. In this situation, it would be strange if the state should not try to solve the dilemma by forcibly increasing demand just as it had forcibly restrained supply. We have, in fact, witnessed in recent decades the development of a special technique for this purpose, a notable example of which is the compulsory use of alcohol as an ingredient in motor-fuel mixtures.* If we add that the agricultural policies of many countries during recent decades have evolved along similar lines, it becomes sufficiently plain that *the formation of prices is the regulator of our economic system and that it cannot be tampered with without requiring, in the end, a reconstruction of the entire economic system.* It is doubtful whether all those who recommend interferences with the formation of prices appreciate the fact that the magnetic pole of such a policy lies in Moscow (and, we should have added a while back, in National Socialist Berlin). "With the first step we are free, with the second we are serfs."

2. *Elasticity of Supply and Demand*

We take now a further important step in our investigation with the establishment of the fact that the degree to which supply and demand react to price changes differs on different markets. On one market a twofold increase in price results in a somewhat less than twofold increase in supply, and reduces demand somewhat less than half; on another market changes in supply and demand will exceed markedly (in quantitative terms) the price changes that have given rise to them. The *elasticity of supply* and the *elasticity of demand* are in the first case low and in the second, high. The degree of elas-

---

*This type of compulsion is found in some European countries. A parallel American example would be the law which requires margarine to be sold uncolored, thus indirectly increasing demand for butter.—*Translator's note.*

ticity of supply and demand (coefficient of elasticity) has, in turn, a significant bearing on the character of price formation on the several markets. A simple example will make this clear.

The Christmas season is hardly a period in which we could expect that people, preoccupied as they generally are with other thoughts, would take the time to reflect on an interesting Christmas problem in economics, namely, the peculiar situation of the Christmas tree market on the day before the holiday. The first thing we find is that the elasticity of demand for Christmas trees is indubitably low. This is so because it would require a very marked rise in price to make the average family give up the idea of having a Christmas tree and, on the other hand, because it would require a very marked decrease in price to induce the average family to buy more than one. The day before Christmas, the supply of Christmas trees is inelastic too, seeing that it cannot be increased by additional cutting of trees nor diminished by putting them in storage. Twenty-four hours later the trees are no more than ordinary cut pines which can be used, at best, only as a covering for rose bushes or as firewood. The effect of this two-sided inelasticity on the Christmas tree market is clear: if there are too few trees on the market, a very marked rise in price is required to equate supply and demand; if there are too many trees a very pronounced fall in price is needed, a fall which may even reach the "firewood" point. Everyone, in fact, has had the experience of discovering that just before the holiday, Christmas trees are ordinarily either very cheap or very expensive. Supply and demand, given their inelasticity, cannot yield. Hence it is the price which must yield all the more in order to reestablish market equilibrium. *The smaller is the elasticity of supply and demand, the greater is the flexibility of prices.* This principle allows us to understand more precisely the characteristics of the several different kinds of market.[2]

Of special interest to us is the *agricultural products market.* Corresponding to the low elasticity of demand for food (of which we have already spoken in Chapter I), the elasticity of demand for agricultural products is generally not very high. Although we should not underestimate the elasticity of demand for the more expensive quality products of agriculture (butter, eggs, vegetables, meat, etc.), this elasticity is certainly low for the various bread grains. Since in the short run the supply of grains is also very inelastic, we can understand why as early as the 17th century an English statistician, Gregory King, could formulate the rule that the price of grains is usually subject to fluctuations greater than the corresponding harvest fluctuations (*King's rule*). If the supply is too great, a sharp fall in price is needed to stimulate demand sufficiently to clear the market, and if the supply is too small an equally sharp rise in price is necessary to restrain demand sufficiently. From which it follows that the farmers, under certain circumstances, may stand to gain more from a poor harvest than from an abundant one. Proof (among others) of this fact is supplied by the American cotton farmers in the state of Alabama who in 1919 raised a monument in honor of a harmful insect, the boll weevil, in gratitude for its partial destruction of the huge price-depressing cotton crop of that year. If we add that the agricultural markets are characterized by still other anomalies, we can readily see that they represent a case apart in the formation of prices, a circumstance which confronts the agricultural policymakers with a number of crucial and important tasks.[3]

The *labor market* must also, as a rule, be considered as presenting a special and difficult type of price formation, though the laws of price can be applied to it in the same way as to the commodities market. While the elasticity of demand for labor differs in the different phases of a cyclical movement, declining to a very low point in the depression phase, the elasticity of supply, at least for the skilled trades, may be said to be decidedly low. This is so because human labor, lacking financial reserves for the most part, cannot be put in "storage" for very long. Then again, due to the time required for its training and to its great immobility, the labor force can be expanded over the short run only within narrow limits. This low elasticity of the labor supply can be increased by all sorts of politico-social measures such as aid to the unemployed which augments their "storageableness," by retraining programs, establishment of more effective communication between the supply and demand sides of the labor market via improvements in employment agencies' techniques, etc. The longer the period of training required for a given kind of labor, the more delayed will be the adaptation of supply to the market situation and, by the same token, the more difficult it will be. A good example of this is the academic labor market, in the several branches of which conditions of oversupply are easily changed to situations of shortage and *vice versa;* and we can appreciate that the advice of a wise uncle to his nephew, to study for the profession most in vogue at the moment, will remain wise advice only so long as there are not too many such uncles and nephews.

There are some special considerations respecting the elasticity of supply which merit our attention here. The most important of these is that elasticity is ordinarily smaller in the short run than in the long run. This is all the more likely to be the case the longer the time required to produce or to transport the goods to market, and the bigger the losses that would be sustained by withholding them from the market. This is why supply on the fish markets is, at any given moment, extraordinarily inelastic and subject to the caprice of demand, while from one fishing day to another, it can recover all its elasticity. The same is true for practically all the food markets— the result of which may be the appearance of vexatious disturbances and bottlenecks in such markets. Their elimination is an important task of economic policy. The stock exchanges, also, offer us examples of markets on which supply, during trading hours, is usually very inelastic, a circumstance which can occasionally lead to unexpected and possibly dangerous fluctuations in stock-market quotations. Such fluctuations are especially likely to occur when brokers are receiving from their clients a large number of orders to sell without any specification as to minimum price. In all such cases of "unlimited" supply, elasticity is reduced to zero, a phenomenon which may be observed with particular clarity at an auction (abstracting from those cases in which the owner sets the minimum bid).

The cases of totally inelastic supply, as well as of totally inelastic demand, border upon the domain of *price curiosities*. Also to be included in this latter category are the cases of *inverse inelasticity* in which supply and demand respond to price changes in a direction opposite to the usual one. It is quite possible, for example, that a fall in agricultural prices may provoke an increase rather than a reduction in cultivation as a consequence of each farmer seeking to compensate for price declines by raising his output. Official exhortations to restrict crop acreage can, in this situation, produce the opposite effect since many farmers would probably expand production in the expectation that all the other farmers would obey the official entreaties. Cases of this kind have actually occurred in the United States. A similar process may be observed on the labor market where price (wage) declines may result in increased labor productivity as each worker strives to maintain his existing income. An example of the inverse elasticity of demand is the familiar case in which an increase in prices causes an increase in demand because of speculation that prices will increase still further in the future.

Let us take note, finally, of the fact that the elasticity of demand can be used in quite another sense than that in which we have thus far used it. Having defined elasticity as the degree to which demand reacts to price changes, we may also speak of an elasticity of demand in terms of the degree to which the demand of individuals reacts to changes in their incomes. We distinguish in this case the *price elasticity of demand* from *income elasticity of demand*. This latter case involves considerations with which have already dealt (Chapter I, Section 2).

3. *Prices and Costs*

Since the majority of economic goods can be increased by the act of production it is clear that the scale on which such goods are supplied reflects their *costs of production*. If prices were insufficient to cover costs, producers would incur losses which would no longer permit them to maintain production to the previous extent; supply, in such case, diminishes, causing prices to climb until they have once again attained the level of costs.

One might suppose that with prices remaining below the level of costs, a given industry would cease operations altogether. This, however, need not be the case, to the extent that the costs of production differ for different levels of output and for the different firms within an industry. When prices decline, only that segment of the total output of the industry is immediately affected whose production costs are highest (*marginal output*). The remaining segments continue to manage on the lower prices. If, however, these remaining segments of output are unable to meet demand, prices will be forced up until marginal production again becomes profitable. Thus, if the costs for each segment of the total supply differ (which is usually the case), it is the highest costs at the time (*marginal costs*) which determine the over-all height of prices (for a given industry). But as the prices offered for all the segments of supply (of the same type of good) are ordinarily the same, the favored producers realize an extra profit which results from the gap between the market price and their low costs of production (*producers' rent*).

It would seem that in making this observation we have once again tapped on that hollow place in our economic system for which we moderns have developed such a sensitive ear. Is it not a provocative notion that at the existing level of prices we are paying fat profits to these privileged producers? The first and most important reply to such a complaint is that insofar as our economic system is not completely permeated with and ruled by rigid monopolies, there will always be powerful forces at work to lower marginal costs. On the one hand, the favored producers will seek to increase their cheaper output in order to drive the marginal producers from the market; on the other hand, the marginal producer will seek to attain the lower cost levels of his more favored competitors. In this way, unrelenting competition gnaws away night and day at producers' rents to the exceeding displeasure of the producers who strive by every available means to curb competition, including the (unfortunately) easy matter of getting the state to lend them a sympathetic ear. But as we shall see later, in detail, this is a circumstance which cannot be charged to the market economy as such. In any case, producers' rents are sources of gains which are sooner or later dried up, even in agriculture, as the experience of the last decades has forcefully made clear. But should these observations fail to remove concern, it need only be pointed out that tax powers are always available to satisfy our desire for social justice without a total overthrow of the economic system.

We can see, then, that the concept of "costs of production" is by no means a simple one. A further complication is that not all of the factors entering into the costs of production have the same bearing on the determination of prices. The influence of these costs on the determination of prices is obviously not due to the fact that a well-meaning authority, out of its love of justice, reimburses producers for their expenses in the same way as the government indemnifies a functionary for expenses incurred on an official journey. If this were true, then it would be only right that the producer agree to a minute examination of his costs by a kind of supreme economic "accounting department" and that for every productive undertaking he secure an official authorization of the kind required by governments for official missions of their functionaries. This is something which the producer, who would like to have a government guarantee for the complete indemnification of his costs, would do well to reflect upon. Only a little thought is required to realize afresh that such a road, once embarked upon, leads straight to Moscow (or, in the National Socialist era, to Berlin). If that is not what the producers want, then they ought, with good grace, to accommodate themselves to the laws of our economic system.

These laws are so constituted that the costs of production exercise an influence on price only insofar as their indemnification is necessary for *future* production. If this indemnification is not assured, the means of production can go on strike in order to find more remunerative employment. This they can do, however, only where there exist alternative opportunities for employment. If the price of coal falls to the point where the owners are unable to retain their workers or to meet current costs, then the mines will close down. The workers, the lubricating oil, and the fuel can be used elsewhere. But for the mine pits themselves there exists no alternative use. The capital invested in them cannot be "retrieved." Normally, the price should be sufficient to cover the payment of interest and amortization on this fixed capital. But if the price falls to the point where the payment of interest and amortization on the fixed capital is no longer assured, the owner of the mine would still do well, as a rule, to continue operations rather than bring them to an abrupt stop, even though the price no longer covers the full costs of production. The fixed capital in such cases may be "written off" either through the depreciation and consolidation of the extant shares of stock or, in the last resort, through bankruptcy proceedings. The certain result of this is that there will be no inflow of new capital to allow for the replacement or the expansion of physical facilities. These consequences, however, will only manifest themselves over an extended period of time. We can, at this point, sympathize with the melancholy utterance of a pessimistic banker that a new hotel is generally profitable only as a "second hand" operation.

The preceding reflections on the nature of the costs of production should serve to stiffen our resistance to laments that this or that branch of production is in imminent danger of collapse because prices are too low, and to harden us a little against the demand that this or that industry be assured a satisfactory level of prices by means of tariff protection or similar measures on the grounds that otherwise it faces "certain ruin." We are now aware of the exaggeration concealed in this extremely popular tactic. *In the first place,* a fall in prices seldom renders a given industry altogether unprofitable and this because production costs for individual producers are not uniform but different. We find that in almost every instance a given industry comprises firms which are graduated in terms of their efficiency: at the top of the scale, the most efficient, capable of weathering severe price declines, and at the bottom, the firms on the margin of existence—those that just get by. Hence, if prices fall, e.g., as the result of foreign competition, the immediate casualties will be confined to the group of marginal firms. What we may expect, then, is not the disappearance of the whole of a particular industry but principally a change in the relative size of operations of the several firms in the industry. Were foreign competition to be eliminated by protective tariffs or import quotas, the state would be guaranteeing, in effect, the profits of the most efficient producers, the very ones who least require protection. *In the second place,* to justify such somber prognostications as the above, the drop in prices would have to be severe enough to affect not only fixed capital costs but variable costs as well.

4. *Monopoly*

Now that we have established that the costs of production (in the sense already used and for the reasons we have indicated) constitutes in the long run the lower limit to which prices can fall, the question suggests itself whether and to what degree they can rise above this lower limit. That they can so rise is undeniable. It is, however, also clear that there is a powerful force which again pushes prices down to the level of costs, namely, the increased supply which results from the competition among the producers to sell at the higher price. The more ineffective this force becomes, the closer we approach *monopoly*. The resulting peculiarities we must now describe.

The characteristic feature of a monopoly, be it a single enterprise or a monopolistic combination of enterprises (cartel, syndicate, trust) is that it (or they) can freely determine the amount of supply; and where supply is sufficiently curtailed, prices can be held above the level of costs. If we proceed on what is probably the not unreal assumption that the monopolist seeks to maximize his profits, the question then is what price should he select to attain his goal? Should he choose a high price, his profit per unit will be high but his total sales small ("small turnover, large per unit profit"). Should he choose a low price, the profit per unit declines, while total sales increase ("large turnover, small profit per unit"). Confronted with these alternatives, the monopolist will select that price which, multiplied by the number of units sold, will yield the maximum net profit. He will seek by a series of experiments to establish the location of this maximum point. This will vary, of course, from firm to firm, and from plant to plant. The decisive factor here is the elasticity of demand; upon it will depend whether an increase in price will induce a sharp decrease in sales or whether a decrease in price will stimulate a sizable increase in sales. If the telephone company can count on a high elasticity of demand for telephone service, it will find that a reduction in its rates will result in an addition to its revenues which exceeds the total of the amounts lost on the bills of the individual subscribers. Thus, the greater is the elasticity of demand the lower is the monopoly price, and vice versa. From this it follows that a monopoly of foodstuffs may have extremely dangerous consequences for the community, especially a monopoly of grains.

Because of the importance of the elasticity of demand in the determination of monopoly price, the managements of monopolistic enterprises—railroads, electric power companies, the post office, state tobacco monopolies—must base their price policies primarily on this factor and have a fairly clear notion of what the coefficient of the elasticity of demand is in the given case. The monopolist must also take into account the fact that the elasticity of demand is decisively affected by possibilities available to consumers to turn to a substitute product (from the railroad to the automobile, from the gas stove to a coal or electric stove, etc.). On the other hand, there are cases where the elasticity of demand is low, e.g., matches or sewing thread, objects which though they possess slight value in themselves nevertheless have great practical importance. Expenditures for such items are imperceptible in contrast to expenditures with which they are associated (for heating and smoking, and for suiting material and tailoring, respectively), while their mass consumption assures to the manufacturers a large profit.

The position of the monopoly price point is further influenced by the structure of costs at different levels of supply. If costs are of the increasing type (i.e., if they increase as output increases), then a higher price is more advantageous for the monopolist; if costs are of the decreasing type, it would be wise to establish a lower price. Mining monopolies (where increasing costs are encountered) may incline to a policy of restricting supply and keeping prices high, while the publisher of a copyrighted book such as this one will find it to his advantage to fix its price as low as possible; the resultant broadening of the market enables him to benefit from the dominant tendency in book production, which is one of decreasing costs.

This last example suggests a further complication in the formation of monopoly price. If, for instance, the present book were a novel or a play, the publisher would have at his disposal still other means of increasing his profit. To begin with, he could publish a deluxe edition of several hundred copies, on imperial Japan paper and bound in vellum, "numbered and signed by the author." These he could sell to collectors at a high price. Next, he could bring out an ordinary edition at a medium price, and finally, a "popular" edition for the masses at a sensationally low price. For our publisher to have brought out the popular edition first would not only have entailed extra risks but a further obvious disadvantage in that those who might have been willing to pay a higher price for the ordinary edition, and even for the deluxe edition, would have profited from the lower price of the popular edition. By beginning with the more expensive type, our publisher puts to use his knowledge of the fact that a uniform price for the entire market establishes itself in accordance with the willingness to buy of the marginal buyers, i.e., those whose desire to buy is the weakest. Thus, the establishment of a single uniform price for a given commodity yields to all the buyers who otherwise would have paid a higher price for it a saving which they owe to the greater reluctance to buy of the marginal buyers. This saving, the counterpart of producers' profits, is designated as *consumers' surplus,* an expression to which, naturally, many will object since it refers not to a positive gain but only to a saving. It is understandable that the producers would cast a covetous eye on consumers' surplus; they are compelled, nonetheless, to cede this much to the buyers so long as a uniform price obtains for all the quantities of a good sold within a given time period. A prime function of competition, we may note, is to ensure, through an easily understood process, such price uniformity.

But the monopolist has the possibility, thanks to *price differentiation,* of increasing his profit at the cost of the consumers. This is accomplished in such a way that the whole of demand is ranged in different classes, according to the different degrees of surcharge possible. Next, prices are adapted to the several classes on the basis of what the traffic will bear in each case, as shown in our example of the different editions of the same book. In this example, price differentiation was rendered possible by artificially dividing the good in question into different qualities, the markets for each of these quality classifications being then successively exploited. The practice of selling a good first at a high price and then, following a progressive saturation of the higher strata of demand, at a low price, is usual even in the case of patented manufactured articles. Consider the example of the so-called zip fastener. When it first appeared on the market, it was regarded as an amazing innovation and commanded a high price. Today, the zipper is so cheap that it has been adapted to thousands of different uses. Similarly, most of the price phenomena connected with the production and sale of articles of fashion are explainable in terms of this principle.

There is an abundant assortment of examples that could be cited to illustrate the process by which a good is divided, artificially, into different subclasses. The transport industries afford a prime instance of such class divisions. The establishment, by the railroads, of a hierarchy of rates for passenger traffic enables the managements of such enterprises to leave to the passengers themselves the business of finding their appropriate classification according to the rates they can afford to pay. Customers in the upper classifications are drawn thereto by the greater comfort, but more especially by concern for their social position and by the less crowded condition of the compartments, things which are precisely the result of higher rates. In this and in analogous cases, (e.g., at the theatre), price classification becomes the equivalent of quality classification; this is true in every instance where the payment of a higher price carries with it a visible social distinction and procures the advantages which result from less crowding in the higher price classes. We shall find this tendency to be the more marked the more crowded are the lower priced accommodations. Otherwise, it would be necessary to install more amenities in the higher price classes. Hence, in the case of a railroad whose coaches are normally filled to capacity, there will be no need for the management to spend much on better equipment for the higher priced accommodations. Quite other considerations, again, must be taken into account to explain the differences in postal rates for letters and for printed matter and, similarly, in electricity rates for the home and for the factory.[4]

The formation of prices on a purely competitive market or on a purely monopolistic one are, in reality, rare occurrences, for these "marginal cases" suppose the existence of conditions which are practically never completely fulfilled. Pure competition occurs only where the number of independent sellers is very great and where there is a perfect market, that is, a market where all the sellers and buyers are simultaneously and always aware of each other's offers and among whom, accordingly, a process of continual adjustment is going on. These conditions are most nearly realized, however, only on *organized markets,* in particular, on the most advanced type of an organized market, the stock market. If free or perfect competition exists anywhere, there is where it must be sought. Rather different is the situation on the *unorganized markets* of which we select retail trade as the best known example. When I enter a store to buy myself a hat, I enter, indeed, the "hat market" in the broad sense that I assert my demand for a hat, simultaneously with the rest of the hat demanders, against the total supply of hats available. But since total supply and total demand in this case coincide neither in time nor in place, a quick over-all view of the market situation is lacking. I must have sought out many shops before being in a position to fairly judge hat prices; many customers must have left hat shops shrugging their shoulders before shop owners bring their prices down and in turn influence the hat manufacturers to do the same. It is to be noticed, then, that the entire mechanism of price formation functions in this instance slowly and hesitantly, a characteristic which explains the many monopoly-like peculiarities of price formation in retail trade.[5]

But the fact that free competition does not really exist in the chemically pure state, and that many prices contain a certain monopolistic element, must not lead us to conclude that our economic system rests, at bottom, no longer on competition but on monopoly. Such a conclusion would be quite wrong. It is to be observed, first, that pure monopoly is an even rarer phenomenon than pure competition. The most important instances in which the monopoly element prevails over the competitive element are: (1) *natural monopoly* where the few existing deposits of certain resources are owned by a single individual or group (e.g., the South African diamond syndicate); (2) *juridical monopoly* based on a grant by the state of an exclusive right to produce or sell a particular commodity (patents, copyrights, etc.), though such a right is usually valid only for a specified period; (2) *transportation monopoly* where the monopolist is protected within his production area against outside competition by the high costs of transport, a situation which may therefore also be termed *area monopoly* (for example, Pittsburgh steel manufacturers); (4) lastly, *trade name monopoly* arising from the susceptibility of consumers to advertisers' suggestions that a given product is unique of its kind (use of brand names). But even in these cases the monopolies, as a rule, must reckon with a number of contrarieties: the possibility that consumers will shift to a substitute product, the tendency for outsiders to move in as the monopoly operations become increasingly profitable, and finally and above all, foreign competition (insofar as the monopolist does not succeed in warding off the latter either by inducing the state to establish protective tariffs or import quotas, or by organizing an international cartel). Finally, the monopolists have to beware of employing their power in such ruthless fashion as to incite public opinion and the state to retaliate; this, however, is an obstacle which may be effectively overcome by the monopolists' skillful influencing of public opinion and of official bodies.

One of the particular accomplishments of modern economic science has been its investigation and definition of the several possible intermediary stages ("market forms") which may lie between pure monopoly and pure competition. But however useful such a procedure, it has had the unfortunate consequence of leading many to conclude that the concepts "monopoly" and "competition" are, for practical purposes, unusable since, in fact, only the intermediate forms exist. Such blurred distinctions serve not only the monopoly interests but also the collectivists who would view only with uneasiness the restoration of a genuinely competitive economy, inasmuch as they need monopoly as a sort of Exhibit A in their arguments for the establishment of a state monopoly as the only remaining solution to the problem. It is certainly possible to define competition and monopoly in such a way that competition can be shown to be unrealizable; consequently, every attempt to take active measures to restore this narrowly defined "competition" to life will be doomed to failure from the start. Such a definition is, however, meaningless. To supply a definition which makes sense, we must begin with what is a decisive question for the ordering of economic life, i.e., how the actual productive forces of the national economy should be allocated as among the several alternative uses. Then monopoly appears as that market form which frees the producer (to the extent to which he controls supply) from the influence of the consumer over the uses of the productive forces. This arbitrary power of the producer attains its maximum extension when production, in accordance with the collectivist program, is concentrated in the hands of the state which then becomes the most dangerous and most powerful of all monopolists. Not the least reason for fearing a state monopoly is the fact that this most powerful of monopolies is simultaneously the one easiest to disguise with slogans.

A criticism which, at the present writing especially, is very widespread is that our economic system is now and will continue to be dominated by monopolies. To this our emphatic reply must be that there is no necessity for such a development. Indeed, it is astonishing how, in every case, competition sooner or later triumphs over monopoly, if only it is given the chance. To say that "competitive capitalism" is necessarily "monopoly capitalism" is simply untrue. The truth is that there is hardly a monopoly worth the name at whose birth, in one way or another, the state has not acted as midwife. Indeed, the history of heavy industry monopolies in Germany has shown that even where the state directly intervened to establish a monopoly, vigorous coercive measures were necessary to force the several producers under one roof. There would probably be few monopolies in the world today if the state, for numerous reasons, had not intervened with all the weight of its authority, its juridical prestige, and its more or less monopoly-favoring economic policy (including the policy of restricting imports) against *the natural tendency towards competition*. Constant and vigorous assertion of this truth is necessary since an exactly opposite view is generally affirmed, and in a manner such as to suggest the inanity of further discussion of the point. Decades of Marxist propaganda have greatly contributed to the diffusion of this bias. The reigning ideology which enthuses over the "monumental" and the "grandiose," and which grows positively lyrical on the subject of "organizing" and "commanding" (at the expense of the natural and the spontaneous), is obviously an ideology favorable to monopoly. Neither do the monopolists fail to make the most of the state of mind of those who go about moaning that "capitalism" is dead or dying, that the competitive system is a contemptible and vulgar business which ought at the earliest opportunity to be replaced by a tightly organized economic system, and more of the same. Nothing, however, prevents governments from shaping their economic policies to the end that the natural tendency towards competition will once again be permitted to play its proper role in the economic system. Such action appears, at the moment, to be rather unlikely. This is certainly not the fault of "capitalism," but a consequence of the dominance of certain ideologies. We have as little reason to suspend the fight against these ideologies as we have to doubt the *economic noxiousness* of monopolies (in most cases) in their ultimate effects.

The principal charge that can be formulated against monopolies is that they do violence, in the fashion already described in Chapter II, to the "business principle" and thus to one of the most essential principles of our economic system. Simultaneously, they introduce into economic life an element of arbitrary power which, in the extreme case of the complete and all-embracing state monopoly (collectivism), becomes absolute. Not only are monopolies in a position to reap super-profits (since competition alone can compel the rendering of a good or service equal in value to payment received) but they cause still further damage by gravely lessening the suppleness and adaptive power of our economic system.[6]

The full perniciousness of monopoly price formation becomes apparent when we remember that prices are the better able to fulfill their *regulatory function* in the economy the more flexible they are and the more faithfully they reflect the costs of production. Every price is a double appeal addressed to buyers and sellers: to the sellers an appeal to increase or restrict their supply; to the buyers an appeal to restrict or to increase their demand. Thus prices regulate simultaneously the use of the productive factors of the economy whose prices constitute, jointly, the production costs of a good. *To sum up, prices are nothing other than continuous appeals to the consumers to decide which of the economy's scarce production goods should or should not be, at any given moment, allocated to the various economic uses which can be made of them.* It stands to reason that prices will the better acquit themselves of the function the less they are manipulated by monopoly power or by interventions of the state.

Only in one case is that situation characterized by the word "monopoly" (which in the strict meaning of its Greek root means "single seller"), viz., the exclusive concentration of the supply of a commodity in a single hand, a consciously pursued objective of economic policy. This is the case of the government's fiscal monopoly by means of which a government (as in the well-known example of the tobacco monopolies of some countries [Austria and Italy]), having forcibly eliminated all competition, openly employs its resulting power to raise prices for the purpose of securing income for which it otherwise would be dependent on excise taxes on the commodity in question.

Precisely this special case makes clear that howevermuch a monopoly position may be desirable from a purely egoistic point of view, it is something which from the standpoint of the general welfare is undesirable, or at least must be regarded with serious misgivings. A consensus may be said to exist on the point that monopoly is basically undesirable because it involves the exercise of a degree of power in the economic and social life of the community which, even where the power is not consciously abused, appears incompatible with the ideals of freedom and justice and in addition creates the danger of disturbances of economic equilibrium and a lessening of productivity. Most people quite correctly associate with the concept of "monopoly" notions of exclusiveness, privilege, arbitrariness, excessive power, and exploitation. These characteristic attributes of monopoly are simultaneously the grounds for one of the most weighty and irrefutable objections to collectivism. As mentioned above, such an economic order, by its extreme concentration of production and distribution in the hands of the state, establishes a complete and all-embracing monopoly against which, in virtue of the apparatus of state coercion on which it rests, there is no appeal. The basic nature of such a system, moreover, is unaffected by possible decentralization of the governmental administration machinery or by the practice of inciting the state-run plants to compete with each other. The idea that in this case the state's exercise of monopoly power provides a guarantee that such power will be employed in the interest of the general welfare is revealed as a fiction.

In a few important instances, monopoly is to be recognized on technical or organizational grounds as superior or even as essential; such instances are the so-called "public utilities" (gas, electricity, water, telephone) in which it is all but impossible to permit the existence of competing firms. All the more unendurable in such cases would be monopoly left to its own devices, particularly since what is at stake here are services which are indispensable to the public. All the more necessary is it, in cases such as these where monopoly is practically unavoidable, to establish a system of control and supervision of the monopolistic enterprises (see Note 6 following this chapter).

Recently, the attempt has been made (in particular, by Joseph A. Schumpeter in *Capitalism, Socialism, and Democracy*) to prove the advantages of monopoly by reference to the special case of public utilities. It is precisely the economic power and capital reserves of the large organization, so runs this argument, which favor technological innovation and progress. What is valid in this argument is that it cannot be known beforehand what use a monopolist will make of the power over which he disposes, whether he will merely extract profits from his enterprise, allowing it otherwise to stagnate behind the sheltering wall of market power, or whether he will seek to enter upon new paths of discovery and invention. What is true in any case is that the promotion of technological progress by means of monopoly can be expected only under specific, and for the most part only infrequently encountered conditions. The decisive fact remains that monopolists dispose of a degree of power over their markets and over the economy which a well-ordered, purposeful economic system based on a just relationship between performance and reward cannot tolerate. To the extent that technological progress is rooted in monopoly privilege, it is at least questionable whether the economic resources of the nation are being employed in accordance with the wishes of the consumer, such as these wishes would have manifested themselves in a context of effective competition.

At the same time, there is one consideration in this connection to which we must pay due regard if we are to arrive at usable definitions of monopoly and competition. Concepts of "pure" or "perfect" competition based on abstract mathematical models, whose assumptions must necessarily remain unrealized in the dynamic reality of economic life, should be replaced by the concept of "active" or "workable" competition in which the continuous striving of the producers for the favor of the consumers is emphasized as the essential note of competition. Where competition of this kind is maintained, it is probable that now one, now the other producer will advance ahead of others and thus acquire a special position. Such a situation is not to be described as "monopolistic" however, so long as other producers have "free entry" into the market in question and thereby the opportunity of themselves acquiring, in turn, such special positions. In this continuous testing and contesting of the protagonists in a given market, and in the incentives provided by the temporary advantages of market dominance, we see precisely that characteristic feature of competition which makes it such an extremely valuable institution. A position of dominance in the market need not be qualified as "monopoly" providing it is temporary and the leader is closely followed by competitors who are free to overtake him in turn. Hence, it does not follow that such progress as is promoted by the expectation and hope of taking the lead in a given industry should be attributed to monopoly. It is legitimate to speak of monopoly only where this competition for the "lead" is eliminated and the "lead" becomes a permanent position of privilege and power—a situation which is calculated more to hinder than to promote progress. On this reasoning, the state's legal sanction by a patent of the "lead," provided by an invention or innovation, constitutes not only just security for intellectual property rights, but also an indispensable economic incentive. Patent rights begin to be problematical, however, to the extent that competition is thereby hindered, and monopoly rights ending in abuses of market power are created.

Where competition is defined as a situation of continuous striving for the favor of the consumers, the concept of monopoly is correspondingly narrowed and limited to those cases in which this striving with its temporary positions of power is eliminated and replaced by a situation of permanently protected positions of power in the market. This makes it possible to set forth all the more unreservedly the evils brought upon the whole community by monopoly. They are found: 1. in the position of dominance of the producer over the consumer achieved in virtue of the elimination of the striving for the favor of consumers who, in turn, lose their appropriate economic role as the "sovereigns" of production; 2. in the resulting possibility of exploitation of consumers and the disruption of the just relationship between performance and reward (business principle), so that the monopoly price lacks the note of the "just price" peculiar to a competitive price; 3. in the weakening of the incentives inherent in competition to provide optimum supply in terms of both price and quality; 4. in the disturbance to the total economic order based on competition and free prices and in the resulting misallocation of resources; 5. in the creation of positions of power which seal off markets from new entrants, thereby depriving them of a fair chance at the economic and social opportunities which otherwise would have been available. Monopoly conditions may exist not only on commodities markets but also on the various individual labor markets in virtue of the power of strong labor unions to establish—by means of techniques such as the closed shop—exclusive control of the supply of labor. The resulting economic evils are analogous to those we have already described.

Applying what we have said thus far to the economic system which predominates in the free world, viz., the market economy, it is clear that such an economy, precisely on account of the central role played in it by competition, suffers a diminution both of its efficiency and its justice (in social terms) where it is plagued by monopoly. If it is desired to reap all those advantages of a market economy lacking in a collectivist economy, if what we wish is a "social market economy" of the type so successfully maintained by the German government since 1948, then the fight against monopoly and the maintenance of effective competition must be recognized as one of the prime conditions thereof.

To properly evaluate the possibilities of a successful fight against monopolies, we must note first that the emergence and even more the duration of monopolies (in the realistic sense used here) are confined within much narrower limits than is popularly supposed and is maintained by social theories which aim at putting the nature of the free economy and its prospects in the most unfavorable light possible. Equally erroneous, we may add, is the view that the development of modern economic life and technological progress tend in ever increasing degree to favor monopolism. If there is an immanent tendency in the free economy it is, today as yesterday, a tendency in the direction of competition, not monopoly. This tendency has been in our time strengthened rather than weakened due precisely to the continuous revolutions in technology and improvements in transportation—with their market-enlarging effects—and the economic development of new areas. Everything is in movement as never before and he who is on top today, whether he be the greatest and most powerful, can maintain his place against his closely following rivals only with the most strenuous effort. If, notwithstanding, monopoly remains one of the greatest problems of our age, this is due not alone to the fact that the conditions favorable to competition are realized only with delay and in any event incompletely, but also to the manifold, often unconscious governmental interventions which frustrate competition. Perhaps the most serious of such interventions are those governmental measures aimed at eliminating foreign competition by means of restrictions on imports.

There is no question but that the outmoded old-liberal view that the desirable situation of free competition is self-perpetuating so long as the state refrains from economic interventions of any kind has been shown to be a fateful error. At the same time, there is a kernel of truth in the notion. Maximum international trade has been shown to be a highly effective corrective for monopolistic tendencies. But it would be unrealistic to count on the realization of this ideal, and even in such case it would be an unjustified simplification to regard the problem of modern monopolism as solved. Consequently, the governments of the free nations of the world cannot avoid the obligation of making the restraint and reduction of monopoly the object of a specific antimonopoly policy. The obligation is indeed one of the most urgent confronting those anxious to defend the free economy successfully against a collectivism whose appeal and propaganda are based largely on the alleged monopoly elements in "capitalism."

Since it happens only rarely that an individual producer can attain and maintain a more than temporary monopoly position (exception being made for the case of natural resources), the existence of monopoly generally supposes that a number of producers have joined together for the express purpose of eliminating competition among themselves (the principal form of such combination is the cartel, though it is to be observed that not all cartels are formed for the purpose of eliminating competition, in particular not such cartels whose interest is the promotion of more rational specialization, scientific research, and the exchange of technological information). In this case, freedom of contract is uniquely and illegitimately misused to restrict contractual freedom and hence economic freedom in general.

At the same time, the inherent difficulties and weaknesses of the cartel ought not be underestimated. As noted above, it is not easy to bring together the firms of a given industry and to keep them together in spite of their persistently divergent interests, and it is still less easy to deal effectively with the omnipresent threat of competition by outsiders who can destroy the cartel by selling below the cartel price. With the intent of overcoming such difficulties the cartels customarily resort to the technique of "compulsory membership," a procedure which must arouse the deepest misgivings. A further disturbing fact is that the difficulties attendant on the formation of cartels vary in severity in different industries (they are least important in those heavy industries which consist of a few large firms, whose fixed capital investments are large, and which are engaged in the production of homogeneous mass-produced commodities), with the result that the less "cartelizable" industries (finished goods industries such as the textile industry) are at a serious disadvantage.

Antimonopoly policy is consequently essentially identical with the legal control of the cartel form of organization. Such control may take three forms. The mildest—and therefore also the least effective —form is the one under which cartels are admitted in principle and only their "abuse" prohibited (principle of prevention of abuse). The second possibility is the prohibition of cartels as such, enforced by the police power of the state (principle of prohibition on the model of the American antitrust legislation of 1890). The third and most desirable form of control is to make cartels subject not to criminal but civil prosecution and thereby to deprive a cartel agreement as an abuse of freedom of contract of the protection of the law (principle of denial of legal protection), without prejudice to the legal exceptions that might made to such a general rule. There is ground for the expectation that the adoption of this form of control would solve the problem of monopolism satisfactorily and silently.

5. *Price Interrelationships*

Up to now we have considered the formation of prices only on a limited market, as if each time we had to do only with a particular market and a particular good. In truth, however, the several markets are more or less closely interconnected and to this fact we must now give a moment's attention.

Markets are related to one another first in the general sense that supply and demand on one market are somehow affected by total demand and total supply on all other markets. If more of one good is suddenly demanded, less of some other good will be demanded. If small plane flying should become a popular sport, it is probable that the demand for baby carriages and baby clothes would decline since the incomes of most people would be insufficient for the upkeep both of an aeroplane and a numerous family. If bread and butter are expensive, the demand for books or furniture will suffer—one could give endless examples of this.

But besides this general interdependence of all markets, we find also a special and narrower interdependence of those markets which, in one way or another are directly "joined."

The *first* example of such a joint relationship is the case of commodities which are *substitutes* for one another: margarine for butter, artificial for real silk, tea for coffee. It is clear that movements in the prices of such substitute goods will show a marked parallelism. These market relationships have an additional importance in that the possibility of substituting one commodity for another provides consumers with alternatives that tend to limit excessive price fluctuations.

Consider now a *second* and still closer interrelationship resulting from the so-called *joint production* of goods. This concept is taken to mean goods which are produced simultaneously by the same productive act, such as gas, coke, and tar in gas (or coke) production, or as iron and slag in foundry operations, or as wool and meat in sheep-raising. All these cases—and they are surprisingly numerous—of joint production present a most interesting variation from the usual type of price formation. Goods of this type are the Siamese twins of the economy, each of whom has its own life and would like to follow its own way but is nevertheless linked inseparably to the other. The salient point is that one of the linked goods cannot be produced without the other; their costs of production are joint and indivisible. It is of course true in this case as elsewhere that total receipts must cover the combined costs of production if production is to be maintained in the long run. The proportion in which the costs of production are shared by the jointly produced commodities (as reflected in their prices) is determined by the intensity of demand for the one and for the other commodity. If there is a greater demand for one of the products than for the other, the one for which there is the lesser demand must be sold at a price low enough to assure the disposal of what amounts to a "waste product." Thus, if the demand for the principal commodity increases without a corresponding increase in demand for the by-product, there may result, by reason of the unavoidable joint production relationship, a marked fall in the price of the by-product. Consequently, those producers who are concerned solely with the by-product, may find themselves in a most vexing situation. A good example of this is silver which, in recent times, has been supplied largely as a by-product of copper and zinc production. Since the demand for copper and zinc has increased much more than for silver, a fall in the price of silver has ensued which—until the rise in silver prices in 1961-62—severely affected operations of mines engaged in the production of silver only.[7]

Consider next, as a final example of market interrelationships, commodities which are complementary to each other and which are consequently jointly demanded. There are many such goods: ink, pens and paper; trout and white wine; collars and ties, etc. The understanding of this market relationship can be of real importance for those responsible for economic policy. If, for instance, it is desired to better the position of a given industry, an efficacious course of action might be to lower the price of a complementary good. One could, for example, bring about a preceptible improvement in the position of the dairy industry in many countries by lowering the tariff on coffee imports.

6. *Foreign Trade and International Price Formation*

For a highly developed country, self-sufficiency remains a dream and, to vary a well-known expression of Moltke's, not even a pleasant dream—all the less pleasant the larger, the richer, and the more powerful a country is and wishes to remain. It is fitting, then, that we include in our survey a brief description of the special characteristics of international market and price relationships.[8]

Technical advances in the transportation and preservation of goods have gradually eliminated the chief obstacle to commerce between widely separated regions, viz., the expenses and the losses connected with the conquest of distance. Indeed, international trade has truly become world trade, linking together not only neighboring countries but also those most remote from one another. To be sure, not all goods are equally suited to international trade, since the resistance of each good to the conquest of distance varies. There are goods which are real globe-trotters, whose motto might be said to be "where I prosper (i.e., where I get the highest price), there is my country." They are of such robust constitution that neither the longest overland trips nor the most fatiguing sea voyages seem to affect them. They do not spoil; moreover, their specific value (i.e., their value per unit of weight or volume) is high enough to remain relatively unaffected by transport costs. These are the goods which are designated as international goods. To this group belong the bulk goods of world trade: wheat, metals, rubber, coffee, textiles, etc., and the majority of manufactured goods.

Other goods are not so cosmopolitan. Their "patriotism" is so marked that only in exceptional cases do they undertake a trip abroad. To this group belong goods which spoil quickly: strawberries, fresh fish, livestock, and finally—the proletarians among goods—paving stones and bricks. The latter could no doubt survive the longest voyage, but their specific value is so slight that they would be unable to afford the travel expenses involved. Lastly, there is a group of goods whose patriotism is truly staunch; there is nothing to be gained in their being shipped abroad. Such are goods which, as in the case of certain household goods, serve solely for the satisfaction of a want peculiar to one country.

In addition to material goods, services have acquired increasing importance in world trade, a proof of which is the ever-growing extension of tourist traffic (the so-called "invisible" imports and exports). The majority of services must, in fact, be procured in a given locality and it is upon this peculiarity that the tourist trade rests. The movement of tourists to Switzerland thus represents a virtual (invisible) exportation, though it is certain that not every Zurich barber realizes that in cutting an English traveler's hair, he is engaging in the export business.

It is, however, not without interest to note the fact that technical progress has made possible the transportation of services which heretofore were available only locally. The motion picture industry, for example, makes it possible for a theatrical performance to be packed in a tin and shipped, ready to be enjoyed, throughout the whole world, a development which has had no small significance for the world economy. Radio and now television-by-satellite render even the film-container superfluous. Whether application of the canned goods principle to art will preserve its quality while increasing its quantity remains an open question.

But international trade is not confined to goods and services alone. It also includes, exactly as trade within a country, every conceivable type of credit transaction and capital transfer. In the course of the development of international trade, the latter activities have acquired ever increasing importance, but they pose problems too complicated to be discussed here.

The importance of international trade can hardly be over-emphasized. The fact is that the nations of the world have, in recent generations, attained a degree of economic interdependence of which few persons have any accurate idea. All countries, all regions are today so closely linked together by economic interrelationships of every kind that a whole has been created in whose successful functioning, as well as in whose decline and destruction, all share. If we do not succeed in rebuilding the structure of the world economy, so heavily damaged by the storms of recent decades, every country will be condemned, in greater or lesser degree, to the ravages of a lingering aenemia. No country can remain indifferent to the success or failure of the reconstruction of the world economy. No country which has its own interest at heart can afford not to contribute its share to such a reconstruction.

A fact which merits the attention of psychologists and sociologists is the astonishing inability of most people to comprehend any matters relating to international trade—a purblindness such as they manifest towards no other aspect of economic life. Surrounded by this incomprehension, the economist's task is a truly ungrateful one. Having in view the welfare of his country, his concern is to explain dispassionately the nature and functions of foreign trade, disassociating these from the extra-economic difficulties arising from such trade. However, the effort to reveal the inanity of the arguments which are invoked in favor of sealing up the country economically, and to expose the superstition behind the fear of an unfavorable balance of trade is one which generally meets with a peculiarly disappointing response. It is not without reason that the great English economist Alfred Marshall could say that for a true economist it was almost impossible to be a good patriot and to have at the same time the reputation of being one.

It is, of course, true that it is precisely in the realm of international trade that we encounter concepts which are especially difficult to comprehend. These concepts can be mastered only when we begin by considering the nature of international trade in its simplest form, starting with the idea that, exactly as internal trade, it rests on the division of labor and on the exchange of goods resulting from this division of labor. No matter how widely extended in space is trade arising from the division of labor, nor how bewildering the tangle of enterprises that compose it, the whole resolves into one process, the nature of which was previously made clear in our discussion of the structure of the division of labor. The fact that in the case of international trade the participants in the process belong to different payment communities does not any more change its underlying character than the fact that they possess different passports and different residences. Nonetheless, international trade encompasses a number of peculiarities which, in a given instance, may give rise to difficult theoretical and practical problems.

Once we have grasped the idea that foreign trade is founded on the principle of the division of labor, the real functions of imports and exports become immediately clear, and a number of misunderstandings are dissipated. Above all, we are in a position to rectify the widespread notion that an export is something good and an import something bad, so that what matters most is to export as much as possible and to import as little as possible. Clearly, exports and imports stand in the relationship of means to end: to be supplied as abundantly as possible with goods is the end, but since the foreigner, alas, generally does not make us a gift of his goods, we must give something for them, and what we give are exports. There are, to be sure, many commodities which we get gratis from abroad, e.g., birds of passage, flotsam, fish, and so forth, and if the concept "abroad" is taken in a vertical sense, we can also include in our reckoning sunlight, meteors, and other presents from Heaven. No one will complain over these cases of "pure" imports, no one will anxiously inquire whether there has been a corresponding export. But the cheaper is a foreign good, the closer it approaches to being a free gift. The less must a country export to pay for its imports, i.e., the higher are export prices in comparison to import prices, the greater is that country's gain from the international division of labor.[9]

This conclusion, however, is so opposed by current opinion on the subject, that we must attempt still a second demonstration of its truth. When a country does not produce everything itself but procures some things through exchange with another country, it adopts a method which—as we learned in a foregoing section of this book (pp. 66-67, 129)—permits it to produce certain products cheaper than before. Let us suppose that foreign trade between Turkey and Switzerland consists in the exchange of Turkish tobacco against Swiss paper. We may then conceive of the paper factories in Switzerland as nothing other than huge machines producing cheap tobacco. Conversely, the eye of the economist discovers that the tobacco fields of Anatolia are, in the last analysis, plantations on which paper is grown more cheaply than if it were produced directly. Foreign trade is similar, then, to a labor-saving machine or to any other method of lowering production costs. The usefulness of this machine is the greater, the more favorable is the ratio of cost to yield, i.e., the less we are required to export in order to obtain a given quantity of imports. The dearer is tobacco and the cheaper is paper, the better it is for Turkey, and *vice versa* for Switzerland. Were the Swiss to put an end to this exchange by prohibiting tobacco imports and growing tobacco themselves, they would be behaving exactly as if they had smashed a labor-saving machine. In addition, the question would arise as to who would now buy Swiss paper, for the Swiss who had up to this point purchased Turkish tobacco had also thereby indirectly purchased their own paper. Conversely, by prohibiting the import of paper, Turkey would not only deprive herself of good and inexpensive paper but would cause a part of the harvest of

tobacco to remain unsold inasmuch as every Turk who had purchased paper had also indirectly purchased Anatolian tobacco.

But perhaps all that we have said thus far is not fully convincing,
since it appears to suggest that there is really no foreign trade problem at all. Should all countries then proceed to pension off their
customs officials? Although worse things could befall mankind, our
preceding reflections have had no such radical objective in view.
Foreign trade, in fact, encompasses a number of problems which are
extremely difficult to solve and which may justify some degree of
state regulation. But these problems are quite other than what they
are usually thought to be. It is impossible, in a few words, to give
any adequate description of them. It must suffice to refer to what
has already been brought out in another part of our inquiry: that
for the increase in productivity which we owe to the division of labor
we must pay a price in the form of possible economic, social, and
cultural disadvantages. The further the division of labor is pushed,
the more proper it becomes to ask the question whether this price
is not too high. This applies especially to the international division
of labor which, for obvious reasons, is possessed of a particularly
unstable and uncertain character. It is for this very reason that the
ideal of obtaining provisions as cheaply as possible is, at present,
frequently thrust in the background in favor of other ideals. We
should beware, nonetheless, of allowing ourselves to be led astray
by those who cite these ideals merely to cloak their own economic
interests. To this we may add that the importation of cheap goods,
though generally advantageous at present, can have a paralyzing influence on the future development of domestic production or can
lead to costly dislocations to which it would be undesirable to see
the domestic economy exposed. These few remarks must suffice to
show that one need not do violence to logic to justify the purpose-
fulness of governmental interventions in foreign trade. Economics
does not teach that every intervention of the state is an evil; it
teaches only that it is necessary to weigh carefully the facts in the
given case, and thereby proves itself to be the indispensable instrument of a far-sighted and genuinely national policy.

In spite of all we said thus far, we have not yet fully clarified the
principle of the international division of labor. Carrying our inquiry further, we discover a difficulty which has already given rise
to many wrong opinions. When I write books and leave to the
carpenter the job of making bookshelves, I provide one more instance

of that division of labor in which every individual is superior in his own field to the nonprofessional and indubitably the better off, economically, for such specialization. But what if it is a question of cataloguing my library? Would it be advantageous for me to engage someone for this task, even though I can do it better myself? Should I engage a gardener to spade my garden although I could do the work just as well myself? There can be no question that it would be to my advantage to employ a librarian and a gardener if my skill in writing books is greater than in cataloguing or spading. It is easy to transpose these simple cases to the level of the world economy. In the exchange of goods between tropical countries and northern industrial countries we have an obvious case of reciprocal superiority in production. We can now also understand how two countries can enjoy a profitable commercial exchange even though one of them is inferior to the other in all branches of production, the proviso being that its inferiority is not the same in all branches of production. Israel for example, is a country which has received a niggardly endowment from Nature. Many infer from this that the Israeli economy should be protected against competition from more favored countries. But there is no reason why Israel should not also enter into advantageous trade relations with countries which are superior to it, if it limits itself to those branches of production in which its inferiority is the least. On the contrary, since Israel can change nothing with respect to its generally rather unfavorable production conditions, the resort to tariff protection to render profitable branches of production in which its inferiority is relatively great can only worsen its situation, to say nothing of the fact that thereby the burden of its productive inferiority would probably be shifted to weaker shoulders. Naturally, such a country must resign itself to having low money costs (meaning, chiefly, low wages), but it would be a still poorer country were it to refuse to share in the division of labor of the world economy. Poor countries can afford even less than rich ones to shut themselves off from the world economy.

In a world where people could move freely from one country to another, equilibrium would result from the fact that people inhabiting the poor countries would flow into the rich countries until average incomes had attained the same level everywhere. There would be, then, no rich countries or poor countries, but only countries with dense or sparse populations. But since there are in fact a thousand and one obstacles to international migration, people must accommodate themselves to unfavorable production conditions by being content with low average incomes. Moreover, their situation could not fail to be considerably improved by the fact that the world economy would allow them to confine their production to the industries in which they can best meet competition. In this way, the international movement of goods acts as a substitute for the now shackled international movement of persons.[10]

NOTES

1. (p. 143) *The Interplay of Supply, Demand and Price*

Price, on a free market, is stabilized only when it has reached a point at which supply and demand are equal. It follows at once that every variation from this equilibrium point acts on supply or on demand in such a way that the price oscillates around the equilibrium point. A diagrammatic representation of this mechanism (in its simplest form) will help us to grasp the relationships involved:

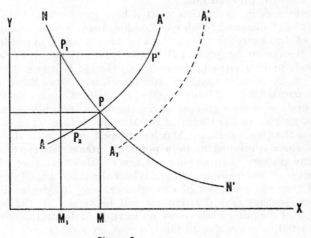

Figure 2.

In this diagram, the unit quantities of a good are inscribed on the X axis while the monetary units are inscribed on the Y axis. The curve NN'—called the demand curve—indicates which amounts of a given commodity would be demanded at different possible prices. This curve is, of course, arbitrarily drawn, but it shows us that the amount demanded tends to fall when the price rises and decreases when the price falls. Correspondingly, the curve AA'—called the supply curve—indicates that supply increases with rising and decreases with falling prices. If we let P denote the point at which the two curves intersect, then the equilibrium price, according to our elementary axiom, is PM. We may establish the truth of this proposition by employing a sort of indirect geometrical proof in which we suppose that a higher price obtains (for example, we may suppose that price lies at the point P_1M_1). From our diagram it is clear at once that this price is untenable, since there will now be an excess of supply over demand (P_1p_1) which will depress the price until it has fallen back to the point P. The same principle applies if we suppose a case in which the price is at a point below P (e.g., at P_2). Hence, it follows that in the long run no other price than the price PM is tenable.

The above diagram ought to be engraved on the memory since it provides an easy and exact demonstration of the simultaneous interplay of supply, demand and price. It shows, moreover, with especial clarity, that supply and demand should never be regarded independently of price; that, on the contrary, every price is, other things being equal, related to specific aggregate amounts of supply and demand. This is what we have referred to in the text as the supply schedule and the demand schedule. Changing conditions (e.g., fashion changes on the demand side, technological progress on the supply side) can, of course, cause supply and demand schedules to change. In this case we must bring about a shift of either the supply curve or of the demand curve. Assume that the market of interest is the market for electric light bulbs and assume further that a new process of manufacture has brought about a reduction in the costs of these bulbs. We shall find that we should have to substitute a new supply curve for the old (e.g., $A_1A'_1$). The new equilibrium price will be found to lie at some point lower than the previous one.

The form of demonstration selected here goes back to Alfred Marshall whose *Principles of Economics* (8th ed.; London, 1922) is indispensable for a thorough study of the interrelationships which we have sketched in outline only. See also: H. D. Henderson, *Supply and Demand* (New York, 1922); E. Barone, *Principi di economia politica* (1st ed.; Rome, 1908); George J. Stigler, *The Theory of Price* (2nd ed.; New York, 1953); H. von Stackleberg, *Grundlagen der theoretischen Volkswirtschaftslehre* (Berne, 1948); W. Krelle, *Preistheorie* (1961). The Marshall study gives us a glimpse of the theoretical difficulties encountered in any careful analysis of the theory of market equilibrium. One of these difficulties, perhaps the greatest, caused Marshall himself no little trouble and has even in recent times continued to be a point of intense interest to economists. The difficulty emerges when account is taken of "time"—a factor which in economic analysis is all too easily neglected. Where the time factor is included, it will be found that while one set of consequences may be yielded in the short run, another, perhaps very different set will be yielded in the long run. As the example of the automobile shows, an increase in demand over a long period can cause a fall in prices due to the fact that, in accordance with the law of mass production, it results in a shifting of the supply curve towards the right.

2. (p. 147) *The Elasticity of Supply and Demand*

The slopes of the supply and demand curves also reflect the degree of elasticity of supply and demand. The less is the amount of slope of the curve, the greater, in both cases, is the elasticity. The particular problems connected with these concepts, which are as important as they are interesting, have received increasing attention in the literature. Cf. Henry Schultz, *Statistical Laws of Demand and Supply* (Chicago, 1928); G. F. Warren and F. A. Pearson, *Interrelationships of Supply and Price* (Ithaca, N.Y., 1928); J. Marschak, *Elastizität der Nachfrage* (1931). The concept of elasticity obviously opens up a fertile field for statistical mathematics, and there is every reason for continuing to follow progress in this field with the closest attention (e.g., the calculation of exact coefficients of elasticity for individual commodities). If it is planned to increase the amount of a consumption tax or of a tariff, to reduce railroad rates or to enact some similar measure, it is generally desirable to have a precise idea of the elasticity of demand in the given case in order to evaluate the possible consequences. To be sure, it should not be forgotten that in the matter of elasticity coefficients we are dealing with historical, and hence changing data, and not with constant magnitudes. On these matters, see L. von Mises, *Human Action* (New Haven, 1949), pp. 347-354, a book which takes a decided and, we may add, justified stand on the issues in question and simultaneously warns of the misuses of mathematical methods in economics.

3. (p. 148) *King's Rule*

It may prove helpful, in trying to grasp the meaning of King's rule, to dwell for a moment on a highly simplified economic situation. Let us suppose that in a given year wheat is harvested to a total of 100,000 bushels and that at the price of $1.00 per bushel it yields a total income of $100,000. Suppose further that in the following year the harvest reaches 125,000 bushels. Will total income be the same, higher, or lower? It is clear that this depends solely upon the elasticity of demand for wheat. If elasticity is such that demand increases in exactly the same proportion in which the price falls (unitary elasticity) total income, where price is $.80 per bushel, will again be $100,000. But let us now suppose that the coefficient of elasticity for wheat is less than 1. Then the total income yielded by the new harvest will be less than the amount received for the previous year's harvest. At a price of $.70 per bushel total receipts would amount to only $87,500. This does not necessarily mean that the farmers will be worse off for it is still required to know what the costs per unit would be for a more abundant harvest. It can be supposed in any event that in not a few instances farmers stand to gain less from an abundant harvest than from a poor one. Cf. W. Röpke, "Das Agrarproblem der Vereinigten Staaten II, *"Archiv für Sozialwissenschaft,* Vol. 59, 1928, pp. 96 ff.

We must proceed, cautiously, however, in attempting to make practical use of *King's rule* in the field of agricultural policy. In the first place, we should keep in mind that this rule applies only to grains. In the case of refined as distinct from raw agricultural products, the coefficient of elasticity of demand is higher (unity and above). This means that, for example, in a period of declining prices (or rising consumer incomes) the prospects for increased sale of butter and similar products may be considered good. There is little cause to fear over-production if the farmer is given the opportunity of obtaining inexpensive cattle feed and, in consequence, finds himself able to get by with a lower price for his butter. The results of over-production may be additionally offset by economic policy aimed at raising the income of the consumers (and thus incidentally favoring the production of the refined agricultural products). In the middle European countries where the production of refined agricultural goods, due to the proximity of markets, enjoys a natural advantage over the production of staple foods (grains), a rational agricultural policy will consist above all in a policy of lowering tariffs on grains. From such a policy, the following will result: (1) cheapening of the costs of production for the refined agricultural products; (2) increase in the amount of consumer income available for such products; (3) fall in the price of the refined commodities and to this extent a sensible improvement in the urban food supply; (4) contracting of advantageous trade agreements, improvement of the situation of the export industries, and increase of consumer incomes; (5) specific improvement of the small agricultural unit (peasant holding)* and, since the production of refined agricultural products requires an especially intensive application of labor, an increase of employment opportunities in agriculture. On these questions see: W. Röpke, *German Commercial Policy* (London, 1934); W. Röpke, *International Economic Disintegration, op. cit.;* W. Röpke, *The Social Crisis of Our Time* (Chicago, 1950); W. Röpke, *Civitas Humana* (London, 1948); W. Röpke, *International Order and Economic Integration* (Dordrecht, Holland, 1959).

---

*The German is *bäuerliche Wirtschaft.* Literally translated this means "peasant economy." But the author writes in his *International Economic Disintegration* (3rd ed.; London, 1959): "I am fully aware that the word 'peasant,' having clearly disparaging connotations, is no real equivalent to the French word 'paysan' or the German word 'Bauer.' Other terms which have been suggested to the author by his Anglo-Saxon friends—like 'agricultural freeholder' or 'farmer yeoman'—sound too artificial and labored. The only possibility left, then, would seem to be to retain the word 'peasant,' and to ask the Anglo-Saxon reader to forget for the moment its pejorative sense until a better term is suggested."—*Translator's Note.*

4. (p. 156) *The Formation of Monopoly Price*

Here again the decisive relationships are best demonstrated with the aid of a diagram. As previously, we inscribe on the X axis the units of quantity, and on the Y axis units of money, and we suppose NN' to be the curve of demand for a given monopolized commodity.

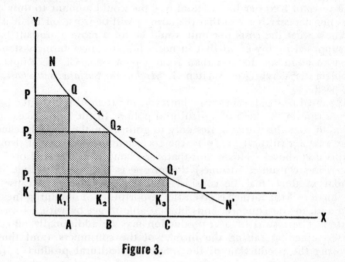

Figure 3.

Moreover, we assume that the monopolist's costs of production per unit remain the same, regardless of the amount of production (constant costs). We designate this cost behavior by the straight line KL. The monopolist will naturally choose a price situated somewhere above OK. But where? Which of the many possible prices will he choose? Should he choose too high a price, he will, as we can see from our diagram, be able to sell only the quantity OA. The whole of his gain will be inscribed in the rectangle PKK_1Q. If, on the other hand, he wishes to sell a large quantity, e.g., the amount OC, it is evident that he will have to lower his price to OP_1. In this case his gain is PKK_3Q_1. Clearly, the monopolist has chosen in this case too low a price. He will now proceed to experiment until he has arrived at the price OP_2, at which the product of the quantity sold times profit per unit attains its maximum. This is shown in the rectangle $P_2KK_2Q_2$. The reader is free to vary the diagram to take account of rising or falling unit costs or different degrees of elasticity. In this way, he can chart for himself the relationships we have dwelt on in the text.

The richly complicated theory of monopoly price belongs to one of the most intensively developed sectors of modern economics. It is a field which is especially suited to mathematical analysis (Pantaleoni, Edgeworth, Pigou, Stackelberg, *et al.*). An excellent survey of the subject of monopolistic *price differentia-*

tion will be found in the monograph of my student Kurt Michalski, *Das Prinzip der Preisdifferenzierung* (Marburger sozialokönomische Forschungen, No. 1, 1932). See also: R. Bordaz, *Coûts constants et prix multiples* (Paris, 1942).

5. (p. 157) *Price Formation under Imperfect Competition* .

Perfect competition may be precisely defined as that situation which obtains when demand for the output of each producer is perfectly elastic. Otherwise expressed, under perfect competition no producer can ask more than another without risking the loss of all his customers; should he demand less than other producers, they would lose all their patronage to him. These being the pre-requisites of perfect competition, it is understandable how rarely such a market situation occurs. In most cases, competition is in fact more or less imperfect. The ensuing problems are just those which have been most searchingly analyzed in recent economic literature. In particular, there has been much attention given to the importance of advertising as a cause of "imperfect (monopolistic) competition." See especially: E. Chamberlin, *The Theory of Monopolistic Competition* (Cambridge [Mass.], 1933); J. Robinson, *The Economics of Imperfect Competition* (London, 1933); R. Triffin, *Monopolistic Competition and General Equilibrium* (Cambridge [Mass.], 1940); A. Kozlik, "Monopol oder Monopolistische Konkurrenz?" *Zeitschrift für Schweizerische Statistik und Volkswirtschaft,* 1941; H. von Stackelberg, *op. cit.;* W. Fellner, *Competition Among the Few* (New York, 1950); *Monopoly and Competition and their Regulation,* ed. W. H. Chamberlin (London, 1953); F. Machlup, *The Economics of Sellers' Competition* (Baltimore, 1952).

6. (p. 160) *The Harmfulness of Monopoly*

To the list of the evils of monopoly already cited we can add still others to which reference will be made in a later chapter. At the same time, we ought not to lose sight of the fact that in a restricted number of cases monopoly is economically superior to competition. We refer here to those enterprises termed "public utilities." Such enterprises have a twofold character: on the one hand they serve to provide the public with goods and services of vital importance (electricity, gas, water, railroads, streetcars, busses, postal services, etc.); on the other, the very essence of these enterprises is such that to permit the establishment of competing units would be uneconomical, if not also technically impossible in view of the large amounts of capital involved as well as the complicated network of property rights which public utilities require (e.g., the underground conduits for wires and cables required by the telephone company).

The politico-economic problem of public utilities resides in the fact that while their monopoly character is more or less unavoidable, it is at the same time particularly dangerous since these enterprises serve to satisfy urgent (i.e., inelastic) public needs. For the solution of this problem there are two possibilities: either we allow the public utilities to exist as private enterprises, though still requiring them to submit to governmental regulation, or we establish in their place official state or community monopolies. Which of the two solutions would be the more purposeful can be determined only with difficulty, since much depends on the special circumstances obtaining in each country and on the particular type of public utility in question. The experience of the United States, where the system of regulated private monopoly prevails, has shown that efficacious supervision is difficult to realize and may well involve serious inconveniences. The over-all disadvantages of state-managed enterprises, on the other hand, argue against the system of state monopolies. (We may note, however, that it is precisely in the case of [publicly operated] public utilities that management is subjected to a salutary scrutiny. The enterprises in question are daily and hourly in intimate and sensitive contact with the public. It is the prestige of the state or of the community which is at stake when complaints are directed against the public utilities of overcharging or poor service, while a well-administered public utility may prove to a particularly effective advertisement of the virtues of public ownership of enterprise.)

7. (p. 167) *Joint Production*

Price formation in joint production is interesting from a theoretical standpoint for it is one of those cases in which the classical economists had already been forced to recognize the impossibility of explaining price behavior by means of a cost-of-production theory and the necessity of returning to the concept of demand for such an explanation. It was Marshall who undertook the first thorough investigation of the problem.

In the text, it was assumed that the quantitative ratio obtaining as between a pair of jointly produced commodities is determined by the technical peculiarities of the productive process in question. However, we find frequent instances in which this proportion can be changed by the producers, for example, by the breeding of sheep for wool instead of for meat and *vice versa*. In these cases, there is a perceptible loosening of the link that binds the jointly produced commodities together. *Cf.* Henderson, *op. cit.*, Chapter V.

The practical importance of joint production is very great and is in the way of becoming even more so. We see its significance with especial clarity in agriculture (Cf. H. Marquardt, *Die Ausrichtung der Landwirtschaflichen Produktion an den Preisen* (Jena, 1934). Indeed, even the different floors of an apartment house can, save the top floor,* be considered as jointly produced goods. Here, too, the production costs of one floor cannot be distinguished from the production costs of another, with the result that rents are graduated according to the intensity of demand, the first floors ("beletage") generally getting more.

---

*In Switzerland, and formerly in Germany, the top floor is used as a storeroom.— *Translator's Note.*

8. (p. 168) *The Theory of Foreign Trade*

International trade has always occupied a large place in economic theory. Even as far back as the classical period, it was a well-developed branch of economic science, its aim being the investigation of those special characteristics of the economic process which derive from the nature of international trade (the conquest of distance, the relative immobility of the factors of production, the differences in monetary systems, political factors, etc.). Much attention has been devoted to analysis of the monetary factors, as we have indicated above (Chapter V, Note 10). In addition to the books mentioned there, see: G. Haberler, *Theory of International Trade* (London, 1950) ; G. Haberler, article "Aussenhandel," *Handwörterbuch der Sozialwissenschaften*, 1954; B. Ohlin, *Interregional and International Trade* (Cambridge [Mass.], 1933), deals especially with the problem of foreign trade as a special case of the general economic problem of distance; W. Beveridge, *et al.*, *Tariffs: The Case Examined* (London, 1931), a very instructive combination of theoretical and practical problems;

J. W. Angell, *The Theory of International Prices* (Cambridge [Mass.], 1926), a thorough treatment of the monetary aspects; R. F. Harrod, *International Economics* (London, 1939); P. T. Ellsworth, *The International Economy* (New York, 1950); W. Röpke, *International Economic Disintegration, op. cit.*; W. Röpke, *International Order and Economic Integration, op. cit.* Outside of what may be said to fall into the category of simple denunciations or invective, the attempts (made in these books) to overthrow classical theory are surprisingly rare. Most such attempts amount merely to corrections, greater or lesser as the case may be, of classical theory. A case in point is Friedrich List's *National System of Political Economy* (1841) which was said to have had the merit of effectively combating, from an historical and evolutionary standpoint, the "long run" formulae of the classical economists. In fact, List's work represented only an important stage in the perfecting of classical theory. A more recent and more radical attempt of this sort is that of M. Manoilesco, *Théorie du protectionnisme et de l'échange international* (Paris, 1929), effectively criticized by B. Ohlin in "Protection and Non-Competing Groups," *Weltwirtschaftliches Archiv*, Vol. 33, January 1931. Those who oppose to the pure theory of foreign trade politico-military arguments will find they are forcing an open door. Adam Smith long since assigned a preeminent place to such arguments. One can subscribe fully to the scientific theory of foreign trade and still take sides for a closed economy; in such case one has at least the advantage of being perfectly aware of the "costs" involved. Most of the attacks against economic theory in general, and against the theory of foreign trade in particular, stem from nothing else than a *fear of clarity*: the attackers try by the sheer loudness of their polemics to give the impression that their arguments are weighty.

9. (p. 171) *The National Gain from Foreign Trade*

Taking a closer look we find that foreign trade procures the following advantages: (1) Certain products are obtainable only by means of foreign trade, viz., those which do not exist inside the country or which can be produced there only at enormous cost (e.g., the greater part of the industrial raw materials used in Europe's industrialized regions). (2) Foreign trade provides us with goods which, though it may be economically possible to produce them at home, will cost us still more than if we imported them from abroad. Hence, it is preferable to import such goods in exchange for those products which can be produced more economically at home. (3) In the distribution of goods through space and time foreign trade acts as a compensatory mechanism by means of which an international balance is established as between the several national markets, thus putting an end to a situation (of frequent occurrence in former times) in which surpluses prevailed in one country and famine in another. It is a sort of escape valve which assures a practically constant "atmospheric pressure," a kind of insurance against the enormous fluctuations to which, otherwise, economic life—were it subject only to the influence of harvests—would be exposed. How important this function is, becomes clear when the mechanism of the world economy breaks down. (4) Foreign trade is an effective antidote to the monopolistic hardening of the arteries of the several national economies, for it subjects the attempts of business units to "coalesce" to the pressure of foreign competition, thus tending to prevent a degeneration of our economic system through "capitalist" exploitation.

Each country participates in these advantages of foreign trade. Naturally, this does not exclude the possibility of one country having a numerical gain greater than that of another country; that is determined by the ratio of export to import prices or, by what amounts to the same thing, the quantity of imports which can be had for a given quantity of exports (the "real ratio of exchange," Taussig's "barter terms of trade"). How important this concept is, is shown by the example of such countries as National Socialist Germany where, thanks to export subsidies on the one hand and the increased price of raw materials (resulting from clearing and compensation agreements) on the other, the barter terms of trade underwent substantial deterioration. The "under-valuation" of a country's currency on the world's exchanges has the same effect. There can be no doubt but that the terms of trade is an important factor in national prosperity.

10. (p. 174) *The Law of Comparative Costs*

The interrelationships which we sought to clarify in our discussion of Israel's economy are usually considered as deriving from the *law of comparative costs*, first formulated by Ricardo in his *Principles of Political Economy and Taxation*, Chapter VII. Strict interpretation of his (in its general outlines still accepted) concept gives rise to difficulties, as shown by the more recent literature on the subject. These difficulties, however, in no way affect the essential truth of the law. It is to be observed that it is also as applicable *within* a country in which there are regions possessing different economic characteristics as it is between different countries. Thus, conditions of production in eastern Germany were certainly more unfavorable, under almost every head, than in western Germany, a fact which in no way prevented both halves of the country from enjoying the benefits of a close economic relationship, unencumbered by any internal tariff walls. No doubt eastern Germany, in order to be able to compete with other suppliers, had to content itself with a lower wage level, but it cannot be denied that if it had erected a customs barrier against western Germany, it would have placed itself in an even worse position. In spite of the almost complete economic inferiority of eastern Germany, both East and West were mutually advantaged by the resulting division of labor, the East limiting itself to that branch of production in which it could best meet competition, namely, agriculture.

CHAPTER VII

RICH AND POOR

"La majestueuse égalite des lois, qui interdit au riche
comme au pauvre de coucher sous les ponts, de men-
dier dans les rues et de voler du pain."
ANATOLE FRANCE, *Le Lys Rouge, VII*

1. *The Distribution of Income*

As he analyzes the mechanism of our economic system, the economist finds himself lapsing easily into the language of GHQ com-
muniqués—those cold, impersonal descriptions of military operations
which leave it to the reader to picture the sum of human resolves,
deeds, and sufferings that lie behind the bare words. We speak
facilely, for example, of the purchasing power of money, although
we know quite well that money does not enter the market by itself
but that it gets there because individual human beings, at once
deliberate, weak, and passionate, have spent it. Similarly, we have
spoken of the demand for a good almost as if it were a physical
quantum, in the certain expectation that the reader would remain
at every instance aware of the abbreviated form of expression which
we here employed. As a matter of fact, the demand for a good is
made up of the demands of all individuals who, with reference to a
specific price, decide to employ a specific part of their income for the
said good. These individual portions of demand, moreover, vary
greatly in amount, not only because of differences in taste but also
because of the inequality of incomes.

Herewith our discussion turns upon that phase of economic inquiry which, in every age, has most deeply interested the majority of mankind. The contrast between rich and poor, between the hovel and the palace, between the haves and the have-nots—this is the great question which for thousands of years has agitated the minds and hearts of men. And, inevitably, the ages in which the contrast was most acute brought forth the champions of justice and equality: the prophets of the Old Testament, the Gracchi of Rome, the founders of the great religions, the peasant leaders and the religious dissenters of the Middle Ages and of the Reformation, the socialists, Communists, and anarchists, the agrarian and social reformers from Solon to the present. In the civilized countries of our own day this problem has lost nothing of its actuality, although it is precisely in the most advanced countries that we find a tendency for it to become less rather than more acute. The distribution of income is everywhere unequal in the sense that as contrasted with the large number of small incomes, we find only a small number of large incomes. While to this law there appears to have been never and nowhere an exception—least of all in Soviet Russia—inequality in some countries has lessened due to the existence of an extensive middle class. Contrariwise, in other countries—and those certainly not the highly developed "capitalistic" countries—we find the bitterest poverty standing directly alongside the most ostentatious wealth. But what arouses doubt about the justice of the existing social order are not only the differences in the size of incomes, but also the differences in the origin and nature of these incomes. While one income accrues from the visible application of effort and hence is intimately connected with the health and well-being of the income receiver, another is made up of interest, dividends, rents, profits and indemnities which reflect no visible work (and frequently no invisible work either) and are independent of the health of the receiver. And lastly, the larger income confers not only a greater power over the use of things but also a greater power over men; it confers on its recipients prestige, influence, and both educational and cultural advantages.[1]

Before entering upon a scientific study of the distribution of income, it remains for us to note the following possible types of income formation: 1. *The extra-economic formation of income,* so designated because income accrues to the recipient irrespective of whether he performs a corresponding service in exchange, i.e., it has no connection with the process of production, be it obtained through violence or fraud, or through governmental charities (welfare and relief payments, gifts, and that "distribution according to need" which doctrinaire Communists would establish for the whole of society). 2. *The economic distribution of income,* which arises from the participation of each individual in the economic process, i.e., from the sale of goods and services of all kinds. In this fashion is formed that type of income referred to previously (p. 120) as original income. Although the extra-economic formation of income is frequently encountered in our economic system, it is the economic formation of income which predominates and upon which the attention of economists is concentrated.

2. *Income Distribution—A Problem of Price Formation*

There are two points of view from which we may investigate the distribution of income. On the one hand, we may ask why one person has an income of this size and another person an income of that size. In so doing we make use of the popular interpretation of income distribution as a *personal distribution of income.* But we may also proceed by relating income to the several factors of production and then examining the amount of income accruing to each of these factors (e.g., a capital of $100), without necessarily concerning ourselves with the number of units of such factor (or factors) possessed by the income receiver. Our aim in using this method is to discover what principle determines the amount of wages paid for an hour of work, the amount of rent paid for a unit of land, the amount of interest paid for a capital of $100 (functional distribution of income). As contrasted with this method of inquiry, there is the analysis of the personal distribution of income in which the fact that interests us is that from the several factorial sources of income, individual A receives a total income of $2,000, B an income of $20,000, and C an income of $1,000,000. The principal categories which we establish for a theory of functional income distribution are wages, rent, interest and profits, corresponding to the factors of production labor, land, capital, and entrepreneurship. In this way, we arrive finally at a theory of price formation for the factors of production. Hence, the explanation of the functional distribution of income involves the application of the general principles of price theory. This indeed is the road which the contemporary theory of income distribution has followed.[2] Let us leave aside, for a moment, the important questions connected with the personal distribution of income and try to put in relief the essentials of the modern concept of the functional distribution of income.

Once it has been recognized that the problem of distribution is identical with the problem of price, it can no longer be doubted that the distribution of income is an integral part of the entire economic process and that it is subject to the same laws as the other parts of this process. Equally little doubt can be entertained about the essential role played by the price-forming process among the factors of production (into which the distribution of income can be resolved). Where it is desired to ensure the orderly progress of economic life, this process can be ignored neither by our economic system nor by a socialist one. That wages in one country stand at such and such a level, that rents, interest, and profits are of such and such an amount—this is hardly to be ascribed to chance. Rather, these situations are the result of specific economic data. Every attempt to alter such data by force will produce disorder in the economic system which, in turn, will engender still greater counter-forces. That the prices of the factors of production stand at any given moment at a certain level is an essential condition of economic equilibrium, in our system as in any other. He who wishes to change these prices—and what economist would not wish to see rewards to the human factor of production at as high a level as possible—is certainly free to attempt to do so. But instead of trying to acquire the facile reputation of a "social-minded" man by vague demands for a "just wage," by railing against "interest slavery" and "profiteering," by emotional outpourings over "gluttonous landlords," and real estate "speculators," and instead of shoving aside as "liberalistic" the objections of those who understand something of these matters, one would serve his country better by applying himself to an unprejudiced study of the complex interrelationships of the economy. The insights thus acquired would enable him to discover what the basic factors are upon which it is necessary to act in order to be able to alter the existing distribution *successfully,* i.e., without provoking a costly disturbance of equilibrium. This is a difficult, thankless, and self-denying task, but one which a genuine social sense and a genuine patriotism oblige us to undertake.

Is it impossible, then, to forcibly raise wages by lowering the return to capital? It is certainly not impossible, but every attempt of this sort leads to a situation which shortly becomes untenable and results in serious disadvantages to the wage receivers themselves. It must be emphasized at the outset that those who promise great things from a transfer of income to the working class are the victims of an optical illusion. Large incomes attract much attention, but most people forget that given the small number of such incomes no particular benefits to the huge number of small income receivers could be expected to result from an equal distribution of the wealth. There would be all the less likelihood of such benefits—and this is the decisive consideration—inasmuch as a forcible transfer of this kind would lead to serious disturbances whose effects would be ultimately borne by the working class. Among the principal disturbances of such a wage policy would be a critical reduction of the economy's supply of capital and a slowing down of investment activity with its consequent effects on employment opportunities. Capital earnings (interest and dividends) go normally to individuals who spend only a small part of them and return the major share to production as fresh capital. It is very doubtful whether this income, once in the hands of workers, would be saved and invested in the same proportion as previously. To this must be added the fact that a collapse of the securities market, which is to be expected from such a policy, would seriously damage one of the most sensitive and at the same time one of the least understood elements in the complicated apparatus which sees to it that the economy is supplied with sufficient capital and that this capital is rationally allocated. Indeed, a policy of this kind would have a depressing effect on the entire economy and from the interaction of these various causes and effects, depression and unemployment could be expected all along the line. That regard for the economy's capital requirements and for its investment activity obliges us to set limits to the extent to which wages can be increased, is not a devilish peculiarity of *our* economic system but— and this is true even of a socialist state—a necessity based on fact. In any case, we have not yet had any information to the effect that the Russian government has fixed wages so high that no surplus funds remain in its hands, nor that this government counts on voluntary savings of the workers for its supply of capital.

Let us take another instance of what happens when wages are increased to a degree which is not justified by the market situation. An arbitrary raising of prices on the labor market will (just as similar arbitrary price rises on other markets) render a part of the "merchandise" unsaleable, i.e., will cause unemployment. If the unemployed are not supported by the state, they will bring their total weight to bear on the wage level (via competition) until an equilibrium situation is again achieved. If, on the other hand, the unemployed are taken care of by the state, their pressure on the wage level will be deflected for the most part. But at the same time there will result such an extreme gap as between the abnormally high wages of those who are employed and the bitter poverty of those condemned to unemployment (not to mention the worsened situation of the tax-paying groups) that we cannot speak of an improvement in the situation of the working class as a whole, but only of an improvement in the situation of one stratum of workers at the expense of the others.

The above picture, of course, has been sketched in broad outline only. In reality, things are, as always, much more complex. Thus, the smaller the forcible increase in wages is, the more prudent and conditional should be our judgment of it. Indeed, there are circumstances under which wage increases may be absorbed without damage to the national economy. We ought also never forget that there is always a degree of "play" between the moving parts of our economic mechanism, making it possible to apply corrective measures without provoking countermovements.[3] On the other side, it is also true that the more macroscopic the relationships are, i.e., the greater the amount of force used to alter the wage level, the more inexorably the disturbance to the economy's equilibrium will claim its revenge. There is a point beyond which a policy of forcible increase of wages may not go without finally provoking inflation and civil war. To deny this is demagogy, which no state, least of all a socialist one, would tolerate.

Or let us take another case in which the *interest rate* is forcibly lowered. Thorny questions of monetary theory are involved here, and the fabric of interrelationships is even more complicated than that which we observed in connection with our previous example of a forcible alteration of wages. Nevertheless, in this case as in the preceding, there can exist no doubt as to the essential outcome. Here, too, there are likely to be after-effects by which the economic system avenges itself when violence is done to it. In the first place, a reduction in, or even a complete abolition of interest by state decree would probably cause those engaged in capital transactions to find ways of circumventing the control of the state or of the community. In devious ways, an illegal interest rate will establish itself, a rate which will not only correspond to the actual ratio of supply to demand on the capital market but one which will be increased by an amount necessary to meet the costs of more complicated transactions, including an indemnity to cover the extra risks run in transgressing the law. But if we posit the rather unlikely situation where the maximum rate of interest decreed by the state is really enforced, we will find that sooner or later an untenable situation will develop on the capital market. As in every instance where a policy of ceiling prices is enforced, a disproportion between supply and demand will develop. In consequence, the state will be forced to take a further step, viz., to ration the available supplies of credit. This means that the state itself will now take over the functions which hitherto had been exercised by the free formation of interest. Can we assume that it will do the job in a satisfactory manner?

To answer this question, we must keep clearly in mind the fact that the rate of interest of the free capital market is, in the first instance, an appeal to all those who are seeking credit to weigh the urgency of their need by comparing the amount of interest they will have to pay with the profit they may expect from their use of the capital. In this way, interest functions as a mechanism which assures a rational allocation of the normally limited quantity of capital. Let us assume now that this function devolves upon the state. Nothing more efficient or better could happen, many will say. At long last, so they think, capital will be allocated in accordance with the needs of the "national economy." But when these persons are asked to state their meaning more exactly, they are thrown into the greatest embarrassment. The only certain notion which can be extracted from them is that each would like to see the largest possible amount of this newly cheapened capital allocated to that branch of production which, for material or idealistic reasons, lies closest to his heart. But how will the state and its agencies, confronted by such a multiplicity of wishes, reach a decision? Let us suppose that the state will really seek after an objective norm, and that it will stop its ears against the siren songs of the special interests or of self-styled benefactors of the people, and let us suppose further that the state takes up the concrete question of whether the shoe industry has greater need of capital than the automobile industry. The authorities must obviously begin with the question of how useful the employment of capital in the one and the other industry will be. Now this usefulness, this utility is measurable and comparable only in monetary terms. But this monetary measure is precisely the one which, via the unhindered formation of interest, would distribute the available supplies of capital. In spite of its imperfections and its weaknesses, such a mode of distribution is far more to be relied upon than one based upon arbitrary estimates of the utility of this or that enterprise by state agencies which, moreover, are not liable for the economic losses resulting from a wrong decision, as are the shoe and automobile manufacturers. The case is, of course, relatively simple when it is a question of comparing industries whose employment of capital, in relation to other factors, is in per cent terms the same (capital intensity).[4] But it remains a mystery as to how the state will make a rational decision in comparisons involving industries with different degrees of capital intensity. Whether, in a given country, more or less capital-intensive types of production should be favored obviously depends on the amount of capital available in that country as compared with the other factors of production, i.e., land and labor. Here again it is only the free formation of interest, in conjunction with the free formation of the prices of the other factors of production, which can furnish us with a fair degree of reliable information.

Next to wages, rent, and interest, there is still another large and important category of income which can be fitted only with difficulty into the framework of our previous considerations. Let us take the case of an entrepreneur who has entered on his books the costs of the various factors of production, employed under the following headings: wages to the workers, rent to the owner of the land (or to himself as the case may be), interest on capital (also to himself should he have contributed the capital), and a normal rate of compensation for his own services (entrepreneur's wage). Assume now that our entrepreneur has been able to dispose of his output in such a way that a surplus income remains to him after he has paid for all of the above "costs" of doing business. This surplus we call *entrepreneur's profit*, i.e., profit in the narrow and proper meaning of the word. To be sure, this income also arises from the process of price formation since the prices of the saleable output and of the factors of production are the resultants of this process. But it is distinguished from the previously considered types of income in that it represents merely a differential gain and not the market-determined price accruing from the sale of a "service" as it is usually understood. The difficult task of a theory of entrepreneur's profit is to explain on general grounds the origin of such pure profit, whereby the hardly less frequent case of entrepreneur's loss (negative pure profit) must also be taken into consideration. Such a theory will also have to answer the question as to whether entrepreneur's profit fulfills a specific positive function within our economic system or whether it is a simple case of enrichment unrelated to any particular function.

Because of the very nature of the phenomenon to be explained, a satisfactory theory of entrepreneur's profit must be broad enough to include the manifold sources of such profit (monopoly profits, speculative or cyclical profits, profits resulting from technical or organizational innovations, pressure on wages, payment of risk premiums, profits arising from disturbances in the economic process, etc.). According to the origin of the pure profit in question, it may be judged either positively as a reward for the performance of a useful function or negatively as an enrichment unrelated to any function. There are, however, two considerations of a general nature which need to be emphasized. *First,* we must not forget that the *possibility* of the entrepreneur making profits as a reward for efficient service is no less necessary to the functioning of our economic system than the possibility of his suffering losses as punishment for being inefficient. To understand the motive power behind our economic system is also to recognize, in principle, the necessity of entrepreneur's profit. This point takes on especial significance when it is realized that a healthy rate of investment (which, as will be shown further on, is intimately connected with the economy's equilibrium) can be expected only if there is the hope of a reasonable profit for the entrepreneur. Denied the possibility of making profits, the entrepreneur would be loath to assume the heavy risks which are invariably associated with the building of a factory, the modernizing of a plant, the expansion of production, the introduction of a technical innovation, even the replacement of machinery. It takes quite a bit of courage to assume such risks in the first place. If we leave to the entrepreneur only his losses and continue to reduce his profits through taxation, wage increases, or other means, private investment activity will be reduced to a game in which one can only lose. The consequence is then stagnation, unemployment, and impoverishment. *Secondly,* it is to be noted that competition furnishes us with a very efficacious means of eliminating entrepreneur's profits in cases where they are only a nonfunctional source of enrichment and of reserving such profits for those who perform useful services.[5]

The masses see only the successful man of business and have but a meager understanding of how such a success is achieved. Equally vague is their knowledge of the silent and pitiless process of elimination which—provided always that competition exists—is carried on among entrepreneurs, a process to which those are sacrificed who are weighed in the scales of the market and found wanting. Thus, the entrepreneur appears in a genuinely competitive market economy as a sort of trustee whom the community has placed in charge of its means of production. Comparing the costs of his services with those of a bureaucratic state-controlled economy, our entrepreneur may be regarded as a very inexpensive public servant, one who really assumes risks, while the politician is apt to be answerable only to God and history. Such a risk-assuming entrepreneur, who disdains the comfortable crutches both of state subventions and of monopoly, should be protected against attacks of a vulgar anticapitalism. From all that we know at present, it is certain that in Communist Russia the differences in income between the economically favored and the workers are far greater than in the capitalist countries, although the population is consoled, from one five-year plan to another, with the promise of a final redemption in which there will be a notable change for the better in its condition. Again, the cliché of the "two hundred families" who are supposed to be secretly exerting an irresponsible control over the free economy's destiny is, when applied to the entrepreneurs we have described above, thoroughly out of place. The difference between the market economy and the collectivist economy rests precisely in the fact that in the first case economic decisions are distributed among very many "families" which, in turn, are bound by the supreme authority of the market, i.e., in the last analysis by the votes of the consumers. In the collectivist state, on the other hand, these decisions devolve upon a single family—assuming that the dictator has one—against which there is no appeal. These statements are valid, of course, only on the supposition that the entrepreneur does not himself become confused and fall into the defeatism of seeking his salvation under the sheltering roof of monopoly or of the state, forgetting that in so doing he destroys himself.

3. Should Interest and Rent be Abolished?

We have seen that the principal categories of income—wages, interest, rent, and profits—are to be regarded as the prices of the factors of production to which each corresponds, that these prices are determined by the economic process as a whole, and that they cannot be arbitrarily changed without causing a more or less radical dislocation of all economic relationships. Although it has already been made clear that this in no way precludes a successful change in price relationships in favor of wages (viz., by acting on the *original* factors), there are many to whom our findings will be a cause of extreme irritation. They reject the idea that interest and rent, for example, should be placed on the same footing with wages, and argue instead that these highly unjust forms of nonfunctional income should be summarily abolished. Are they not right? And if such abolition is not possible within the framework of our economic system, is this not reason enough to make an end once for all of this system and its execrable "laws" about which economists make such a great to-do?

To add some light to all this heat, it will be useful to distinguish once again between the personal and the functional distribution of income. In truth, we must sharply distinguish between the one fact that rent and interest are paid at all, and the other that they are paid to individuals in such unequal amounts. If the distribution of property were more equal than it is today and if, in consequence, the masses were to receive a larger share of the income accruing from the ownership of land and capital, the attitude of the average person towards rent and interest would probably be much less hostile. We have here, then, two different questions to answer. Let us for the moment confine our attention to the first: whether interest and rent are justified at all, regardless of to whom and in what amounts they are paid. In answering this question we can under no circumstances ignore the fact that rent and interest are not meaningless sources of enrichment but institutions which have a specific significance and function. Although we have already discussed the functions of interest in the preceding paragraph, the point seems to be important enough to justify a fuller and more general explanation. Such an explanation should, above all, secure recognition of the fact that behind rent and interest is concealed a complex of relationships, knowledge of which is just as important in a socialist as in a "capitalist" state.

We know that interest and rent are nothing else than the prices which are paid for the services of the corresponding factors of production. These factors of production are available, however, only in limited quantities, while the demand for them may be measured on a scale which extends to infinity. The formation of prices, which leads in this instance to the phenomena of rent and interest, is thus only a special case (although a very important one) of the general principle of equilibrium which, as we saw previously (pp. 26ff., 33ff.), rules our economic system.

All economic systems, of whatever kind, are confronted with the task of effecting a rational allocation of land and capital as among the various possible uses open to them. This task can be accomplished in different ways. Our economic system is distinguished from others in that it seeks to solve this eternal human task by placing prices on land and capital; in this way, he who wishes to employ one or the other factor is compelled to give way to the person who believes he can put the factor in question to a better use. This is certainly not an ideal solution but it is all the same a solution. It was not thought up by anybody in particular, but came into being in a thoroughly natural way over a span of time which extends back thousands of years. In this long probationary period, it has demonstrated its practicality. A *socialist* state would have to find some substitute for it. As a matter of fact, such a state, if it wanted to have a rational economy, would have to invent rent and interest even if this were only with the purpose of providing itself with calculating devices to guide it in its use of these scarce factors of production. Otherwise, it would run the danger of having them appear on its books as free goods, thereby opening the doors wide to waste. If the economic calculations of the socialist state were to fail to take account of the scarcity of land and capital by means of some sort of index, these calculations would be hopelessly wrong. But it is to be feared that having destroyed the free market economy, such a state will have deprived itself of the mechanism which alone can solve the mathematical problem involved in calculating an index of this kind.[6]

In order to appreciate fully the difficulty which would face a socialist state in solving this problem, we must visualize the decisions which the government would have to make every hour of every day. These decisions are far more complicated than those described above in our example of the shoe and automobile industries. To bring us somewhat closer to the realities of the situation, assume that a large number of other industries are simultaneously pressing their claims for capital (e.g., the phonograph industry), that farmers are complaining about shortages of reaping-machines, and that besides all this there is talk of adopting a new-type locomotive. The method which the socialist planned economy usually falls back on in such case is to have the government itself decide, quite arbitrarily, where the capital can be most usefully employed. (It may happen, for instance, that a majority of the decision-making commissars detest phonograph music, in which case they will go over the heads of the only really competent judges, viz., the consumers, and decide that the capital requirements of the phonograph industry will not be met). The other alternative is for the government to leave it up to the population to decide where its capital can be most usefully employed. In such case, as we have seen, the population makes use of a scale which, in our economic system, results in a more or less efficient distribution of capital. Nevertheless, there are grounds for believing that such decisions by the people would be impossible in a socialist state.[7] This all goes to prove that interest is not a stupid and provocative device for the impoverishment of some and the enrichment of others, not an organ like the appendix which can be removed with impunity, but a vital organ which in every economic system has an essential function to fulfill.[8]

The same is true of *rent,* whose existence is predicated on the necessity of making demand for land conform to the degree of need in each case, and of equating this need with the limited supplies available. Rent fulfills in our economic system a function which must be fulfilled in every economic system, viz., the introduction of reasonable order into the allocation of the limited supply of land. A very vivid appreciation of this function of rent may be had by observing the countryside from the vantage point of an airplane. The division of the land into residential and farm areas, forests and meadows, railroads and highways, the silhouettes of the cities with the skyscrapers in the center and the villas in the outskirts—all this is, fundamentally, the work of rent which through a series of gradations in its amount causes one piece of land to be used for this purpose and another for that purpose. Just as interest—to express this idea in more drastic form—ensures that subways will not be built in every country town, so rent acts to prevent the planting of potatoes in Regent Street or on Fifth Avenue. Rent is a warning, as it were, that land of a given quality or in a given location is scarce, and that therefore it should be entrusted only to those who are able and willing to make the best and most profitable use of it. The general regulatory principle which rules the whole of our economic system comes here, as elsewhere, into full play. That land is reckoned among the production costs of every economic good (since a price in the form of rent must be paid for its use) is an expression of the truth that the use of a piece of land for one purpose precludes its use for another purpose. In consequence, we see that rent differs in no wise from other cost elements.

This, of course, does not prevent rent from exhibiting certain peculiarities which, though the theoreticians of another day gave them undue importance, cannot be ignored. Although it would be an error to speak of an absolutely fixed or even of a monopolized supply of land, it is nonetheless true that land of a given fertility or location is more or less fixed in amount. Hence, where there is increasing demand for land there is a tendency for its price to rise, with no possibility of reestablishing equilibrium between supply and demand through increased production. Consequently, rising standards of living and an increasing population undoubtedly have a tendency to force up rents. On the other hand, we should be careful of over-estimating the strength of this tendency. It would be wrong, for instance, to believe that rent, like a ripening fruit, will wax bigger while the landowner contentedly sleeps. It is too easily forgotten that the rent of a specific piece of land can, in spite of increasing population and economic development, just as easily fall as rise, since there may occur shifts in demand for the several classes of land. With respect to land, one can lose as easily as one can gain, just as in every other form of capital investment. As one share of stock differs from another share, so does one piece of land differ from another due to its location or its quality. It often happens that even within a rapidly expanding urban area considerable losses may be sustained as the result of rent declines in what were once fashionable quarters, whereas they may be sharp increases in rents in areas that had been hitherto neglected. The same principle holds true for agricultural rents which, in spite of population growth, are equally subject to fluctuation. Naturally, we must guard against exaggeration in considering any of these possible alternatives. Still, it often happens that thanks to the sudden development of a city, to improvements in communications systems, or to construction of railroads and canals, those who happen through coincidence to be the owners of the land in question, may be legitimately regarded as the beneficiaries of an "unearned increase in value." In cases of this kind, special taxation may be justified. But here we are anticipating our discussion of the personal distribution of income.[9]

4. *Changing the Distribution of Income*

After a considerable detour we have finally arrived at that decisive stage in our investigations where we may take a position on the burning question of a just distribution of income, without being sucked into a torrent of blind passions. Several times in the course of this book we have been at pains to explain the purpose and the character of our economic system. On each such occasion we saw ourselves obliged to admit that the equilibrium mechanism we had described functioned only under a certain condition—and one which can be criticized from many angles—viz., the existing and unequal distribution of income. While the "capitalistic" economic process can be compared to a continuing plebiscite in which each piece of currency represents a ballot and in which the consumers, via their demands, are constantly voting to decide what types and amounts of goods shall be produced, this right of the consumers to vote partakes of that "majestic equality" to which Anatole France alludes so ironically in the motto to this chapter. The ballots are in truth very *unequally* distributed. It is right that the mechanism of our economic system should be so constructed that it synchronizes production with the wants of the consumers, and it is an objection which holds no water to say that producers seek to influence these wants by advertising their goods in the same way that political parties make propaganda for their programs and their candidates.[10] But since what counts are only those wants which are backed up by money, we have not the right to regard the outcome of the consumers' plebiscite as a complete and satisfying one. While our voting mechanism ensures, in the long run, that the production of houses will correspond to that *demand* for houses which arises from the existing distribution of income, it does not of itself prevent the production of houses from lagging behind the *need* for decent and healthful living accommodations. Outright condemnation of our economic system would seem to be the next logical step, and there are many who take it. The considerations upon which we have dwelt throughout this book make it possible for us to recognize the confusion which lies at the bottom of this popular condemnation, and to find a way to avoid the ruinous consequences of unreasoning anger.

Even the adversaries of our economic system do not, as a rule, deny that the services which it renders in the sphere of production are deserving of considerable respect. A number of them were not even dissuaded by the economic crisis of the thirties from holding that in this regard our economic system is very much superior to a communist one. Only because it is so unjust, they say, should it be done away with. To criticisms of this sort one must resolutely affirm that it is thoroughly possible, and even necessary, to bring about changes in distribution so long as such action does not result in the destruction of the high achievements of our economic system in the realm of production. To accomplish this purpose, three courses of action are available: 1) an "organic" change in the functional distribution of income; 2) a change in the personal distribution of income; 3) the use of extra-economic means to offset a change in the distribution of income.

We have already established that for a change in the *functional distribution of income*, it is not required to employ force, but rather to effect an "organic" change by acting on the original factors. To describe these factors in detail would require a whole book, the reading of which would not be easy since it would be necessary to treat of the very thorny questions connected with the theories of wages, interest, and rent. What must here be stressed is only the most essential consideration, viz., that both theory and experience point to productivity as being the final determining cause of the average level of wages in a country. All the differences in national living standards—between the United States and Europe, between Sweden and the countries in the Danube basin—can be traced back to this single factor. Everything which increases the productivity of labor, increases wages. Of decisive importance is the fact that the productivity of labor is greater, the larger are the quantities of capital and of land with which the labor factor of production can be combined. This depends, in turn, on the quantitative ratios of the three factors of production to one another, a circumstance whose importance has already been made clear to us (pp. 133 ff.). We can doubly understand now why the level of wages is high in a country where the labor factor of production is scarce in relation to capital and land. Because labor is scarce, a higher price must be paid for it, and because it is combined with a greater quantity of capital and land, its productivity is increased. This much established, it can be easily demonstrated that both points are reducible to the same common denominator. Of especial importance in this connection is the quantitative relationship between the productive factors of labor and capital, a fact corroborated by the classical theory of wages (wages fund theory), if not in its premises, nevertheless in its conclusions. At the same time, the truth is once again borne in upon us that an unrestricted increase of population will almost certainly cause a change in the distribution of income to the detriment of the wage income of the masses. A waste of capital caused by unproductive government expenditures has, in the long run, an identical effect.

Last but not least, we must make mention of the role played by foreign trade. The more completely a country participates in the international division of labor, thereby making the most rational use of its factors of production, the more favorable are the terms of trade which it can obtain on international markets. The less restricted a country is in buying foreign goods where they are cheapest and in selling its own where they are dearest, the higher will be the wage level of that country. This is a factor which plays an especially big role today in the surprising prosperity of certain small countries such as Switzerland and the Scandinavian countries.

We have thus arrived at a strange but suggestive result. It turns out that the functional distribution of income is the more prejudicial to wage income the poorer—i.e., the more unproductive, the more "proletarian," and capital-poor—a country is. On the other hand, the greater a country's average wealth, the more equitable will be its distribution of wage and property incomes. There is some truth to Uncle Bräsig's famous thesis in Fritz Reuters *Ut mine Stromtid* "that poverty comes from being poor."* We can see from the foregoing that it is possible to formulate a policy of raising the national level of wages which will have a real chance of success. Such a policy will consist of the following: increasing capital wealth (by means, if need be, of capital imports and a rational organization of credit), allocation of the factors of production to their most productive uses, intelligent participation in the international division of labor, exploitation of technological and organizational prog-

---

*"Armut kommt von der 'Poverteh.'"

ress, restrained increases in population, a reasonable economic policy in all fields, peace, security, confidence and order—such are the bases of national prosperity.

A change in the functional distribution of income in favor of wages will result at the same time in a more equal *distribution of personal income* since it will give to the masses of wage receivers the increasing possibility of obtaining—via wealth formation—income from the ownership of property of all kinds. The consequence will be a "de-proletarianization" which ought to be close to the hearts of those who need no propertyless masses for the fulfillment of their political ambitions. This process can be assisted by a number of direct measures, above all by an economic policy which sees to it that the equalizing effects of the competitive principle are not frustrated by manipulations which lead to an undeserved enrichment of the few at the expense of the many. An antimonopoly policy is thus always a good income policy, as is also the suppression of abuses born of the competitive struggle. Other measures that would help to reduce excessive concentration of wealth are housing programs, encouragement of independent farming, easing the difficulties encountered in progressing from one social class to another, attention to the credit needs of small industries, and numerous other measures.

As a last resort, there is available the *extra-economic correction* of the distribution of income. This consists in the state awaiting the results of the economic distribution of income as they are crystallized in the market processes, and then correcting these results by taxing the rich and spending for the poor. As a matter of fact, a considerable portion of the public finances is devoted to such rectification, supplemented by the efforts of private welfare groups. Obviously, there are certain limits here which may not be overstepped if paralyzing effects on the process of production are to be avoided. It is, of course, clear that the state can go much further in employing such corrective measures the smaller are its expenditures for other purposes.

NOTES

1. (p. 184) *The Unequal Distribution of Income*

The unequal distribution of income in all the civilized countries raises a host of economic, statistical, sociological and political questions for which we must refer the reader to a special—although not too extensive—literature. For the conceptual and statistical clarification of the phenomenon we are indebted to V. Pareto (especially in his *Cours d'Économie politique* (Vol. 2 [Lausanne, 1897]). He found that the inequality of income distribution in all advanced countries exhibited such regularity that it could even be expressed in a math-ematical formula (Pareto's first law). He believed further that it could be shown that inequality of income distribution lessens as average income per capita increases (Pareto's second law). This second law of Pareto is in agree-ment with what we established on pp. 192 ff. For excellent work in this field see also Edwin Cannan, especially *Wealth* (London, 1914), and the work of his pupils: Hugh Dalton, *Some Aspects of the Inequality of Incomes in Modern Communities* (London, 1920); F.C. Benham, *The Prosperity of Australia* (Lon-don, 1928); W.H. Hutt, *Economists and the Public* (London, 1936), pp. 313 ff. See also the standard work of A.C. Pigou, *The Economics of Welfare* (4th ed.; London, 1932); Bertrand de Jouvenel, *The Ethics of Redistribution* (Cam-bridge, 1951) ; *Einkommensbildung und Einkommensverteilung*, papers at con-ference of Verein für Sozialpolitik at Cologne, 1956. A collation and interpre-tation of statistical data from several countries may be found in: Colin Clark, *The Conditions of Economic Progress* (2nd ed.; London, 1950).

2. (p. 185) *Evolution of Distribution Theory*

Although we find little awareness in classical theory of the distinction between the personal and the functional distribution of income (classical theory was concerned almost exclusively with the latter), the classicists succeeded, never-theless, in laying the foundations for a scientific study of the problem of dis-tribution by breaking down individual income into definite income-types (wages, rent, and "capital profits"). In this regard, we may point to the still accepted classical view that production and distribution (formation of value and forma-tion of income) are closely connected with one another, and that income for-mation is subject to the laws governing the whole of the economic process. This idea was developed with especial vigor and clarity by Ricardo. The classical doctrine, of course, did not progress so far as to conceive of the individual cate-gories of income as being in themselves price phenomena. Consequently, it was constrained to construct a number of special theories, but without being able to join these together into a coherent whole. The weakness of these special theories was subsequently one of the main reasons why the classical concept of an economically determined distribution (by categories) had to give way almost completely to that agnostic-activist view which was defended throughout the nineteenth century by the adversaries of the classical school, the socialists and the historical school. The belief that the established power relationships in society are the determining factors, and that consequently a change in distribu-tion could only be effected by state decree or the pressure of labor unions, found increasingly wide acceptance. The result was that progress in the theoretical analysis of the problem of distribution, which the classicists had carried rather far forward, was halted for a considerable period of time. Ultimately, modern theory, applying the marginal principle in this field as it had in others, arrived at solutions which, though largely confirming the results of classical theory, established the problem on a new and broader foundation. For the first time it was possible to have a total view of income distribution deduced not from arbitrary special theories but from the general principles of value and price theory. The concept which has proved itself of the greatest usefulness in this connection is that of the "marginal productivity" of the factors of production. The classicists, it must be admitted (especially Ricardo and J.H. von Thünen), did have an inkling of this concept, but the first complete exposition of the principle and its establishment as the basis of distribution theory, we owe to the American J.B. Clark in his *The Distribution of Wealth* (New York, 1899). The "imputation of costs" theory developed by the Austrian School leads, fundamentally, to a similar set of conclusions. As a result of the recognition that functional distribution (or factorial distribution) is really the outcome of the formation of the prices of the factors of production, the classical doctrine of an economically determined distribution was proven in a most convincing way. How sound this modern theory of distribution is can be ascertained by its readiness to concede the more or less considerable degree of "play" which must be allowed to the undetermined factors in distribution, and its willingness to admit such corrections and adjustments as may therefore be necessary. One of the accomplishments for which are indebted to modern distribution theory is its clear distinction between the personal and the functional distribution of income. This is shown most notably in E. Cannan, *History of the Theories of Production and Distribution in English Political Economy from 1776 to 1848* (London, 1893).

3. (p. 188) *The Theory of Wages*

On the many and complex aspects of the theory of wages the following literature is recommended: R. von Strigl, *Angewandte Lohntheorie* (Vienna, 1926); J. Marschak, *Die Lohndiskussion* (1931); J.R. Hicks, *The Theory of Wages* (London, 1932); W.H. Hutt, *The Theory of Collective Bargaining* (London, 1930); P.H. Douglas, *The Theory of Wages* (London, 1934); Ch. Cornélissen, *Théorie du salaire et du travail salarié* (Paris, 1908); A. Amonn, *Das Lohnproblem* (2nd ed.; Berne, 1945); D. Robertson, *Wages* (London, 1955). On the relationships between wage theory and cyclical theory see Wilhelm Röpke, *Crises and Cycles, op. cit.* On the interrelationships of wage and interest theory see the classical study of F.W. Taussig, *Wages and Capital* (first published in 1896, new ed., London, 1935).

Of the many complexities of the theory of wages we shall select only one for mention here. Repeated efforts have been made to get around the fact that wages are economically determined. Thus it has been argued that an arbitrary increase in wages will of itself so change the known economic determinants (the "original" factors in our text) that the new wage increase ceases to be arbitrary. What the proponents of this view try to prove, in other words, is that a rise in wages can increase the productivity of labor. This "theory of high wages" is met under two forms. According to the one, high wages cause an increase in the productivity of labor since it increases both the capacity and the will to produce of the workers. Insofar as this idea is not simply a product of the confusion of cause and effect, it involves a thesis which has no general validity in the first place and is unprovable in the second. The other variant of the "theory of high wages" reposes on the notion that high wages will indirectly cause an increase in mass purchasing power, thus stimulating mass production with a resultant increase in productivity (purchasing power theory of wages). In spite of the numerous errors with which this theory (most popular in the United States) bristles, it contains a modicum of truth, especially in connection with certain findings of cyclical theory. But this bit of truth in purchasing power theory cannot be considered as anything more than as a kind of broadening of the "zone of indeterminism" in wage determination.

With the extension and solidification of modern labor union power the problem of the wage as a "monopoly price" has assumed increasing importance. See Henry C. Simons, "Some Reflections on Syndicalism" in *Economic Policy for a Free Society* (Chicago, 1948); Fritz Machlup, *Monopolistic Wage Determination as a Part of the General Problem of Monopoly* (Washington, D.C.: Chamber of Commerce of the United States, 1947); J.A. Schumpeter, "The March into Socialism," *American Economic Review,* May 1950; Charles E. Lindblom, *Unions and Capitalism* (New Haven, 1949); *The Impact of the Union,* ed. D.M. Wright (New York, 1951).

4. (p. 190) *Interest and Differences in Capital Intensity*

The existence of manual labor alongside machine production shows us how different, even within the same industry, is the "intensity" of capital (to which Marx applied the somewhat confusing appellation "the organic composition of capital"). Whether the one or the other kind of production is more suitable is something which, in our economic system, is decided by the ratio of interest to wages. In East Asia, for example, this ratio is so unfavorable to the use of machinery that human labor power (ricksha coolies) plays a role even in the transport of persons, a thing which would be impossible if wage levels were higher. The varying intensity of capital is a fact which Ricardo himself found embarrassing in constructing his theory of profit.

5. (p. 191) *Entrepreneur's Profit*

Entrepreneur's profit is differentiated from other kinds of income in that it does not constitute an integral part of the costs of production (and hence is not a determining cause of price). Rather, it is itself a product of the process of price formation, a sort of *ex post facto* income as it were. It is just because of this that we experience difficulty in assigning to entrepreneur's profit its proper functional importance. In all such cases in which a surplus profit remains after the costs of doing business have been paid, we speak of *rents.* Since rent in the usual sense (ground rent) also contains such an element, the term came gradually to be applied to this phenomenon exclusively. Strictly speaking, however, this usage is incorrect and distracts attention from the essential character of ground rent as a type of cost income. Literature: H. von Mangoldt, *Die Lehre vom Unternehmergewinn* (1855), a pathmaking book by a German economist who only now is receiving his proper due; J. Niehans, article "Unternehmereinkommen", *Handwörterbuch der Sozialwissenschaften,* 1959; J. Schumpeter, *The Theory of Economic Development* (Cambridge [Mass.], 1934); A. Amonn, "Der Unternehmergewinn" in *Die Wirtschaftstheorie der Gegenwart,* Vol. 3 (1928); D.H. MacGregor, *Enterprise, Purpose, and Profit* (Oxford, 1934). There is, finally, a copious and especially high level American literature on the subject, in particular, F.H. Knight, *Risk, Uncertainty, and Profit* (New York, 1921), a standard work, especially on the element of risk in entrepreneur's profit; A.E. Monroe, *Value and Income* (Cambridge [Mass.], 1931); F.B. Hawley, *Enterprise and the Productive Process* (New York, 1907); Clare E. Griffin, *Enterprise in a Free Society* (Chicago, 1949).

6. (p. 194) Economic Calculation in a Collectivist State

It is to a group of non-Marxist economists that we owe thanks for drawing attention in recent years to the problem of economic calculation, that is, to the method by which the economic system makes a rational allocation of its productive resources. This is, in fact, the central problem of a collectivist state: how to arrive at a halfway rational method of economic calculation in the absence of the free formation of the prices of the factors of production, especially of land and capital. See L. von Mises, *Socialism* (London, 1936); T.J.B. Hoff, *Economic Calculation in the Socialist Society* (London, 1949); Pohle-Halm, *Kapitalismus und Sozialismus* (4th ed.; 1931); B. Brutzkus, *Die Lehren des Marxismus im Lichte der russischen Revolution* (1928), a book which combines penetrating analysis with an interesting evaluation of the Russian experiment (an English translation is contained in the first part of *Economic Planning in Soviet Russia* [London, 1935]); F.A. von Hayek (ed.), *Collectivist Economic Planning* (London, 1935); F.A. von Hayek, *Individualism and Economic Order* (Chicago, 1948); W. Röpke, article "Sozialisierung," *Handwörterbuch der Staatswissenschaften*, 4th ed.; R.L. Hall, *The Economic System in a Socialist State* (London, 1936); W. Röpke, *Civitas Humana* (London, 1948). The immensity of the problem of rational economic calculation in the collectivist state, with which the above literature is concerned, finds additional confirmation in the failure of all efforts in Russia to establish a genuine collectivist system. On the realities of collectivism see: W.H. Chamberlin, *A False Utopia: Collectivism in Theory and Practice* (London, 1937); W. Lippmann, *The Good Society* (Boston, 1937); L.E. Hubbard, *Soviet Labour and Industry* (London, 1942); A. Baykov, *The Development of the Soviet Economic System* (London, 1946); J. Jewkes, *Ordeal by Planning* (London, 1948); W. Eucken, "On the Theory of the Centrally Administered Economy: An Analysis of the German Experiment," *Economica*, May and August, 1948; A. Müller-Armack, *Wirtschaftslenkung und Marktwirtschaft* (Hamburg, 1947) ; W. Röpke, *Mass und Mitte* (Erlenbach-Zurich, 1950), pp. 86-134; W. Röpke, *The Problem of Economic Order* (Cairo, 1951).

7. (p. 195) Socialism and Democracy

A continuing plebiscite or popular referendum in a socialist state must be considered as impossible, from which it follows that socialism is incompatible with genuine democracy and individual freedom, and hence necessarily presupposes a totalitarian state. Extensive and still unrefuted argumentation for the truth of this highly significant thesis, one confirmed also by all previous experience, may be found in the following works: W. Lippmann, *op. cit.;* F.A. von Hayek, *The Road to Serfdom* (Chicago, 1944); W. Röpke, *Civitas Humana, op. cit.* The effort made by J.A. Schumpeter in *Capitalism, Socialism, and Democracy* (2nd ed.; New York, 1947) to refute these arguments must be regarded as unsuccessful (see F.A. von Hayek, "The Use of Knowledge," *American Economic Review*, September 1945; W. Röpke, "Kapitalismus, Sozialismus und Demokratie" in *Gegen die Brandung* [2nd ed.; Erlenbach-Zurich, 1959], pp. 354-362).

8. (p. 195) The Theory of Interest

The essence of interest may be understood from a study of the essence of capital (see Chapter V, pp. 130 ff. and Note 9). The difficulties of capital theory reappear in the theory of interest; current scientific discussion of the one and the other is equally intense. The point of departure for the study of these matters is still the pathmaking work of Böhm-Bawerk on capital and interest theory, (Eng. tr. by George D. Huncke and Hans F. Sennholz, *Capital and Interest*, 3 volumes [South Holland, Ill.; 1959]); see also the article "Zins", *Handwörter- buch der Staatswissenschaften*, 4th ed., revised and expanded by F.X. Weiss. Until Böhm-Bawerk, theories of capital and interest were thoroughly unsatis- factory. He set the theories on their proper foundation by stressing as the cen- tral fact of his explanation the time dimension of capital and interest (the sac- rifice of the present in favor of the future, "waiting"). The underlying idea to which Böhm-Bawerk gave expression dominates all of modern interest theory. The form in which he expressed himself, however, has left his findings open to many legitimate criticisms, especially since they do not comprise a complete or unified theory. In point of fact, the "agio" theory of Böhm-Bawerk, the "scar- city" theory of Cassel *(The Theory of Social Economy* [1932]), the "impatience" theory of Irving Fisher, the marginal productivity theory of interest (a model explanation of which is to be found in E. Cannan, *An Economist's Protest* [London, 1927], pp. 285 ff.), and related theories are, at bottom, only varia- tions on the same fundamental theme. It is to be noted that the modern time- difference theory, which is the leitmotif of all these variations, should not be confused with the abstinence theory of Senior to which we drew attention in another section (Chapter II, Note 4, p. 38). Interest ought not to be paid as a reward for a sacrifice, but because "waiting" is necessarily scarce by reason of the greater attractiveness of current consumption and the unlimited demand for capital which would develop if there were no interest. Nor should it be thought that interest is something which is required to induce men to create capital. The supply of capital is more often than not inelastic, i.e., largely in- dependent of the rate of interest. A certain amount of saving would take place without interest. It is even possible that not a few individuals, in their desire to draw a given amount of interest-income, would save more where the interest rate is low than where it is high (see W. Röpke, *Die Theorie der Kapitalbil- dung* [1929]). From the foregoing we may conclude that the function of inter- est is more to regulate and to sift the *demand* for capital than to regulate its supply. We may summarize by saying that the existence, rate, and function of interest are explainable in terms of the time factor. In our economic system, interest is the *"time gland,"* so to speak, which balances the present and the future in the national economy, and which ensures that scarce capital in each case will be rationally distributed among the several competing uses for it. Its counterpart is rent which, as a sort of *"space gland,"* has the function of ensur- ing *spatial* order in the economy. Most recent literature: F.A. von Hayek, *The Pure Theory of Capital* (London, 1941); J.R. Hicks, *Value and Capital* (Ox- ford, 1939); J.M. Keynes, "Alternative Theories of the Rate of Interest," *Eco- nomic Journal*, June 1937, pp. 246-248; J.M. Fleming, "The Determination of the Rate of Interest," *Economica*, August, 1938, pp. 333-341; W. Eucken, *Kap- italtheoretische Untersuchungen* (1934); R. v. Strigl, *Kapital und Produktion* (Vienna, 1934); F.A. Lutz, *Zinstheorie* (Zurich-Tübingen, 1956).

Quite outside the contemporary explanation of interest in terms of the time dimension are two other theories of interest: the dynamic theory and the theory of exploitation. According to the dynamic theory, represented chiefly by J. Schumpeter *(The Theory of Economic Development, op. cit.)*, interest is pos- sible only in a progressing and developing economy and not in a static one. According to the exploitation theory, held for the most part by socialists (Marx, Franz Oppenheimer, and most recently Hans Peter in *Grundprobleme der theo- retischen Nationalökonomie*, Vol. 1 [1953], pp. 85 ff.), interest is interpreted as an enrichment arising from changing power relationships. For a critique of both theories see F.X. Weiss, supplement to the article "Zins," *Handwörterbuch der Staatswissenschaften,* 4th ed.

From the beginning it was recognized that the problem of interest is not only a real (natural) problem, but also a *monetary* one. It is precisely this fact which adds to the complexity of interest rate theory and which has been too long ignored in the literature. The *monetary theory of interest* has become nevertheless increasingly important. A pioneer in this field is the Swede Knut Wicksell (originally in his book *Interest and Prices* [1898], more recently in his *Lectures on Political Economy,* ed. Robbins, Vol. 2, [London, 1935]). Additional readings: L.A. Hahn, *Volkswirtschaftliche Theorie des Bankkredits* (3rd ed., 1930); L. von Mises, *Theory of Money and Credit* (New York, 1934); F.A. von Hayek, *The Pure Theory of Capital, op. cit.*; Frank A. Fetter, "Interest Theory and Price Movements," *American Economic Review,* Supplement, March 1927; D.H. Robertson, *Banking Policy and the Price Level* (3rd ed., London, 1932); J.M. Keynes, *A Treatise on Money* (London, 1930); J.M. Keynes, *The General Theory of Employment, Interest and Money* (London, 1936); F. Machlup, *Börsenkredit, Industriekredit und Kapitalbildung* (Vienna, 1931); W. Röpke, "Kredit und Konjunktur," *Jahrbücher für Nationalökonomie,* March-April 1926; W. Röpke, *Crises and Cycles* (London, 1936), pp. 111 ff.; Hans Gestrich, *Kredit und Sparen* (2nd ed., Godesberg, 1948); W. Lautenbach, *Zins, Kredit und Produktion* (Tübingen, 1952); F.A. Lutz, *op. cit.*

9. (p. 197) *The Theory of Rent*

Here again we are confronted with difficulties which were passed over in the text in order not to distract the reader's attention from fundamentals. We may best begin with the Ricardian theory of rent, the extraordinary durability of which is proven by the fact that it still holds an important place in contemporary theory. Ricardo laid the greatest possible stress on the differential character of ground rent. Rent for Ricardo is not an element of costs; hence it is not a cause but a consequence of the prices of agricultural products. Since for all producers the price of grain in the market will be the same, whether it is produced on rich or poor land, on land far removed from the market or near to it, or with much or little labor and capital, a differential gain will accrue to the land having the lower costs of production. If there should be, perchance, a rise in the price of grain, this will not be because rent has increased; rather, rent increases because the price of grain (perhaps on account of increasing population) has gone up. In this way, Ricardo believed he had completely eliminated the land factor of production as an element in the formation of prices of agricultural products.

Ricardo's theory of rent remained for a long time the most durable part of his work and is still regarded as correct by many economists. It cannot, however, be accepted any longer within the framework of modern theory; at least not in the form which Ricardo gave it. The fact is that rent appears in quite another light if viewed in the theoretical scheme of modern economics. Rent is now seen to be the price paid for the use of the factor of a production "land"; like every other price, it is determined by the scarcity of the factor. This price which is paid for the use of land is also a real cost element and corresponds to the modern view of costs as a reflection of the utility which could have been obtained from another use of the factor. In other words: rent expresses the fact that land which is used for one purpose cannot be used for another; it indicates that land of a certain type is scarce and by its amount shows the degree of that scarcity. The function of rent, then, is to make these facts known and to see to it that the best possible use is made of land of a given quality or location. Consequently, rent will always appear where land of a given quality or location becomes scarce. It follows that differential rent is basically nothing else than the price of a factor of production which, just as the prices of other factors of production, is an integral part of value (price) calculation, since it represents an element of cost in the subjective sense of a sacrifice of alternative uses (opportunity cost). Even a socialist economy must take the scarcity of land into account since if it did not, land would be treated as a free good and the state itself would be in the position of having abetted the ensuing waste. The difficulty, however (which was spared the reader in the text), lies in the fact that the real cost character of rent is revealed only insofar as a piece of land actually has an alternative use. If, however, the land in question has a specific use, e.g., the land of a famous vineyard, we cannot explain the rent which is paid for it in terms of the other uses to which it could be put, since these other uses practically do not exist. In this case, the pure rent character (differential gain) of rent cannot be denied. See Franz X. Weiss, "Die Grundrente im System der Nutzwertlehre," *Die Wirtschaftstheorie der Gegenwart*, Vol. 3 (Vienna, 1928); A. v. Navratil, "Rentenprinzip und Grundrente," *Zeitschrift für die gesamte Staatswissenschaft*, Vol. 94, 1933; O. v. Zwiedineck-Südenhorst, *Allgemeine Volkswirtschaftslehre* (1932), pp. 234 ff.; Hubert D. Henderson, *Supply and Demand, op. cit.*

On urban rents: Adolf Weber, "Die städtische Grundrente," *Die Wirtschaftstheorie der Gegenwart*, Vol. 3, (Vienna, 1928); F. von Wieser, "Die Theorie der städtischen Grundrente," *Gesammelte Abhandlungen* (1929), pp. 126 ff.

10. (p. 197) *Advertising*

Advertising limits the freedom of economic choice of the consumer no more and no less than election propaganda limits the freedom of voters. Nor is this freedom of the consumer constrained by the fact that his decisions are guided by a whole set of motivations and influences of which advertising is only one. The choice of the consumers remains always free in the sense that in the economic democracy of the market we cast our votes in accordance with our preferences. But this freedom, it should be noted, exists only in the market economy, not in the collectivist "command economy." Of course, it is true that advertising frequently causes a want to appear where none existed before, and induces us to purchase something which we otherwise would have done without. Surely, however, it does not conflict with our concept of a rational human economy if the producer steps out of his role of a waiter standing by for his orders and recommends something new on the menu or wine list. Even orange juice originally achieved its popularity as the result of advertising. But who has bitter thoughts about advertising when he drinks a glass of orange juice? Be this as it may, advertising has aroused many severe criticisms which may be found elsewhere. In this connection, see: W. Röpke, *Mass und Mitte* (Erlenbach-Zurich, 1950), pp. 200-218; W. Röpke, *A Humane Economy, op. cit.*, pp. 137-138; E.A. Lever, *Advertising and Economic Theory* (London, 1947); Herbert Wilhelm, *Werbung als wirtschaftstheoretisches Problem* (1961).

CHAPTER VIII

DISTURBANCES OF ECONOMIC EQUILIBRIUM

1. *The Sources of Disturbance*

The differences between rich and poor are a very understandable cause of dissatisfaction and criticism, and all of us have reason to give our serious attention to the demand for greater social justice. No less challenging is the fact that our civilization seems to be stricken with the curse of instability and recurrent mass unemployment. Here again we confront a problem to which a better solution must be found in the future than has been found in the past, if our civilization is not to be placed in the greatest jeopardy. Thus, we touch once more upon a theme to which we have had to give our attention over and over again in the course of this book. And although it is impossible to investigate the problem from all angles within the framework of the present discussion, it is nevertheless too important for us not to make the effort in this chapter to survey the basic issues involved.[1]

We know already that our economic order rests upon an incalculable number of freely taken decisions in production, consumption, saving, and investment, and we are aware also of the forces which shape a definite order out of this seeming chaos. How enormously complicated this operation is was made clear in our discussion of the developments attributable to the modern division of labor. By the same token, we are now in a better position to appreciate how extremely unstable such an economic system must be and how easily disturbances can occur now in one sector, now in the other, their elimination requiring a process of continuous adaptation.

We can also understand how these disturbances may become so serious and so extensive as to impair the entire economic process and bring about extensive unemployment (depression.) The greater the degree of division of labor, the greater will be the growth of productivity but, at the same time, the more susceptible the economic system will become to equilibrium disturbances. This instability is still further increased due to the fact that the production of consumer goods does not follow a direct path, but rather takes a detour via the anterior production of producer goods. In other words, the modern process of production is not only a labor-dividing one but simultaneously an indirect, detour-making, and therefore time-consuming process. Just as the division of labor requires that producers mutually arrive at a correct estimate of their needs for goods, so too the greatly increased importance of capital goods production requires that the need for fore-products be rightly estimated, and that the extent of fore-production be kept in proper proportion to the extent of end-production. These relationships, moreover, must be preserved in spite of the difficulties which the characteristic time-consuming nature of our production process entails.

Again, all this takes place in a world in which politics, the caprices of consumers, the inventive spirit and a thousand other things daily create a new and unforseen situation. Keeping all these things in mind, there it seems more reason for astonishment over the high degree of order in the economy than over the fact that this order is continually disturbed.

Also, since a socialist state will have to reckon with the same sources of disturbance (the division of labor, advances in the technology of production, and instability of the outside world), it would be erroneous to assume that it would be spared the problem of equilibrium disturbances. So long as there is division of labor and a highly developed technology, so long as man, nature, and society have not become rigid machines, so long as there are new inventions, harvest fluctuations, changes in consumption habits, migrations, fluctuations in births and deaths, wars and revolutions, optimism and pessimism, trust and mistrust, every social order will be confronted with the problem of disturbances in economic equilibrium. Wherever these disturbances occur, one must adapt oneself to them in order to overcome them. The difference between the market economy and the collectivist economy in this respect lies fundamentally in the fact that the process of adaptation in the market economy is, in accordance with the essence of this economy, spontaneous; in the collectivist economy, however, adaptation is "commanded."

If we now assume that our economic system is afflicted by that severe disturbance which we call depression, we will find ourselves faced with the melancholy picture of idle factories and unemployed workers—although just a short time before (in a boom) production may have reached record figures. Thus, the situation would appear to be due to a generalized condition of over-production. But we will not arrive at the underlying causes of this situation simply by saying that total production has exceeded consumption and that excessive quantities of *all* goods have been produced. Further reflection will show us, in fact, that there is no rational basis for this popular concept of generalized *over-production*. One awaits in vain an answer to the question: over-production in relation to what? The living standards of the masses are almost everywhere so low that not even a tenfold increase in present levels of production would serve to raise these standards noticeably. Until these standards are so raised, it is meaningless to even question the necessity of putting all the productive forces at our disposal into the fight against scarcity. In this light, we are faced not with a general oversupply of labor power but with a deficiency of it, not with too many machines but rather too few, not with too much rationalization of production but rather with too little. This constantly recurring *fear of production* is absurd.

But how does this square with the indisputable fact that in a depression factories are shut down and workers made idle? The question may best be answered by means of the following comparison. The battle against the scarcity of goods, which we are condemned to fight with chronically inadequate forces, is like the battle of an army against a superior opponent. Every soldier is used in such a battle and every technical advance in armaments is welcome. And yet because of the organizational disturbances which are inevitable in the enormously complicated apparatus of a modern army, it is a common occurrence for individual units to be withheld from action even though they may be bitterly needed on some other sector of the front. Temporary surpluses of soldiers in individual sectors does not mean that there is not a shortage of soldiers as a whole. Hence, no reasonable man will conclude that these momentarily unemployed troops should be sent home or that the army as a whole should adopt a "spread the fight" program by increasing the number of furloughs or by reverting to the use of halberds. The close connection between "too little" on the whole and "too much" in parts is so obvious here that even a person of the most limited capacities cannot fail to recognize it. But understanding of the fact that we are confronted with this very same problem in the economy appears to be extremely difficult for most people. A depression cannot be defined as generalized over-production of all goods simultaneously, nor as the overtaking of consumption possibilities by production possibilities. It is to be defined, rather, as a disproportion among the individual branches of production: an equilibrium disturbance within a productive system which—on the whole and over the long run—is as yet clearly unable to satisfy all the possible needs of consumers.

The total quantity of goods which we may profitably produce is not a cake of a certain fixed weight or size which those willing to work are required to divide up among themselves in a spirit of mutual jealousy; it is rather, superficially considered, something which is dependent on total demand. Now we know that total demand results, in the last analysis, from the successful disposal of goods on the market, so that the total amount of demand is determined by the total amount of production. Thus it follows that consumption is determined by production and not the other way around. This means that there are no limits to profitable production on the whole (assuming that the composition of total output is "right") since the saturation point for human desires is not in sight; there is only one limit to consumption and that is set by the existing production technology. All else is nonsense: the fear of production, the belief that we must always be prepared to "spread the work," the opposition offered to every attempt to improve production methods. It is inconceivable that all producers will produce surpluses which they are unable to exchange with one another, provided they have correctly adjusted their production to their mutual needs. As to the question of what will become of unemployed workers and idle factories in a period in which markets are choked with goods and every branch of production overstocked, we make the following answer. In a depression, productive facilities are lying fallow, so to speak; these facilities will come to life and a market for the resultant goods will be created when those who have been shut out of the productive process win back their former purchasing power by being reinstated in this process, a chain of events which will occur once economic equilibrium is reestablished. Unused production reserves correspond, then, to an equivalent amount of unused reserves of purchasing power. *The reestablishment of economic equilibrium creates purchasing power.*

To understand that total equilibrium disturbance which we describe as the alternation of prosperity and depression (the business cycle), we must begin with two fundamental ideas. One is that the real cause of depression is not to be found in the depression period itself but in the preceding boom. The other idea is that the boom mechanism, which finally leads to depression, produces a sharp rise in capital investments (conversion of money capital into real capital), which in our economic system are financed by an expansion of credit (credit inflation) and which set the whole economy in motion in a network of changes acting and reacting on one another. Expansion and contraction of investments, which go hand in hand with expansion and contraction of the supply of credit, constitute the real core of the cyclical movement.

If we wish to understand more fully why the "full employment" of a boom period—after it has exceeded a certain critical point—leads to ever greater tensions which ultimately induce a depression, we must take into account a number of circumstances which are described in the special works dealing with cyclical theory. Long before the entire labor force has found employment, scarcities will develop with respect to certain important types of skilled workers. These scarcities, in conjunction with other difficulties, will lead to production bottlenecks in industries which have a decisive bearing on total production. Wage increases and rising prices for raw materials, machines, or other goods will sooner or later paralyze entrepreneurs' incentives, speculation will make the price and rate structure more and more unstable until, finally, it needs only one slight touch to cause it to topple. Above all, however, the sudden and abrupt increase in investment is itself a source of disturbance and one which would also give trouble to the collectivist state, involving as it does problems of a technical nature. The phenomenon in question may be designated as the "acceleration principle." Thus, a rise in investments is itself the occasion of still greater investment activity since an increase in capital goods production presupposes, in its turn, an increase of capital goods. A boom in poultry farming, for example, is a self-reinforcing process which will continue so long as new farms are established, resulting in an increased demand for fowls for breeding purposes. However, a point is finally reached at which the need for basic equipment for new farms has been satisfied. Further poultry production will then be at a level in excess of normal requirements for fowls for consumption and breeding purposes. This situation will arise as soon as there is a decline in the previous rate of increase in the number of new farms. It is evident that once the poultry boom has gotten underway there will come a certain moment when a "bust" can no longer be avoided since one cannot go on forever producing fowls for the sake of producing fowls. There is equally little justification in the economic system at large for producing capital goods at an ever-increasing rate for the sake of the capital goods. One cannot keep on forever building and "rationalizing," erecting new electrical plants, and installing new machinery. Above all, one cannot do this in a geometrical progression since the strength of the credit system needed to finance this flood of investments would in the end be enfeebled to the point of breakdown. So soon as it proves impossible to avoid a shrinkage of the capital goods industry, collapse of the boom is inevitable.

All of these reflections make it clear that a too abrupt and extensive rise in investment (*over-investment*), with its attendant disturbance of the economy's equilibrium, is a possibility which must be reckoned with in any highly developed complex system. A rise in investment will remain within safe bounds, however, so long as investments are financed by the voluntary savings of the population, for movements of the latter are themselves generally even rather than erratic. Only when investments are pushed beyond the boundaries set by real savings can they constitute a threat to equilibrium (total investment > total savings). To produce this situation, some sort of compulsion will be required to loosen the bond which ties capital goods production to the voluntary savings of the population, and to raise the relative restriction of consumption above the point which the population itself is prepared to undergo via its savings. This compulsion can take the form of the openly brutal methods of the collectivist state which, on the model of the Russian many-year-plans, stimulates investment activity by keeping the consumption of the population at a low level through taxation, manipulation of prices, and the planned economy. In our non-collectivist economic system this compulsion is replaced by credit expansion of the kind we have already dealt with in a previous section. Credit expansion fulfills a double function: it provides the entrepreneur who is prepared to invest with the additional credits he needs and, by increasing the prospects for profit, it stimulates the desire to invest generally. Investment activity of this type, in contrast to that which prevails in a collectivist state, is dependent on the voluntary decisions of the entrepreneur. It is only such credit expansion which, constituting as it does the motive power behind every boom period, makes it possible for investments in our economic system to exceed regularly the total amount of real savings.

Now it is to be observed that the economy will enter the boom period with a reserve of unused labor power and productive means inherited from the previous depression. This reserve will for a while permit investments to be financed by means of credit expansion, without any of the above-mentioned consequences. Obviously, the investment of capital means that productive power is being used for the erection of factories, the installation of machinery, or the building of houses instead of for the production of consumption goods. The greater the amount of investment, the less the quantity of productive resources which remains for the production of consumption goods. Hence, a nation must save if it wishes to augment the number of its machines, factories, and roads. If it does not, its consumption will have to be restricted forcibly (via the authoritarian forced saving of a collectivist economy or the monetary forced saving of a noncollectivist economy). The greater the amount of investment, the less the quantity of goods that can be consumed. This mutual competitiveness of investment and consumption does not obtain, however, so long as resort can be had to unused production reserves for the additional amount of investment. In the latter case, investments, far from disturbing equilibrium, are the indispensable means needed to reestablish it and thus to put an end to the depression (investment in such case is complementary to, not competitive with consumption). If, during the depression, investments were less than savings, additional investments will result in the reestablishment of equality between total investment and total savings. Hence, until a state of equilibrium is attained, investments are not in competition with consumption for the economy's factors of production; on the contrary, such investments have a salutary effect on the economy by their mobilization of unused productive resources. What in fact happens is that, thanks to the increase in total production brought about by investments, consumption is even greater than before. As long as the unused productive resources are not fully absorbed, total production may not be regarded as the usual cake which, as is well known, one cannot eat and have too; on the contrary, it is a cake which actually becomes bigger the more we eat of it. This seems paradoxical unless it is realized that it is precisely the claim on the factors of production resulting from an increase of investment which, by re-establishing equilibrium (quantity of investment = quantity of savings), sets the whole productive apparatus in motion.

As long as the upswing of economic activity can draw on the reserves of unused factors, credit expansion will not bring about a rise in prices since the increase in purchasing power is compensated for by a corresponding increase in goods. Credit expansion, then, serves the salutary purpose of compensating for the decline in purchasing power which had come about because of the fact that in the depression more was saved than was invested (deflation); in this case, credit expansion is *compensatory*, not *inflationary*. This idyllic phase will come to an end, however, as soon as the unused production reserves are exhausted and when there is no more unemployment worth mentioning (a condition imprecisely described as "full employment"). As a rule, however, the end of this phase of "safe" expansion is reached somewhat earlier than might be expected on account of the aforementioned "bottlenecks." The more intensive the demand by labor for wage increases during the upward movement is, the sooner the critical point will be reached, since in this case, credit expansion is converted into an increase in prices instead of an increase in employment.

When this *critical* point in the upswing is reached, credit expansion becomes inflationary instead of compensatory. Investments once again enter into competition with the production of consumption goods, and the magic cake which simply grew bigger the more we ate of it, is changed back into a quite ordinary cake of which we cannot eat a single piece and still have it. Investments made after this point is attained are equivalent to a real subtraction from the means of production available for consumption uses. From this moment on, we are traveling in a danger zone: the factors originally responsible for the boom mutually reinforce each other in a cumulative process which must end, finally, in a new depression. The stronger one's determination to prolong this process for the purpose of maintaining the "full employment" situation, the worse will be the final and inevitable collapse. We should not forget that the last great crisis of 1929-32, whose consequences were so enormous, was a collapse of this type. The crash of '29, however, was not only a consequence of the extraordinary piling up of investments which preceded it (notably in the United States) ; a whole constellation of other mishaps conspired together to intensify and extend the catastrophe.

In what light, then, are we to regard *depression?* We can understand why a depression must come, once free rein has been given to a cumulative process of over-investment via an inflationary expansion of credit during the boom period. After being built up to too high a level, the tower of investments crashes down, and makes necessary a painful and costly process of readjustment and rearrangement of the economy. Extravagance and unsound speculations come to an end; close reckoning becomes necessary once again and all economic structures which are interiorly unstable collapse. There is, however, the grave danger that this, in itself inevitable reaction, will far exceed the character of a mere cleansing operation and that henceforth, a cumulative *process of decline* will develop, representing the counterpart of the preceding cumulative process of expansion. The inevitable primary depression may be followed by a *secondary* depression which it should be the first object of policy to avoid. It is indeed quite possible that in the unfavorable psychological climate of a depression (to which many other more or less fortuitous circumstances, political and other, may contribute) , entrepreneurs' incentives may be weakened to such an extent that investments will sink below the level required to convert the continuing savings of the economy into investments and thereby into demand for goods (total investments < total savings).

To understand the above, two things have to be kept in mind. *First,* it is to be observed that the act of saving, or the putting aside of a part of one's income, means nothing else than nonconsumption, i.e., the absence of demand, and thereby a minus in the sale of consumer goods. Savings are once again converted into demand when they are invested, i.e., used for the purchase and production of capital goods. *Secondly,* we must realize that these two actions—saving and investing—do not necessarily synchronize with one another; on the contrary, they are two distinct processes, each of which takes place independently of the other. Savings are not necessarily converted into investments; at the same time, such conversion is not necessarily excluded, a fact which deserves to be emphasized in opposition to certain excessively pessimistic theories of the present day.[2] The extent to which such conversion—with its decisive bearing upon economic equilibrium—takes place depends upon numerous and varying circumstances of a psychological, legal, institutional, or political nature. It is understandable, of course, that this process of conversion will run into severe difficulties following the collapse of the boom. Should investments, at this juncture, continue to lag behind savings (*under-investment*), a decline in demand will take place (deflation) which, should it assume large proportions, can bring about a secondary depression of that dangerous type which afflicted the world after the crisis of 1929. Then we are faced with a very severe disturbance attended by the well-known phenomena of mass unemployment and drastic price declines, effects which may be aggravated by the mutual reinforcement and multiplication of the effects of a fall in demand. The disturbance will be brought to an end only when total savings and total investments are again harmonized with one another, be this through an increase in investments or a decrease in savings.[3]

2. *Stabilization Policy*

In order to discover the right methods for the attainment of the vitally important goal of economic stabilization and to distinguish these from the wrong methods, we must make a scrupulously conscientious effort to picture—in this instance in outline form only—the extraordinarily involved nature of the economic process and the conditions necessary for the maintenance of equilibrium. Competence in evaluating a given economic situation requires a fairly clear understanding of what really goes on in the economy in terms of production, saving, investment, and consumption, of the way in which the flows of money and goods are related to one another, of the significance of prices, wages, interest and profits, of how and where credit enters the picture, of how banks and stock exchanges work together to keep the economic process functioning, etc. If we are all agreed that the real issue at stake is to attain and maintain as high a level of employment as possible, such a study of the dynamics of economic life should put us in a better position to recognize the dangers of a policy of forcible stabilization which, under the label of "full employment," has become popular in all countries. It is a policy which is shaped exclusively by reference to the question of how total demand, by means of the continual creation of new money (and with complete disregard for the deeper causes of equilibrium disturbances), can be maintained at a level sufficient to ensure the sort of "full employment" which existed in peacetime in National Socialist Germany, and in all countries during and after World War II. In reality, of course, full employment of this type would be more accurately defined as abnormal "over-employment." For those eager to establish such a policy of "constant inflationary pressure," the problems arising from disturbances of economic equilibrium with which we have concerned ourselves seem hardly to exist. The only circumstance that interests them is that these disturbances lead to a fall in demand which they hasten to push up again through the creation of money, without inquiring into the deeper causes of disturbance and the means of overcoming them. It is this radical simplification which gives rise to all of the grave dangers of such a policy of constant "full employment."[4]

We have been dealing here with a wrong policy whose dangers, as seen in the National Socialist full employment experiment and in contemporary economic tensions, have received far too little attention. We should take note of the fact, however, that there are other ways of attaining the goal of a stable economy with a high level of employment; these ways may be more unpleasant, but on that account can be recommended with a clearer conscience by the economist. In this connection, there are four principal points to keep in mind:[5]

1. Given the inevitable fluctuations in economic conditions and associated fluctuations in employment, the necessity of continual adaptation and adjustment is of the first importance. This is only possible, however, if the economic apparatus is, in all its parts, as flexible as possible. The more rigid this apparatus becomes—a trend which has increased noticeably over the past decades, and which will become even more pronounced in the future if certain politico-economic tendencies of our time are perpetuated—the more difficult will adaptation and stabilization become, and the more severe the fluctuations of the economy will be. Simultaneously, the greater will become the temptation to keep employment high by resort to the mechanical method of increasing the money supply—recommended by the "full employment" school, cost what it will. Then only will it become clear how apt is the apparently paradoxical statement:

the more stabilization, the less stability. We can make this very clear to ourselves if we compare the economic apparatus to a bicycle. A bicycle can be ridden securely only if the handlebars are movable, thus allowing us to adjust the vehicle to every small disturbance of equilibrium. Were the handlebars to be "stabilized," the bicycle rider would fall. So also is it in economic life, where the handlebars steering the economy is the free market. Every price and cost rigidity, every official restriction of market freedom, every arbitrary collective contract, every monopoly, every immobility of the factors of production, every quantitative limitation of output—all are additional accessories screwed onto the handlebars of our economic apparatus, encumbering it so that it can no longer remain upright and gives us one spill after another unless the state provides ever increasing support.[6]

2. If it is true that the changing ratio between total savings and total investment is a principal cause of disturbance, then the proper course of action is to forestall both the *over-investment* of a boom period and the *under-investment* of a depression. As soon as the boom enters the danger zone of inflation, investment must be braked by taking appropriate measures with respect to money, credit, and budget policy. In a depression, on the other hand, investment should be stimulated (when absolutely necessary, but only then!) by resort to those radical methods advocated by the "full employment" school as suitable at all times.

3. Such stimulants, however, as are given to investment in a depression period may prove to be of little avail. Indeed, the outdistancing of investments by savings can become a permanent tendency if *entrepreneurs are dissuaded from investing* by a combination of exaggerated wage and social demands, a government policy of increasing arbitrariness and restrictiveness in respect to economic life, and monopolistic rigidities. In this situation, investment, which even in normal times requires a great deal of daring on account of the uncertainty of all calculations regarding the future, will become an increasingly risky business in which one can lose a great deal but win only a little. Heavy taxation, forcible reduction of dividends, ruthless exploitation on the part of labor-union monopolies (the consequences of which have to be borne by the less ruthless and less tightly organized workers), abandonment by governments of fixed principles in the making of their economic and social policies, the

routine granting of subventions, threats of further socialization as the result of which one can no longer be sure whether one will reap tomorrow what one sows today, disregard of individual rights and freedoms, complete arbitrariness in the matter of international trade policy and monetary policy—all of this can be regarded as very progressive and the opposite branded as "reactionary." But then there should be no surprise if in such a climate investments fail to come up to expectations, with the consequences for employment opportunities with which we are familiar. From these remarks may be inferred what the ingredients of a positive policy of stabilization should be.

4. We would be very much mistaken were we to regard the problem of stabilization as solved by the measures to which we have thus far alluded. Even in the most favorable case, we shall have to reckon with considerable fluctuations in economic conditions. The task which confronts us in consequence can best be made clear by an illustration. Smooth driving depends on two conditions: the smoothness of the road and the quality of the springs with which our car is equipped. A road can never be so smooth that we can dispense with springs; the bumpier the road, however, the better must the springs be. Applying this illustration to our problem of economic stabilization, we find that up to now we have concerned ourselves with the smoothness of the road and with the means needed to make it still smoother. But just as we cannot expect to find roads which will render springs unnecessary, neither can we hope to attain complete economic stability. Indeed, it is to be expected that the economic highway of the future will be spotted with a number of bad holes. Hence, with respect to economic life, we must take care to provide ourselves with a better set of springs and in this way ensure that individuals will be better able to resist the shocks that will be inevitably encountered. And herewith we glimpse the outlines of a policy —going beyond cyclical policy—which seeks to mitigate the sensitivity and instability of our proletarianized, centralized, mass-type society through *decentralization, de-proletarianization, the anchoring of men in their own resources, encouragement to small farmers and small business, increased property ownership, and the strengthening of the middle classes.* In this way, it would be possible to equip society, internally, with a set of springs with whose help it could withstand even the strongest economic shocks without panic, pauperization, and demoralization.

3. The Impact of Keynesianism

John Maynard Keynes, who died in 1946 at the age of 62, is not only the best known economist of our times but also a man who by any standards must be reckoned as one of the leading personages of the first half of the twentieth century. The history of the era which followed World War I can no more dispense with the name of this singular individual than it can with the names of Einstein, Churchill, Roosevelt, or Hitler. It is only in this broad perspective that Keynes' full importance becomes visible. How ought we to judge the influence of this man? Is he the Copernicus of economics, as so many claim, the man who banished the ghosts of economics grown rigid in the chains of tradition, who opened the door to prosperity and stability? Or did he destroy more than he created and has he summoned into being spirits that today he possibly would be gladly rid of?

It is difficult to make a simple answer to these questions. A fair judgment would have to take into account not only the manifold talents and personal charm of the man, but would require also the dissection of issues which have nourished most of the economic controversies of our time and which have given even the experts pause. We may begin by noting a characteristic trait of this animated, impulsive, and artistically sensitive man: his virtuoso-like ability to change positions on important questions, positions which he had only shortly before defended with intelligence and vigor. It is difficult to recognize in the author of *The Economic Consequences of the Peace* (1919) and of the famous series of articles on reconstruction in the *Manchester Guardian*—works which at the beginning of the '20's stood for a program of free trade and Malthusian liberalism —the same man who later announced the "end of laissez-faire," who, using extremely weak arguments, took it upon himself to champion economic autarky and so prepared the ground intellectually for the transition to economic and monetary nationalism on the part of his own and other countries. Indeed, it was his fate—one in which, initially, he even appeared to find some visible satisfaction and which at any rate he did not explicitly disavow—to become the intellectual authority for economic policy in National Socialist Germany. A fund of nervous energy, great productivity, temperament, virtuosity in debate, a cavalier nonchalance in changing positions—these were the chief notes of Keynes' personality.

In two fundamental respects, nevertheless, Keynes was more consistent than he appeared to be. In spite of all his criticisms of "capitalism," he never became a socialist. He remained a liberal, professing devotion to democratic freedoms and convinced that in his singular way, he was promoting them. Another constant in his career was his belief, derived from his expanding researches in monetary theory, that the real defect of our economic system must be sought in the organization of its finances and its monetary institutions. To improve this organization, he made proposals ranging from the moderate ones of his *Tract on Monetary Reform* (1923) to the radical ones of his last great work, *The General Theory of Employment, Interest and Money* (1936).

This is not the place to evaluate in detail the services which Keynes, in these works, rendered to the advancement of theory. Unquestionably, they are considerable. At the same time, it is precisely because he so deeply influenced his time that it is necessary to ask whether the practical results of his theories and proposals, which were intended to improve the working of the existing economic system, did not ultimately have the effect of weakening its foundations—so that Keynes, in tragic opposition to his own intention, must be numbered among the grave-diggers of that very order of liberal democracy to which his innermost allegiance belonged.

One may believe that there are times in which vigorous measures to increase the money supply will prevent disaster; but not with impunity can a leading scientific figure like Keynes bestow the mantle of his authority on the chronic propensity of all governments to inflate. One may believe that under certain circumstances an increase in government debt is the lesser evil; but not with impunity is such a temporary measure transformed into a maxim. It can happen—as in the Great Depression of 1931-32—that all efforts to put a quick end to unemployment prove useless, so that recourse must be had to an increase of "effective demand" by the expansion of the money supply; but not with impunity can one treat, with hardly concealed contempt, the established rules and institutions upon which, in the long run, the ordered conduct of economic life depends if it is not to be held under constant inflationary pressure. One can uncover in the mechanism of saving many a problem requiring special attention, overlooked by earlier and more fortunate generations; but not with impunity can one take away from men the feeling that it is right to save, to put aside a reserve for them-

selves and their families, instead of spending everything and then
calling upon the help of the state—the greatest spender of all—in
time of need. Just as a storm on the high seas may require that masts
be cut down and freight thrown overboard, so too in economic life
there will be hurricanes which will require us temporarily to suspend the principles of free international trade; but not with impunity can one declare these principles to be "out of date" so soon
as they get in the way of a policy of "full employment," a doctrine
which, following the shock of the Great Depression, has become as
inflexible as any of the views ever held by the despised "old economics." To be sure, competition, freedom of markets, wage flexibility,
and a prudent fiscal policy do not necessarily guarantee prosperity
and stability; indeed, there are extraordinary situations in which
exceptions to these excellent principles must be made; but not with
impunity can one announce to the crowd that henceforth they may
in good conscience be trampled upon.

These bitter-sweet reflections come to mind as one attempts to
fill in the impressive outlines of Keynes' full and immensely influential life. Because he was possessed of such an acute intelligence and
such an attractive personality the damage he inflicted was all the
greater, for his teachings were rendered all the more seductive
thereby. Thus, he accustomed a new generation to a kind of economic logic which revolves solely about the question of how "effective demand" can be most securely maintained at the highest possible level, whereas the real problem of the postwar era was how an
inflationary boom can be braked in time. Other things he did were
of still graver import in their ultimate consequences. He not only
demolished that which was decayed, but by his preaching of economic pragmatism and his attack on deeply rooted principles in the
moral-political sphere, he became one of the principal agents in that
general decay of standards, of norms, and of principles which constitutes the real core of the social crisis of our time. At bottom, his
economic policy program consisted in saying: *pecca fortiter;* that is,
do with a light heart what you have hitherto regarded as a sin!
Whether and to what extent Keynes' accomplishments on the level
of economic theory and economic technique are right, will be a
subject of debate for a long time to come; but that on the higher
level of social philosophy and political ethics he was very wrong, is
already sufficiently clear.

That Keynes not only preached these things but preached them apparently in good conscience, indeed with the same messianic fervor which has become so characteristic of his numerous disciples, is something which has a deeper explanation, an explanation which must be sought in the type of man and the type of philosophy which he represented. How is it that such an extraordinary man (in the best sense), whose intellect was so wide-ranging and who was just as much artist and organizer as he was scholar, could at the same time be so blind to moral-political postulates (which even in the narrower domain of economics are more important in the long run than clever monetary formulae) without which human society cannot exist?

To fully appreciate the kind of man and the kind of philosophy we are here concerned with, it is useful to compare Keynes with Adam Smith. In the depth and extent of their influence at least, the two men were strikingly similar. Moreover, both Smith and Keynes had interests which extended far beyond the confines of economics. But whereas Smith left us, in addition to his magnum opus on the *Wealth of Nations* (1776) a book on the *Theory of Moral Sentiments* (1759) which exposes the full moral-philosophical foundations of his much-misconstrued economic doctrines, Keynes has left us, in addition to his economic works, a monograph on the theory of probability (*A Treatise on Probability,* 1921). For Smith, whose book on the *Wealth of Nations* was planned as a segment of a giant opus on the cultural history of mankind, economics was viewed as an organic part of the larger whole of the intellectual, moral, and historical life of society; for Keynes, economics was part of a mathematical-mechanical universe. The one man was a representative of the humanist spirit of the 18th century; the other a representative of the geometric spirit of the 20th century; a deistic moralist was the one, an exponent of positivistic scientism the other. For the one, the cosmos of human society and the human economy was the result of the working of an "invisible hand," a living order with an immanent logic of its own which the human mind could comprehend and even destroy but could not duplicate; for the other, economy and society were the result of mechanical *quanta* subject to precise measurement and direction by an omnicompetent technical human intelligence. The teachings of the one were a promising beginning; those of the other the end product of a process of distintegration in which the crisis of an exclusively rationalistic society finds its ultimate expression. On the lesser level of economics, the road from Adam Smith to Keynes has doubtless been one of progress in many respects; on the higher level of total intellectual and spiritual development, it is equally certain that the road has been one of reaction and regression.

There is little consolation in the fact that Keynes at the close of his life worriedly endeavored to dampen the overzealousness of his followers. And it is tiresome, after a while, to have to listen to the repeated affirmation that Keynes himself, had he lived, would have contributed the necessary correction of "Keynesianism." This may well have been the case. On the other hand, the real tragedy of the Keynesian legacy is that what Keynes regarded as intellectual "working capital," i.e., ideas easily shifted from the service of one ideal to that of another, became for his less flexible disciples intellectual "fixed capital," the profits of which were protected by every means available, including that of monopolistic exclusion. Keynes cannot be spared the reproach of having failed to take this fateful result of his writings and teachings into account.

A fact of the postwar era, which is as singular as it is compromising for Keynesianism, is that the more determinedly the Keynesians have sought to enthrone the teachings of the master as the only legitimate economics, the more decisively have actual economic events moved away from the Keynesian postulates. Most governments, if not most economists, have become painfully aware of the inadequacy of Keynes' teachings in dealing with the chronic inflation of the postwar years; nor was this teaching able to shed any light on the fact that it was precisely the noninflationary economies of this period, least influenced by Keynesianism, which achieved the most remarkable rates of growth, employment, and stability, whereas it was the inflationary (in particular, the Anglo-American) economies which, by comparison, stagnated. Indeed, so compromising for Keynesianism were these postwar developments that the efforts to transform the ideology into a mere logical apparatus, capable of being shifted with cool detachment from the fight against deflation to the fight against inflation, are quite understandable. Of course, when this is done with the claim that it is still the pure light of Keynesian teaching which informs the new approach, we scientific legitimists will be excused for showing some astonishment at so much flexibility. After having for years pointed out to the representatives of the "new economics" the threat (inflation) which finally became reality, we find it difficult to accustom ourselves to seeing our analysis and prescriptions tricked out in the language of this same "new economics." This being the case, it may at least be permitted to make a few comments thereon.

To begin with, we will readily concede that the use of Keynesianism as a logical apparatus, as a simple technique in the struggle against inflation in the full employment countries is (and was) thoroughly legitimate in one respect at least. Non-Keynesians themselves make use of the apparatus when they say that such countries were "living beyond their means," i.e., that their aggregate expenditures for consumption and investment generated more purchasing power for the output of the economy than could be supplied at current prices, with the consequent emergence of inflationary gaps and balance of payments deficits. Such insights could have been derived from the "old economics" as well, although it is conceded that macroeconomic concepts have been improved and refined by the "new economics."

But having made these concessions and with them a step toward conciliation, it would be reasonable to expect that the representatives of the "new economics," in turn, would frankly admit: first, that their passionately-held ideology has turned out to be, in truth, a mere logical technique; and secondly, that if in the postwar period it became necessary to apply the technique to a situation diametrically opposed to the one Keynes had in mind, this in itself was largely due to the ideological influence of Keynesianism with its emphasis on fear of deflation, full employment at any cost, and unrestrained government spending.

It is the latter circumstance which points to the great difficulty of applying the logical apparatus of the "new economics," in admirable nonpartisanship, to either inflation or deflation, depending on the situation. Keynesianism, even in the most favorable case, tends to be latent inflationism. This inflationism becomes virulent so soon as disturbances occur, especially those accompanied by unemployment and business contraction, which appear to constitute "deflation." In fact, the disturbances may be due not to disproportions between the gross magnitudes of the economy (as the "new economics" would have it) but (in terms of the "old economics") to false values—prices or wages—and to a false allocation of the factors of production. What then? What of the case in which wage increases cause unemployment? Above all: how is it planned to cope with the fact that the reduction of inflationary over-employment is usually accompanied by pseudo-deflationary phenomena?

We see that even where the new economics is reduced to a mere neutral logical technique, and even where it happens to find itself in agreement with the prescriptions of the "old economics," the desired synthesis is considerably more difficult to achieve than at first appears. Such a synthesis will at all events not take place unless the representatives of the "new economics" determine to give up their claims that their theories and methods are the only valid ones, and until they abandon still more positions than they have already done.

The idea that by a continuous manipulation of macroeconomic variables it is possible to offset now a deflationary, now an inflationary tendency is extremely attractive. The "new economics," however, has by no means an exclusive patent on it; from the beginning it has been the signpost of a reasonable economic policy. But it will remain a misleading and a dangerous idea so long as it is not purged, far more completely than hitherto, of all traces of "Keynesianism." For inevitably the Keynesians will be found looking at inflation through the wrong end of the telescope and deflation through a magnifying glass. Hence, this otherwise useful idea—so long as it remains in the grip of the "new economics," with its exclusive concern with macroeconomics—will be the captive of an intellectual outlook which distorts the nature of both deflation and inflation. The very circumstance that in the postwar period so much time and argument and so much inflation were required before even the more observant of the representatives of the "new economics" were persuaded to change course from anti-deflation to anti-inflation, shows the inner tendency of this whole school of thought. In the logical machine so cleverly devised by Keynes and his followers we find, to be sure, an inflation brake. But the machine is so constructed that the brake is depressed only when a breakneck rate of speed has been attained; and the brake has the further fatal tendency of being released as soon as the braking action is the least bit effective.

In summary, we find in the teachings of Keynes the social philosophy of a man who, proud of his alleged modernity and progressiveness, believes himself capable of "making over" society and the economy. We find a man who has forgotten those mysterious powers of the human soul and of human society which cannot be expressed in mathematical equations, nor confined within an assemblage of statistics or the rubrics of economic planning. It is in no small degree this character of Keynesian teachings which explain their large success in those countries and with those political parties in which a preference for social planning and active suspicion of individual freedom is especially marked. The greater the extent to which a person's milieu, habits, way of life, and social environment prevent him from seeing that the real evil of our civilization lies in the profoundly unnatural character of our lives, our society, and our way of thinking—not in any still imperfect ability to increase government budget deficits, keep interest rates down, pump up "effective demand," make rates of exchange flexible, and manipulate balances of payments—the greater is the likelihood of his susceptibility to the doctrines which Keynes made fashionable. Conversely, the success of these doctrines shows us how many people there are who find them appealing, and how sick is an age which could spawn them in such numbers. For all these reasons, we may expect to be able to measure the progress of the recovery of society (the first signs of which we believe to be already visible), in part, by the number of men who succeed in freeing themselves from the spell of Keynesianism and in recognizing not only its economic weaknesses, but the errors of its social philosophy as well.[7] Then it will be possible to evaluate, objectively and unemotionally, the real contributions of Keynes, infused as they are with the elements of both grandeur and tragedy. On this note we may proceed to the last chapter of this book.

NOTES

1. (p. 208) *Economic Fluctuations*

The reader is referred to the following additional publications of the author:
W. Röpke, *Crises and Cycles* (London, 1936); W. Röpke, *Civitas Humana*
(London, 1948). See also: G. Haberler, *Prosperity and Depression* (3rd ed.;
Geneva, 1941); Hans Gestrich, *Kredit und Sparen* (2nd ed.; Godesberg, 1948);
J. Schumpeter, *Business Cycles* (New York, 1939); League of Nations (report),
Economic Stability in the Post-War World (Geneva, 1945); G. Haberler (ed.),
Readings in Business Cycle Theory (Philadelphia, 1944); W.A. Jöhr, *Die Kon-
junkturschwankungen* (Tübingen-Zurich, 1952); G. Schmölders, "Konjunkturen
und Krisen," *Rowohlts Deutsche Enzyklopädie*, Vol. 3.

2. (p. 217) *Inadequate Investment—A Matter of Fate?*

Under the influence of Keynes (*The General Theory of Employment, Interest
and Money* [London, 1936]) and of the American economist Alvin H. Hansen
(*Full Recovery or Stagnation?* [New York, 1938]), widespread currency was
given to the notion that the rich industrial countries have entered the phase of
relative investment saturation ("mature economy") and that consequently a
permanent tendency for savings to outstrip investment will develop unless appropriate measures are taken to forestall this. This theory of latent chronic stagnation must, however, be abandoned as unproven. See W. Röpke, *Civitas Humana*
(*op. cit.*, pp. 218-220); Howard S. Ellis, "Monetary Policy and Investment,"
American Economic Review, Supplement, March 1940; Henry C. Simons, "Hansen on Fiscal Policy" in *Economy Policy for a Free Society* (Chicago, 1948);
Willford I. King, "Are We Suffering from Economic Maturity?" *Journal of
Political Economy*, October 1939; George Terborgh, *The Bogey of Economic
Maturity* (Chicago, 1945). The above-mentioned League of Nations report also
rejects the mature economy thesis; in the interim it has long since been dis-
proved by events, and its place taken by the concern as to how rapid rates of
growth can be achieved without inflation.

3. (p. 217) *Secondary Depression*

See W. Röpke, *Crises and Cycles, op. cit.;* W. Röpke, "Die sekundäre Krise
und ihre Ueberwindung," *Economic Essays in Honour of Gustav Cassel* (London,
1933).

4. (p. 218) *"Full Employment"*

For criticism of the "full employment" school see: G. Haberler, *op. cit.;*
Howard S. Ellis, *op. cit.;* Hans Gestrich, *op. cit.;* W. Röpke, *The Social Crisis of
Our Time* (Chicago, 1950); W. Röpke, *Civitas Humana, op. cit.;* Allan G.B.
Fisher, *Economic Progress and Social Security* (London, 1945); Henry C. Simons,
op. cit., especially Chapter XIII, "The Beveridge Program: An Unsympathetic
Interpretation"; L.A. Hahn, *The Economics of Illusion* (New York, 1949);
W. Röpke, " 'Vollbeschäftigung'—eine trügerische Lösung," *Zeitschrift für das
gesamte Kreditwesen*, 1950, No. 6 (discussion on the same in No. 11). For the
practical application of these thoughts to the case of German economic policy
since 1948 see W. Röpke, *Ist die deutsche Wirtschaftspolitik richtig?* (Stuttgart,
1950), a monograph prepared at the behest of the German government, the

essentials of which have been reprinted in Wilhelm Röpke, *Gegen die Brandung* (Erlenbach-Zurich, 1959). An extreme example of the "full employment" ideology and one in which its principal errors may be particularly well studied is the United Nations report by five economic experts entitled *National and International Measures for Full Employment* (Lake Success, New York, 1949). For criticism of this document see: Jacob Viner, "Full Employment at Whatever Cost," *The Quarterly Journal of Economics*, August, 1950; W. Röpke, *The Economics of Full Employment* (New York, 1952).

5. (p. 218) *Cyclical Policy*

In addition to the above-mentioned League of Nations study, *Economic Stability in the Post-War World*, see my own book *Crises and Cycles* and also: Charles La Roche, *Beschäftigungspolitik in der Demokratie* (Zurich, 1947); B. Ohlin, *The Problem of Employment Stabilisation* (London, 1950); Paul Binder, *Die Stabilisierung der Wirtschaftskonjunktur* (1956).

6. (p. 219) *Flexibility of the Economic System*

This extremely important theme has been the subject of investigation by: H.L. Keus, *De ondernemer en zijn social-economische problemen* (Haarlem, 1942) ; Allan G.B. Fisher, *op. cit.;* League of Nations, *Economic Stability in the Post-War World, op. cit.;* Madeleine Jaccard, *La mobilité de la main d'oeuvre et les problèmes du chômage et de la pénurie de travailleurs* (Lausanne, 1945); W.H. Hutt, *Plan for Reconstruction* (London, 1943) . For discussion of current problems in this area see also my book *A Humane Economy, op. cit.*

7. (p. 228) *"Keynesianism"*

The theories of Keynes ("Keynesianism") which long dominated economic debate and policy with respect to economic fluctuations, and which produced many uncritical analyses of the problem of "full employment," have been subjected to increasingly sharp, even devastating criticism. See L.A. Hahn, *Common Sense Economics* (New York, 1956); L.A. Hahn, *Geld und Kredit* (Frankfurt am Main, 1960); Henry Hazlitt, *The Failure of the "New Economics," An Analysis of the Keynesian Fallacies* (New York, 1959); Henry Hazlitt (ed.), *The Critics of Keynesian Economics* (New York, 1960); W. Röpke, *A Humane Economy* (Chicago, 1960); W. Röpke, "Was lehrt Keynes?" in *Gegen die Brandung, op. cit.;* David McCord Wright, *The Keynesian System* (New York, 1962).

CHAPTER IX

STRUCTURE OF THE ECONOMY; ECONOMICS AND THE WORLD CRISIS

> "It is a pity that the philosopher and the reformer cannot set up models of their republics and of their reforms, for it requires a high order of talent in philosophical speculation to be able to predict that such schemes will not work. On the other hand, it needs only a combination of boldness and enthusiasm to cause the more naive members of the public to barter their ancestral acres for a share of stock in the riches of the South Sea."
>
> G.CH. LICHTENBERG (1742-1799)

1. *Structure and Mechanism of Our Economic System*

This book has set itself the difficult task of describing the several parts of the economic system and the way in which these parts work together. The author's task would have been easier and do doubt he could have ingratiated himself with many a contemporary reader if he had given free rein to his feelings and, out of his own antipathy to the many degenerate features of our economic system, had constructed an arsenal of charges against it, culminating in a demand for its complete overthrow. But these degenerate aspects are so obvious to everybody, they are the subject of such an extensive and overly emotional literature, that it is the duty of the scholar to emphasize the other side of the picture and to lead the discussion back to an understanding of the *foundations* of our economic system. And thereby it becomes clear that a number of these degenerate features

231

are, in fact, closely linked to fatal lack of understanding of what constitutes the real character of our economic structure.

Sheer indignation, no more than impassioned pleas for economic revolution, can accomplish very little. The urge to surrender to emotions of this kind is very strong, for it is a normal human trait to set small store on what one already possesses and to clothe with the romantic aura of perfection what one would like to possess. The first duty of an economist aware of his immense responsibility is, nevertheless, to oppose with all his strength this natural inclination and to establish an exact understanding of two things: the economic system which we have and the one which we would establish in its place. The next step is to apply this deepened insight into the real nature of the economic structure to the discovering of ways by which it can be freed of its imperfections and degeneracies, and its power to function increased instead of diminished. Only when this step has been taken are we at liberty to choose between our economic system and a more or less collectivistic one, for only then will we have the full awareness of all that we would give up, and all that we would receive, in choosing the one or the other. If the welfare of our fellow men means anything to us, we should not risk the surrender of an economic system whose structure we have not even taken the trouble to study, against one which has existed up to now only in our over-stimulated imagination and which might cruelly deceive our hopes.

It is, indeed, disquieting to find how small a minority in any country really understands the essence of our economic system. Actually this should occasion no surprise, for such understanding is gotten only by patient and thorough study of the science which investigates economic interrelationships, unruffled by the attacks to which it has been subject at all times—today more so than ever (a point to which we shall return later on). But how many bother to make this effort? That the number is so small is in itself a cause for concern, since the overwhelming majority of those who are engaged in passing random judgments on our economic system seek to disparage the minority who do understand it as ignorant and biased— a spectacle to be met with in no other science. Probably the very fact that our time has so little understanding of its own economic system is not the least of the reasons why the world finds itself in its present lamentable condition.

Our economic system is misunderstood by most people probably because they regard certain of its more puzzling phenomena as harmful and senseless outgrowths of "capitalism." The truth is that the phenomena in question may conceal a certain useful function which must be fulfilled in every economic system, or they may simply prove to be the more or less inevitable ingredients of any economic system whatever.[1] Certain things are regarded as unique historical occurrences which, in fact, we find reappearing in every age and at every stage of economic development. We have encountered this logical error so often in the course of our inquiry that a few remarks should suffice to dispose of it. Thus, in a previous chapter, we discussed at length all the dangers and disturbances which arise from an extreme division of labor. Now, since our economic system is the first in history to be characterized by an extraordinarily differentiated division of labor, many are easily tempted to blame the resulting disadvantages on our economic system, and to seek a solution in collectivism (socialism) without realizing that in so doing they are guilty of confounding two different things. They confuse the principle of a highly differentiated division of labor (which, in contrast to the pre-capitalistic economic system, characterizes both our economic system *and* the collectivist one) with the mere method of coordination in respect to which a collectivist economic system would be distinguished from our own. They have an antipathy to our economic system on account of its centralization, its artificiality, its complexity, and its impenetrability. Since collectivism appears to be the opposite of this economic system, they regard it as a foregone conclusion that it will deliver us from these evils. They fail to realize that a collectivist economic system can no more avoid the evils flowing from exaggerated differentiation than our own, since both are outgrowths of the same economic-historical epoch. Still less are they aware that a collectivist system would, in all probability, also carry us still farther away from that idyllic stage of economic history which the world left behind it when it passed over to capitalism. Thus we arrive at the height of confusion when the same people who untiringly attack the rationalist, mechanical, and artificial character of our economic system with its industrialization, its proletarianization and urbanization, seek salvation in planned economy and centralized organization, i.e., in an economic structure which will be still more rationalist, still more mechanical, and still more artificial than the existing one. Does this not suggest the plight of avalanche victims struggling to dig their way out of the snow, but burying themselves ever deeper because they have lost their ability to sense which way is up and which is down? A large portion of mankind seems to find itself today in this unfortunate situation.

As these reflections show, there will always be a tendency to misjudge our economic system in the absence of a clear realization that its replacement by a collectivist system would change the form, but not the substance, of many phenomena. This fact makes it more than questionable whether such a change would be for the better. Thus, the great to-do which is made about advertising and distribution costs is coupled with a failure to take into account the fact that a collectivist economic system would also have to reckon with the corresponding costs connected with the setting up of an apparatus for the distribution of goods (including propaganda). The only question would be, then, whether these costs in a collectivist economic system would be lower than under the existing system; and there are enough reasons for assuming that they would be higher. Still another instance of where complaints are brought to the wrong department is found in the case of big industry, among the less happy features of which the depersonalization of work and the dependence of the worker stand foremost. It is, however, clear that the techniques of production such as are found in big industry would certainly be taken over by the collectivist state, with the result that the dependence of the worker would actually become even greater since he would no longer be able to choose among different employers. As the collectivization of agriculture in Russia demonstrates, we must actually expect an extension of mass-production techniques to areas which, in our economic system, have this far successfully preserved the form of the small enterprise. This is an expectation which is supported by the fact, among others, that every totalitarian state has for political reasons a burning interest in the agglomeration of dependent, easily fanaticized and controlled masses.

Finally, we know from preceding chapters that phenomena such as costs, prices, profitability, interest, and rent can in no way be construed as devilish inventions of "capitalism." On the contrary, they constitute an ingenious and thoroughly intelligible mechanism and serve for the fulfillment of tasks with which any economic system whatsoever is faced. Together they comprise that apparatus needed to achieve general economic equilibrium for which the collectivist state must find an equivalent, though, as we have already seen, the probability of its being able to do so is remote.

It appears that there are many people who, even though they have a clear understanding of the regulatory mechanism of our economic system, experience especial difficulty when it comes to a proper appreciation of the dominant role played by the profit principle in the sphere of production. In their legitimate indignation over everything that seems to them to emphasize self-interest at the expense of the community, in their anger at cupidity and usury, they sense behind the dominance of the profit principle something vaguely immoral. In reality, things are far more complex than they appear. True, men today, as always, strive for maximum satisfaction of their desires, but these desires, as always, are very different from one another. Some seek honor and power, others a modest degree of happiness, still others are most content when engaged in the service of the commonweal, and the rest have ambitions only to satisfy to the maximum their purely material needs. But all fear poverty and social degradation. The dominance of the profit element in production is no proof, therefore, that the springs of economic activity are less diverse today than at other times. This circumstance shows only that in the profit principle we have a sure and indispensable criterion for determining whether or not any given enterprise may be fitted into the context of the national economy or not. The dominance of the profit principle merely brings it about that an entrepreneur who fits into this context is rewarded by the market; he who does not is punished by the market. The reward is as high as the penalty is severe, but it is precisely in this way that we are assured of the selection of persons qualified to direct the process of production. And since the fear of loss appears to be of more moment than the desire for gain, it may be said that our economic system is (in the final analysis) regulated by bankruptcy. The collectivist state must find an equivalent regulatory principle: in the place of profitability it will have to establish another criterion of success and another system of selecting the managers of production. It is very doubtful if such an equivalent can be found. In any case, the fact that those who direct the process of production (the entrepreneurs) personally enjoy the fruits of success and personally suffer all the losses incident on failure is one of the most important (if unfortunately often abused) principles of our economic system. It would be difficult to prove that it is either unnatural or unpurposeful.

But all of this is valid only under one condition, whose importance we must make every effort to grasp if we would understand the structure of our economic system and the true extent of the *distortion* which it has undergone in recent times. The road which leads to profit may be entered only the condition that an *equivalent economic service is rendered in return*. At the same time, there must be assurance that deficient performance will find its inexorable punishment in the losses and finally in the bankruptcy proceedings which remove the incompetent persons from the ranks of those responsible for production. Similarly, the use of underhanded methods to obtain income (without corresponding service) and the avoidance of penalties for deficient performance (by shifting losses to others' shoulders) must be prevented. For the fulfillment of this condition our economic system disposes of two devices. The *first* is that responsibility and risks (chances for gain and loss) are coupled closely together. Here we encounter one of the most disturbing disfigurements of the modern economic system. The fact is that the growth of the corporation with its much discussed but unfortunately too seldom remedied abuses has led more and more to the assumption of risks by the community ("socialization of losses"). This and many other developments have resulted in a considerable weakening of the *coupling principle,* a situation which obviously must receive primary attention in any plan of economic reform which is to be truly effective. No less vexing problems arise with respect to the *second* device, with which the reader is already familiar, viz., *competition*. All the hardships that it implies and all the admittedly serious problems which it encompasses cannot get rid of the fact that our economic system stands or falls with competition, since only competition can tame the torrent of private interests and transform them into a force for good. It is competition which sees to it that the high road to profit is entered only by the rendering of an equivalent service (business principle). To restrict competition, then, is to jeopardize the principle of economic reciprocity. If this much is clear, then the conclusion can no longer be avoided that the growth of monopoly represents an extremely serious disfigurement of our economic system. The state can effectively fight monopoly by energetically opposing restrictions of competition and by carefully avoiding economic policies which favor the formation of monopolies.[2] For this, however, it is necessary to have a strong state—impartial and powerful—standing above the mêlée of economic interests, quite contrary to the widely held opinion that "capitalism" can thrive only where there is a weak government. The state must not only be strong; unmoved by ideologies of whatever brand, it must clearly recognize its task: to defend "capitalism" against the "capitalists" as often as they try to travel a more comfortable road to profit than the one indicated by the sign "principle of service" and to shift their losses onto the shoulders of the community.

These reflections should help us to clear up another prevailing misunderstanding. This is the notion that our economic system is one based on "production for profit" in which mere profitability determines what should be produced, whereas the collectivist economic system ensures "production for use," i.e., production oriented to the needs of mankind. Our investigations up to now, however, leave no doubt that insofar as the principle of service is safeguarded by competition, our present economic order guarantees "production for use," since the delicate and incorruptible scales of the market determine what is profitable and what is not. This means, simply, that the *dominance of the service principle is synonymous with the sovereignty of the consumers.* Can our economic system be described as anything else than as production for use when, through the simple working out of its principles, the desires of the consumers incite producers to attain maximum levels of output? And have we not even a greater right to so describe our economic system, the more doubtful it has become (upon mature deliberation and in the light of the experiences undergone in the meantime) whether a collectivist economy, even conceding that its leaders have the best of intentions, can be oriented to the "needs" of the population? If we examine the real conditions obtaining in the collectivist countries, both those that have collapsed and those still carrying on, does it not appear to be a cutting bit of sarcasm to describe collectivism as "production for use"?

The point of view from which this time-worn question must be answered has shifted decisively within the last decade. When this book first appeared there still existed in the developed countries a market economy which functioned after a fashion. Then the question at issue was how, on the one hand, to improve this economic order in spite of its numerous defects and to demonstrate the possibilities of a satisfactory reform of the market economy; on the other hand, it was imperative that the deceptions which lay in wait for those who pinned their hopes on collectivism be unmasked. In the interim, collectivism has changed from the phantasy-adorned ideal it once was to the hard and sober reality seen in the middle twentieth century. He who praises it speaks no longer of a utopia, of some distant paradise, but of an experiment which has been carried out repeatedly in a most thoroughgoing way and under the most diverse conditions, and which has shown itself to be the "grand illusion" of the postwar era. Hence, it is no longer the spokesman for the market economy but the collectivist who has been placed on the defensive. He finds himself compelled to clear collectivism of a five-fold charge: 1) that it is unable to solve satisfactorily the problem of order and productivity in the economy; 2) that it conflicts with our elementary ideals of freedom and justice; 3) that instead of showing the way to a solution of monopoly it leads us into an ineluctable and all-embracing state supermonopoly which is worse than private monopoly; 4) that it is incompatible with the prerequisites of an international community; 5) that it makes inevitable chronic inflation. On the one hand, there has been no serious effort up to now to refute this fivefold charge. On the other, we have had no example as yet of where collectivism has eventuated in a genuine order which would be compatible simultaneously with a government grounded on the principles of freedom and law and with a free international community.[3]

2. *The Collectivist Alternative*

Since the collectivist alternative owes a good part of its allure to a lack of understanding of the competitive system and the possibilities which it encompasses, the subject need not detain us too long. As the example of the slogan "production for use" has already shown, many of the labels tacked on to collectivism are hopeful but misleading. The same holds true for the fashionable comparison of the collectivist "planned economy" with "capitalist anarchy."

Since everyone today uses *planned economy* in a most imprecise way, an exact definition of this term should be our first order of business. The expression is frequently used in such a general way as to include every politico-economic activity of the state since in every such instance a plan of some kind is involved. Thus, the imposition of a tariff is part of the government's plan to build up the productive potential of the country. Streets and railroads are always built according to a given plan drawn up for the economy as a whole, so that it is incorrect to designate as examples of planned economy the public works projects which are initiated in many countries as emergency measures to combat depression. Cities, too, have, as a rule, been built according to a certain plan without its being necessary to resort to the term planned economy. Finally, the monetary and credit policies of many countries have for decades been based on certain principles aimed at regulating the economy, and they too have nothing to do with the concept of "planned economy." If all of this is planned economy, the concept loses all meaning. In such case, we would have had planned economy as far back as the beginnings of human economy, for economic life has always been subject to certain norms and influences at the bottom of which was the idea of some sort of purposeful direction. In this sense, the present-day market economy is, of course, also a "planned economy"; for the legal-institutional framework of this economic system was also constructed on the basis of systematic deliberations respecting the whole of the national economy.

But even if we take the concept of planned economy in a narrower sense and understand, thereby, a centrally administered economy as distinguished from a self-regulating one, we cannot deny that the present-day economic system possesses the attributes of a planned economy. For although our economic system, as we have seen in an earlier part of this book, may lack the conscious central direction of a collectivist economy, it is nevertheless directed in a certain way by the market and the formation of prices. In an undistorted competitive system, the plan of production is established by persons whose qualifications for the job we cannot very well question, viz., the consumers. The collectivist state, on the other hand, is placed before the dilemma either of imitating the competitive system, more or less, and basing its production plan on the wishes of the consumers (however ascertained) , or of establishing a plan based on other considerations to which the consumers will be compelled to submit. In the latter case, the decisions as to what will or will not be produced will be made on the basis of the thoroughly subjective notions of the leaders of the collectivist state; consumer freedom is at an end, and the population must agree to that use of the productive forces of the country which the dominant group in the government of the moment has decided is good. This, as can be easily shown, is how every planned economy in fact ends up. What results then is a thoroughgoing economic dictatorship which is inconceivable without a simultaneous political dictatorship possessed of the necessary means of coercion. So incompatible is the collectivist planned economy with freedom and the development of personality that this very statement would be added to the long list of crimes meriting death which the penal code of the collectivist state must include. Hence, to want to fight simultaneously for freedom and for planned economy would be to give evidence of a serious degree of mental confusion.

The collectivist planned economy differs from the "plan" of the market economy not only because it forces the population to submit to a plan designed to operate over a long period of time but also by reason of the particular methods with which it carries out its plan. Whereas the market economy is founded on the complicated interplay of the decisions freely made by all groups entering the market, the collectivist planned economy aims at replacing this spontaneous process by commands from above, and at turning over to a group of government officials the responsibility for decisions respecting the use to be made of the economy's productive resources. The collectivist planned economy thus substitutes a government fiat for the spontaneous reaction mechanism of the market, so that in the interest of clarity it might better be designated as *economy of the bureaucrats* or *command economy*. It is not necessary to list here again the enormous, even insurmountable difficulties which such a system would have to struggle with. We can sum up in one sentence all that we have thus far said: the uncorrupted market economy is the functioning planned economy of those whose business it is; the collectivist economy is the non-functioning planned economy of those whose business it is not.

That the collectivist economy is indeed the non-functioning economy of those whose business it is not, thus combining inferior economic performance with serfdom, is shown by the continuous failure of the Soviet Government's propaganda efforts to prove the contrary. In order to avoid being misled by this propaganda, and by the judgments of those who consciously or unconsciously lend themselves to Soviet purposes, the following facts must be stressed.

The Iron Curtain, with its barbed wire, mined border strips, machine guns, walls, and dire penalties for every attempt to escape from the prison, proves that the Communists seek by all possible means to hide two things: on the one hand, they endeavor to prevent their own subjects from learning about real conditions in the non-Communist world, and on the other, they permit the non-Communist world to learn only so much about life in Communist countries as is considered useful. In both cases, an unhindered investigation of the truth is prevented wherever possible.

But those who are so anxious to conceal the truth admit their own weaknesses in so doing. If the Communist state could proudly point to economic accomplishments as can the United States, France, Italy, Switzerland, or Germany, there would be no reason for it to shun the light like a night owl. This circumstance alone makes it probable that economic conditions in the Communist world are, today as yesterday, as bad as economic theory would lead us to expect they would be. Nowhere is this more apparent than in that part of the Communist empire which—to the vexation of Communists everywhere—is not able to completely seal off the truth, viz., the Soviet Union.

Only this isolation of the Communist world, joined with the thoughtlessness of the Western world, can explain the recent success of Communist propaganda in spreading the idea that Communism is at the threshold of economic achievements which can stand comparison with those of the free countries and the free economy. Here and there the suggestion is even taken seriously of the possibility that the Communist Assyrians may one day overtake us. This intellectual confusion in the free world—exhibited even by many whose economic training should have made them know better—has been all the more successful to the extent that Communist propaganda has been able to beat the drums for such technical marvels as Sputnik and its successors. But is it not obvious that while such enormously costly individual accomplishments give evidence of a number of things, for example, of special abilities in certain areas (and the ruthless concentration of scarce means in these areas), they are no proof at all of the existence of an efficient economic system? Do not such "accomplishments" in a country where the most basic consumer goods are lacking represent the pinnacle of waste? Is it not clear that they are no more useful in terms of the people's welfare than the Egyptian pyramids (which were the result of the same combination of technical genius and inhuman concentration of economic power), but considerably more ugly and ephemeral? And what are we to think of the streams of naive tourists to Russia who repeat with the pride of a Marco Polo that they were not required to do without anything?

In the light of such confusion in the evaluation of the Communist economic system, it is urgently necessary to draw attention to the following fundamental considerations. It is clear in the *first* place, that such a regime will make every effort to create as favorable an image as possible of its economic accomplishments and that in its dressing up of the facts, it can go much farther (thanks both to its insulation from the outside world and to the circumstance that no internal contradiction of the official line is permitted) than many a statistician of the free world would believe imaginable. Every piece of information originating in the Communist world must be regarded as colored by propaganda (unless the opposite can be proven), if not as plain swindle. In the interpretation of these data, expert detective techniques are required and even then there is no assurance of being able to extract the truth from such slippery witnesses.

But sufficient evidence is available, and this is the *second* point, to put a very unfavorable light on the Communist economy. What is undeniable, and more or less openly conceded by the Communist despots themselves, is the failure of Communism in agriculture, i.e., in precisely that branch of production upon which the population depends for supplies of the most elementary and essential goods. What this failure, which is tantamount to catastrophe, really signifies may be seen in figures published in a recent issue of the American *Monthly Labor Review* and derived from official Soviet sources. The data show that the Russian population constitutes a pyramid of wage earners—the base of which, equaling two-thirds of all wage earners, consists of 40 million persons earning the lowest wages (less than 600 rubles a month)—who even in 1960 were hardly able to buy more than the barest essential foodstuffs. For these foodstuffs, moreover, the wage earners in question had to work longer hours than in 1928 (18 per cent longer for bread, 153 per cent longer for milk, and 190 per cent longer for eggs). All experience shows that the totally inadequate performance of Communist agriculture is a result of the application to this sector of the Communist principle of collectivism (collective farming), with a resulting paralysis of incentives to produce. Tito proved himself cleverer in his decision to abandon this Communist principle and to restore the individual peasant economy.

But with respect to industry—and this is the *third* point—it is equally undeniable that in the Communist economy, even apart from the efforts at statistical prettying-up, very substantial increases in output have been registered in steel, coal, cement, oil, and electricity. These increases are very unequally distributed in the individual industrial sectors, but that changes nothing with respect to the fact that what has occurred is what is today referred to as economic growth. And since Russian growth commenced from a very low level, it is not unexpected to find this growth showing exceptionally large increases in *relative* terms. But only those will be astonished by such figures who have failed to note the statistical illusion involved. When, for example, we are told that the production of electrical energy in Russia is expected to increase between 1957 and 1965 by 123 per cent but in the United States by only 68 per cent, the significant neglected fact is that in the United States the percentage increase is measured from a much higher initial level. In truth, the absolute increase in electrical energy in the United States turns out to be more than half again as large as the Soviet increase, yielding an expected total output of energy in 1965 2½ times the expected Soviet total in that year.[4] Nor may we overlook in this connection the extraordinary help provided by the free world (in the form of the highest quality equipment and machinery) to a Communist empire dedicated to its destruction.[5] That Western entrepreneurs are so conscienceless as to strengthen our deadly enemy in this way, and Western governments so weak as to permit this, is one of the most humiliating and incomprehensible evidences of our intellectual and moral weakness.

But even when the illusions of statistics are disregarded, the very concept of economic growth which underlies all these comparisons is one which must be regarded with serious misgivings. Many persons—among whom the American professor W.W. Rostow must count as having made a particularly egregious contribution to the prevailing confusion—conceive of the process of growth as one in which the prime consideration is to increase investment in industry as much and as rapidly as possible so that the economy, like an airplane, will "take off" and climb ever higher. This is a purely technical concept in which the problem of economic order is completely overlooked. The belief that a functioning economic system results from the simple addition of individual production statistics betrays little thought and little real training in the fundamentals of economics. Apart from the fact that such statistics tell us nothing of the quality of the commodities in question (which in the Communist economy is usually notoriously poor), they relate merely to purely physical productivity. But this is of no help in answering the question of whether the problem of economic order has been satisfactorily solved: whether the factors of production have been properly allocated, whether the right things have been produced in the right proportions, whether the various branches of production are properly coordinated one with another so that the well-known "bottlenecks" are avoided; or whether, on the contrary, there are not continuous wastes and mistakes with the result that physical increases in output are converted into a general improvement in living standards only at great cost and after long delay.

Here then we discover the reason—this is the *fourth* point—why the exceptionally large increases in the output of important raw materials in the Communist countries have produced only very small improvement in their general living standards. Substantial shortages of every conceivable sort of commodity and bottlenecks of all kinds are a matter of course in the Communist economy. The foreign tourist customarily receives only a very inadequate impression of these conditions since he is continuously shepherded through model developments and never learns what it is like in a Communist country to have to buy a pail or to have a broken pane of glass replaced. He never learns what it means in such a country to have to find food, shelter, and clothing and to be plagued day in and day out by insufficiencies of every sort. He will receive even less information about the fact that wherever the Communist economy functions well to some extent, it is due only to manifold concessions made to the market economy (more or less legally free markets, free migratory workers, etc.) and to a substantial degree of corruption and bribery. Without these departures from "planned economy" the system would function even worse than it does.

In the *fifth* place, the tourist, like many others, is inclined to measure Communist development against the wrong yardstick. For the person who is condemned to dwell in such countries, and who has the misfortune to be cut off from the rest of the world, it is not unnatural to compare the present provision of commodities in his country with some earlier period, and to be impressed by what may seem to be a noticeable improvement. It would indeed be very surprising if decades of striving and sacrifice to improve the apparatus of production had not produced some kind of result. Something, in the end, must come out of such a machine. But if we want to know whether the Communist economic system has justified all the struggles and all the sacrifices we must apply to it an entirely different yardstick. We must not compare the present situation with some prior situation, but rather we should ask what a free economy would have achieved with such striving and such sacrifices, or by how much less effort and how many fewer sacrifices the present (Communist) living standards could have been attained in such a free economy. Otherwise expressed: that an improvement has occurred is undeniable, but it is an improvement which is not only pitifully inadequate to the need, but accomplished at a cost to the people that a free economy would have made unnecessary. Still otherwise expressed: the Communist economy suffers from a huge disproportion between outlay and yield because it is burdened with enormous losses, diseconomies, and wastes.

Therewith we arrive at the *final* and most important point. No reasonable person has ever maintained that a Communist economy is an impossibility, but the proofs have always been overwhelming that a Communist economy—as a system designed to serve the needs of the people—is a tragic failure. Conversely, however, Communism's very ability to operate without regard for the people's welfare enables it, with slave-driving techniques, to extract the uttermost both from workers, who are subject to the edicts of the sole employer, the state, and from consumers who are deprived by a variety of cunning devices of the fruits of their labor to the end that state investments shall increase.

The real accomplishment of Communism consists in the fact that it can concentrate economic resources wherever it appears politically purposeful to do so, be this in spectacular buildings and industrial projects, in the propagandizing and undermining of the rest of the world, or in armaments with which it can simultaneously hold the world in the spell of its threats.

If the results of the Communist economy are to be judged negatively in respect to its services to the welfare and happiness of mankind, it is equally necessary to give it positive marks for its unexampled concentration of economic effort in the service of a policy whose openly avowed objective is the conquering of the world. Communism—"The greatest organized unhappiness of the greatest number," as it was called recently by the London *Times* in a parody of Jeremy Bentham's well-known aphorism—represents on these selfsame grounds an immense and still increasing danger for the whole world.

All of us have the feeling that a fair judgment of Communism must avoid both underestimating it and overestimating it. Many incline, on the one hand, toward *underestimation* because they wish to avoid supporting the efforts of Communist propaganda, because they believe complacently in the superiority of the free world, or because they welcome reasons which dispense us from the need for vigilance and for constant effort to keep pace militarily and economically with our Communist rivals. Many incline, on the other hand, to *overestimation* because they are anxious to avoid self-deception, or because without being Communists they are collectivists, to the extent of feeling a certain sense of satisfaction at alleged proofs of the economic capabilities of Communism, and finding therein reasons for promoting their own collectivist ideas. Still others incline in this direction because they are intellectual snobs, and yet others because they are looking for a new reason for slackening the vigilance and efforts of the free world: viz., the alleged hopelessness of ever being able to match the Communist colossus.

What this amounts to is an extremely confused and therefore dangerous situation which must be put to an end. We must avoid overestimating Communism as an economic system serving mankind. But it is equally incumbent on us not to underestimate it as a system of the most extreme concentration of economic power in the service of politics—in the service of a politics whose ultimate goal to destroy and enslave the free world can be ignored only by the hopelessly blind among us. To our misfortune, most of those who in the free world belong to the Left, conspire to do the exact opposite in that they vastly overestimate the Communist economy as an economic system but simultaneously woefully underestimate it as the instrument of a world imperialism. The result is that they refuse to draw the hard conclusions required for the strengthening of our own economic counter-weapons. To allow ourselves neither to be bluffed nor lulled—that is what is required if we want to learn how to deal with Bolshevism.

3. The German Experiment in Noninflationary Market Economy

It would seem as if one of the world's most important industrial countries deliberately subjected itself to the experiment of demonstrating in succession (1) that collectivism requires not only political unfreedom but leads to disorder, waste, and low living standards, and (2) that the opposite economic system of the market economy is not only a prerequisite for political and intellectual freedom, but also the road to economic order and to prosperity for all the people as well. The country in question is Germany. Under the rule of the National Socialists it gave the world the example of a collectivist economy—which of necessity became increasingly inflationary and of which the chief marks were planned economy, price control, wage control, capital control, and exchange control. And the whole world showed great zeal in endeavoring to follow this example as rapidly as possible. Indeed, until quite recently the almost universally encountered brand of economic policy was, in essence, the National Socialist variety; and in not a few countries— the so-called underdeveloped ones—it is a policy which is still very much in vogue. Where this system led in Germany has been described in an earlier section of the book (Chapter IV, Section 4) which dealt with the phenomenon of repressed inflation.

It was the complete bankruptcy of this inflationary collectivism which (as indicated earlier) made possible the subsequent legendary economic revival of the non-Communist half of Germany. The success of this reform was so extraordinary, and the transition from poverty and hopelessness to prosperity and feverish economic activity so sudden, literally from one day to the next, that the term "German economic miracle" gained world-wide currency.

But the German accomplishment was nonetheless—in economic terms—no miracle at all, if the essence of the reform of 1948 is clearly understood. Its success was on the contrary precisely what its architects had expected. The real miracle lay in the fact that in this particular country and in a world still under the spell of inflationism and collectivism, it proved possible politically and socially to return to the economic reason of the market economy and to monetary discipline. It was then that the spectacular success of this reform which, from election to election, broadened the initially narrow political base of the market economy and finally compelled even the socialists to throw away, more or less convincingly, most of the planks in their economic platform.

It was, to be sure, a long time before the inflationists and collectivists of every kind and degree bowed to the irrefutable evidence of the facts and abandoned their attempts, as numerous as they were scientifically untenable, to minimize or even deny the unexampled and historically unique success of the German economic reform of

1948. Outside Germany there still appear to be some diehards who —either out of ignorance of the facts and interrelationships, or against their better judgment—resist admitting that here is to be found the most convincing case in all history against collectivism and inflationism and for market economy and monetary discipline.

In what did the German reform consist? A complete answer to this question cannot be given here since it would necessitate the analysis of many and in part complex issues.[6] It is sufficient for our purposes, however, to limit ourselves to a simple observation. The essence of the German economic reform corresponds to the sickness which it was intended to cure. If the sickness was that combination of collectivism and inflation which we have designated as repressed inflation, the therapy for it had to consist, on the one hand, in the elimination of inflationary pressure and, on the other hand, in the elimination of the apparatus of repression (maximum prices, rationing, controls and other interferences with free prices) and the restoration of market freedom, free prices, competition, and entrepreneurial incentives. Freedom in the realm of goods, discipline in the realm of money—those were the two principles upon which rested the German economic revival from 1948 onwards, and they have remained the foundation of German prosperity in spite of all the many concessions made to interventionism and the welfare state.

The reform of 1948 was constituted, then, of two parts: the overcoming of inflation and the dismantling of the apparatus of repression. The first was accomplished by the monetary reform, the second by the economic reform represented in the restoration of the market economy. Thus were the twin pillars of genuine economic order reconstructed from the chaos and the paralysis of the inflationary planned economy: the steering and motive power of free prices and the stability of the value of money. Both made it possible in a few years for a war-devastated rump state, swollen with refugees, whose cities had been destroyed to the extent of 50 per cent and more, to develop a "hard," fully convertible currency, to become the chief creditor nation of Europe, and finally, even to be found worthy of helping the leading power of the free world, the United States, out of its balance of payments difficulties with credits of one kind or another. German foreign trade, after having fallen to zero during and after the war, expanded within a decade to the point where Germany assumed the number two position in world trade (after the U.S.). Later, Japan—using the same recipes—achieved similar results.

In reality, as we have suggested, the situation was more complex than we have presented it here. It was not always easy to maintain, uninterrupted, the course of such a noninflationary market economy. The temptation was strong to give in to an anchronistic Keynesianism and to fight the persisently high level of unemployment, due to the continuing stream of refugees from the East, with a program of inflationary investments. The American occupation authorities exerted, over a considerable period, strong pressure on the German government and the German central bank in this direction. Fortunately, the Germans withstood both the pressure and the temptation, so that Germany was preserved from a relapse into the National Socialist policy of repressed inflation. But it was a long time before this problem of structural unemployment was solved by a patient policy of adaptation and adjustment. An essential prerequisite for this policy, as well as for the enormous increase of investment (which represented the real motor of the German revival), was the restrained wages policy of the German labor unions, who had the good sense to wait upon the fruits of real prosperity, and a tax system which provided the necessary incentives for entrepreneurs to invest.

Thus it was that Germany, with its particular version of market economy (termed "social market economy"), gave the world an example of a constructive and internationally responsible economic policy, following its prior repellent example, under the National Socialists, of an economically destructive and internationally disintegrative economic policy. This was a not ignoble way of attempting to make good the damage caused by the former bad example. It is certainly not at all flattering to our age that the world—so quickly, zealously, and obstinately—determined to follow Germany's former bad example of a collectivist-inflationary policy, that the occupation authorities in Germany in the immediate postwar period insisted on the continued implementation of such policies in the conquered country, and that this same world delayed as long as possible in following Germany's new good example, and then only with mistrust, incomprehension, and hostility. But the weight of the evidence and the sheer logic of the situation finally won the day. The events of the German case spoke too clear and compelling a language to be misunderstood, with the result that one country after another followed the German lead, more or less faithfully, more or less successfully, but unquestionably in the direction of more market economy and greater monetary discipline. A particularly impressive example of this general development is the case of France which, by finally (end of 1958) adopting the German recipes of monetary discipline and market economy, succeeded in converting its chronic balance of payments deficit into a sizable surplus.

4. *The Third Road*

Having had a glimpse of the rather unattractive future which the collectivist alternative holds in store for us, let us return now to our own economic system. We find that this system is composed of a complicated network of contractual relationships which, however, join together to produce an ordered whole—thanks to the mechanism of the market. It is a combination of freedom and order, representing what is probably the highest level to which these two ideals can simultaneously attain. Moreover, it is a combination which has bestowed on the human race an unparalleled increase in its standard of living. Obviously, this combination of freedom, order and progress is far from being perfect. Often the three principles are found to be in conflict with one another so that frequent compromises must be made among them, sometimes at the cost of the one, sometimes at the cost of the other.

To the admission that our economic system is characterized by unstable equilibrium, we must hasten to add the fact that small disturbances, affecting a limited sector of the economy, can generally be overcome with ease and with hardly perceptible effort by means of the steering mechanism of the market. The market economy is also able to adjust with surprising rapidity and elasticity to most changes in economic "data" (methods of production, size of population, consumption habits, etc.). However, from time to time grave and total equilibrium disturbances take place: we have spoken of them in the previous chapter, and we have seen how they may be most effectively overcome.

The admission that our economic system undoubtedly contains within itself the seeds of crisis does not really signify too much. For the admission must be qualified by two circumstances, neither of which we can afford to overlook. The first of these is the undeniable fact that the disturbances, which for decades have affected the economic life of most countries and which finally culminated in the Great Depression (1929-33), owe their severity and extent primarily to the *external* shocks which have afflicted the world since 1914. It is a real miracle that our economic system has not completely collapsed in consequence, and we have the right to ask whether another sort of economic system would have exhibited similar powers of resistance. The point is that our economic system ought not to be made the scapegoat for the political sins of our generation. Moreover, it is a fact that in this same period our economic system has been deformed in ever-increasing degree by interventions and degeneracies of every conceivable sort, to the point where it is almost unrecognizable. The result is that the system has become increasingly less able to fulfill its functions, less elastic, and less maneuverable. It has lost this adaptability and this flexibility precisely at a time when these qualities are most urgently needed, since economic conditions are changing more quickly and more radically than ever before. But in a fatal chain of reactions, the disproportion between the need and the ability to adapt have led to measures of policy and to interventions which as an end result have served only to widen the gap.

To find a way out of this vicious circle is one of the most important of the many crushing responsibilities which our generation has to shoulder. This is so difficult that not a few have turned away from their responsibility in despair. It remains, nevertheless, one of those problems upon the satisfactory solution of which hangs the fate of our Western civilization.

There is no doubt about the fact that our economic system needs a complete "overhaul," if we wish to arrest the process of degeneration before it ends in an intolerable degree of unproductivity and —what is worse—corruption and injustice. To accomplish this, something more is required than a mere freeing of the system from "non-assimilable" interventions of the state. The job cannot be done by merely adopting a negative approach and abstaining from action, i.e., by a return to simple "laissez-faire" methods. Of much more significance in the shaping of a constructive policy are the abundant proofs that the structure of the market economy is not nearly as simple as its friends, as well as its enemies, have maintained. We now know that its functioning depends upon a whole series of economic, juridical, moral, psychological, and political conditions, none of which are simply "given," and which, in any event, must be largely restructured to fit the changed needs of the present. Above all it will be necessary to overhaul, with the help of trained economists, the legal framework of our economic system (bankruptcy laws, corporation laws, patent laws, monetary and banking laws, and anti-trust laws).

Just as we ought not to let ourselves be led astray in the execution of this task by ideological name-calling, so ought we to take care not to allow ourselves to be paralyzed by the weak-willed fatalism of those who would have us believe that the dissolution of our economic system is a matter of fate, to struggle against which would be mere quixotism. This belief that economics is subject to ineluctable laws of evolution—a part of the abundant residue of *Marxist thought* still current in our time—is no more justified today than it was previously, and is all the less appropriate to a generation which prides itself on possessing more courage and energy than did its predecessor.

There is in our time hardly a more urgent task than to find a way out of the sterile struggle between the champions of a "free" economy, as it was formerly known, and the protagonists of a socialist economic order which, with its endless disappointments, we have come to know so well. It is the economist who is especially inclined to warn against over-emphasis of the economic factor in history; but he may nevertheless be permitted the observation that our whole civilization is everywhere entangled in seemingly insoluble problems because it has not succeeded in the elementary task of constructing an efficient and humane economic order. We may add that our world has failed in this task precisely because it has not clearly understood what the issues really are.

Our first duty, then, is to determine precisely what the problems are which must be solved. The truth is that it would be hard to exceed the confusion which today prevails on this point. The origin of the confusion is rooted in two basic fallacies. In the first place, there is too little regard for the fact that there are a number of *different* problems to be solved, most of which must be kept separate from one another. Stemming directly from this fallacy is the second fallacy, viz., the belief that all these different problems can be solved once for all with a single ready-made solution, be it that of the flagwavers for the free or for the socialist economy. Both errors must be avoided.

If we now examine the present condition of the Western world, and ask ourselves where we must begin in reforming our economic and social system, we find but four cardinal problems, each of which is different from the others and each requiring its own solution:

1) the problem of order; 2) the social problem; 3) the political problem of the distribution of power and 4) the moral-vital problem, as we may describe it in brief.

As far as the *problem of order* is concerned, the reader of this book is now sufficiently aware of what is at issue. Just as the individual farmer must reflect on the use he will make of each unit of his land, capital and available labor power—in order that the right items will be produced and in the right proportions—so too must the national economy as a whole reflect on the use it will make of its resources. Not only individuals but society as a whole is faced with the question: what use shall be made of the given productive resources? Ought we to produce this or that, and how much of this or that? It is unnecessary to comment again on the enormous difficulty and complexity of this task. Suffice it to say that a well-ordered economy results in the right things being produced in the right proportions at the right time in the right place and with the right methods of production. It ensures simultaneously that an optimum effort will be made by all those engaged in the process of production, so that the right goods will be produced, and that they will be of the best possible quality and available in the largest possible quantities. It also sees to it that people will take heed of the future, that they will save and invest.

We can clarify what has been said with an illustration. Just as a watch needs not only a balance wheel to regulate its running, but also a spring to keep it running, so is a satisfactory economic system not possible without an efficient system of *regulatory and propulsive forces*. The present condition of many countries is characterized by a serious lack of these regulatory and propulsive forces. Because the problem of economic order familiar to previous generations is no longer understood, our contemporaries have destroyed the existing system of regulatory and propulsive forces and are unable to find a substitute for it. Indeed, they have failed to realize that anything has been destroyed. Inexperienced fingers have been meddling with the delicate machinery of the watch: they have bent its spring and balance wheel. It makes little difference how much the watch is shaken; it will not run properly as long as the spring and balance wheel are not repaired.

Order and incentive in the economy—these, then, are the two cardinal problems around which everything revolves and which from minute to minute must be freely and noiselessly solved. We find, however, if we extend our inquiry back to first principles, that there are only *two possible solutions* to these problems (if we exclude the special case of the self-sufficient peasant economy). The two possible solutions, as we know already, are those of freedom and command. That of *freedom* means the strict adherence to an order functioning with astonishing regularity through the medium of the free market with its freely fluctuating prices. That of *command*, however, means an economic order in which order and incentive are placed in the hands of the consciously ordering, planning, inciting, commanding, and command-enforcing state. The one we call market economy, the other command economy, planned economy, centrally administered economy, collectivist (socialist) economy. It cannot be too strongly emphasized that as far as the task of ordering economic life is concerned, we have only this exclusive choice between market economy and command economy. We cannot take refuge in some third alternative, in cooperatives, trade unions, in undertakings patterned after the much-cited but much misunderstood Tennessee Valley Authority, corporatism, industry council plans, vocational orders, or any other form of "ersatz" socialism. We must choose between price or state command, between the market or the authorities, between economic freedom or bureaucracy. Having tried out both systems, however, we know only too well that, in fact, we have no further choice in the matter. It has been shown that Western man is not free to opt for a collectivist system, since the latter is unable to guarantee an effective system of order and incentives which would be compatible with freedom and with the existence of an international community. He who chooses the market economy must, however, also choose: free formation of prices, competition, risk of loss and chance for gain, individual responsibility, free enterprise, private property.

This choice—and herewith we return to the heart of our argument—has nothing whatsoever to do with what was formerly understood under the terms "free economy" or "capitalism." The new orientation of economic policy—along a path which the author has designated as the "third road"—consists precisely in this: that we recognize the impassibility of the socialist road without our feeling it necessary, on that account, to return to the old worn-out road of "capitalism." Two important planks must be included in this new program whose aim it is to ensure the existence of a natural order. The *first* calls for a stable framework which, as already observed, is indispensable to a well-ordered market economy. This in itself means that the state has a number of important tasks to fulfill: the establishment of a healthy money system and a prudent credit policy which together will serve to eliminate an important source of economic disturbances. Such a framework will also necessitate a legal system carefully constructed to prevent, as far as possible, abuse of the freedom of the market and to ensure that the road to success will be entered only through the small door of reciprocal service. In a word, this framework should be designed so as to reduce to a minimum the numerous imperfections of the market economy.

This is the first part of the program, one which of itself will provide the state with enough to do. The second becomes necessary due to the fact that, in addition to solving the problem of order, there are further tasks to be done. The market economy, of itself, will furnish a solution only to the problem of order. To determine whether it can provide answers to the other problems, even if only partially, requires more exact investigation. We want not only to produce maximum quantities of the right goods as economic order prescribes, but also, once this problem has been satisfactorily solved, to see other ideals realized as well.

And herewith we come to the other three key problems with which we began our main discussion. There is, to repeat, the *social problem*. This means that we are not satisfied with the existing order as a whole, but are concerned to provide security and protection to the weak by a certain correction of the distribution obtaining under the market economy. It is not necessary, however, to sacrifice order for the sake of social policy, nor social policy for the sake of order. There is, further, the political problem of the *distribution of power*. This, too, should be carefully distinguished from the problem of order, though it is necessary to add that the problems connected with the distribution of power are to a large extent solved by the whole process of the market economy, in which no economic and consequently no political power groups can long prosper.

There remains what we have called the *moral-vital problem*. This expression is to be understood as meaning that although it is very important that we have a well-ordered, productive, and just economy, it is at least as important to ask what the effects of such a system are on the moral and spiritual condition of man—on those intangibles which constitute the real meaning of his existence and the foundation of his happiness. How does this system affect man in his capacity as a person called to revere the Most High, as neighbor and citizen impelled toward community with his fellowmen, as member of a family and as worker? The material goods with which a well-ordered and highly productive economy furnishes us are indispensable, but they are only a means. The end, on the other hand, is a life which is complete and meaningful, adapted to the nature of man. In our time this kind of life is most gravely menaced by mechanization, depersonalization, proletarianization, breakup of the family, the growth of a mass society, and other items on the debit side of our urban-technical civilization. The rejection of the market economy by many on these counts appears to stem from the most worthy motives. Such persons must bear in mind, however, that the market economy makes no pretense of providing solutions to the problems described above. It merely supplies the framework within which we must seek the answers to these last and most fundamental questions. In the absence of a market economy these problems are, in fact, insoluble; only such an economy can guarantee us order in freedom, without which all the rest is in vain. This is not the place to describe in detail an economic policy of this kind; in any case, it will be one which has freed itself from the "idolatry of impressive-sounding slogans".[7] Its outlines are denoted, first, by the fact that instead of regulating and commanding—doing violence to the laws of the market economy—it seeks to attain its goal by cooperating with these laws: to reestablish a genuinely competitive economy, thereby providing an offset to the frictions, hardships, and difficulties inherent in a developed economy. Such a policy will distinguish sharply between measures which are adapted to our economic system (conformable), and those which are in conflict with it (nonconformable), and will favor the former with the same resolve with which we choose to drink ethyl instead of methyl alcohol. This means that it will follow as far as possible the indirect, organic method of exerting influence on economic life, and not the direct method which consists in the promulgating of decrees. It means, further, that economic policies as such will be designed so as to avoid, as far as possible, interferences with the process of price formation, and that they will be applied either before or after this process.

This "third road" of economic policy is, above all, a *road of moderation and proportion*. It is incumbent upon us to make use of every available means to free our society from its intoxication with big numbers, from the cult of the colossal, from centralization, from hyper-organization and standardization, from the pseudo-ideal of the "bigger and better," from the worship of the mass man and from addiction to the gigantic. We must lead it back to a natural, human, spontaneous, balanced, and diversified existence. It is incumbent upon us to end an epoch in which mankind, in the triumph of its technological and organizational accomplishments and in its enthusiasm over the vision of a future of unending growth and unrestrained progress, forgot man himself: forgot his soul, his instincts, his nerves and organs, heedless of the centuries' old wisdom of Montaigne (*Essays,* Book III, Chap. 13), that even on the highest stilts we must still walk with our legs and even on the world's highest throne we must still sit on our bottom.[8]

Such a "road" signifies, above all, the favoring of the ownership of small and medium-sized properties, independent farming, the decentralization of industrial areas, the restoration of the dignity and meaning of work, the reanimation of professional pride and professional ethics, the promotion of communal solidarity. The prospects for the success of such a policy would be not too good, were it not for the fact that a slow-down in population increases is eliminating one of the principal causes of the rise of the proletariat, and were it not obvious that the advantages which up to now have been attributed to large scale enterprises have been seriously exaggerated. The notion that we are faced with an irresistible trend toward large-scale enterprise has been shown to be completely inapplicable to the broadest and most important segments of the economy, particularly agriculture, the handicrafts, and small business. Even with respect to industry, it can be assumed that the notable increase in average-sized enterprises in recent decades is explainable less in terms of the technical-economic advantages which would be thereby gained, than as a reaction to that megalomania to which the world has so heedlessly surrendered. It is everywhere apparent that the dimensions of many areas of our lives—economic as well as noneconomic—have expanded far beyond the optimum, and that they must be deflated to more reasonable proportions, a process which will prove to be painful but, in the long run, beneficial. In this connection, there must be due recognition of the fact that contrary to a widely held opinion, technological development itself has very often had the effect of strengthening the viability of the small as opposed to the large-scale enterprise.

But whatever specific form the economic policy of the future will take, it will stand no chance of success if it is not shaped by experts thoroughly acquainted with the structure and mechanism of our economic system and if it is not executed with the understanding, the support and the cooperation of the broad masses of the population who know what is at stake. To bring this to pass is the great practical task of the science of human behavior which we call economics. Economics can successfully accomplish this task only if it is not itself sucked into the vortex of the contemporary crisis of civilization, and if it does not finally fall victim to the uncomprehending attacks to which it is exposed at present. It is reported that Napoleon once took umbrage at the obstinate behavior of one of his officials and reprimanded him for it. The honest servant replied: Sire, one can support oneself only on that which offers resistance. The same may be said of the science of economics.

NOTES

1. (p. 233) *"Capitalism"*

The reader will have noticed that this popular description of our economic system has been employed only seldom in our text, and as a rule in quotation marks. There are good reasons for this. As coined and circulated by Marxism, the term has retained up to the present so much of its hate-filled significance and class-struggle overtones that its usefulness for the purposes of scientific discussion has become extremely questionable. In addition, it provides us with only a very vague notion of the real essence of our economic system. Instead of promoting understanding, it merely arouses the emotions and obscures the truth. Walter Eucken deserves especial credit for his efforts to arrive at a clear definition of the economic system and thereby of the term capitalism as well; see his *The Foundations of Economics* (London, 1951). See also: Alexander Rüstow, *Ortsbestimmung der Gegenwart*, Vol. 3 (Erlenbach-Zurich, 1957), pp. 159 ff.; W. Röpke, *Civitas Humana* (London, 1948).

2. (p. 236) *Competition as a Problem of Economic Policy*

The problem of competition—its function, its conditions, its institutional framework and its evolutionary tendencies—is being given an ever-increasing amount of attention in the most recent literature, and rightly so, since it is this central problem which gives rise to all the other symptoms of the present crisis of our system. Increasingly, the confusion erected about this key question of our economic system by some confused persons, and by some very unconfused monopoly interests, is being summarily dispelled. Hearteningly, it is now recognized —in opposition to alleged ineluctable processes of evolution—that our economic system can in the final analysis continue to exist only as a competitive system. See: F. Böhm, *Wettbewerb und Monopolkampf* (Berlin, 1933); F. H. Knight, *The Ethics of Competition* (London, 1935); C. J. Ratzlaff, *The Theory of Free Competition* (Philadelphia, 1936); W. H. Hutt, *Economists and the Public, a Study of Competition and Opinion* (London, 1936); L. Einaudi, "Economia di concorrenza e capitalismo storico. La terza via fra i secoli XVIII e XIX," *Revista di Storia Economica* (Turin), June 1942; W. Eucken, *Wettbewerb als Grundprinzip der Wirtschaftsverfassung* (Munich, 1942); Monographs of the Temporary National Economic Committee (Washington, D. C.; 1940/41); J. M. Clark, *Alternative to Serfdom* (New York, 1948); T. W. Arnold, *The Bottlenecks of Business* (New York, 1940); C. v. Dietze, "Landwirtschaft und Wettbewerbsordnung" *Schmollers Jahrbuch*, 1942, No. 2; W. Röpke, *The Social Crisis of Our Time* (Chicago, 1950); W. Röpke, *Civitas Humana, op. cit.;* Walter Lippmann, *The Good Society* (Boston, 1937); L. Miksch, *Wettbewerb als Aufgabe* (2nd ed.; Godesberg, 1947); C. D. Edwards, *Maintaining Competition* (New York, 1949); C. E. Griffin, *An Economic Approach to Antitrust Problems* (New York, 1951); ORDO, *Jahrbuch für die Ordnung von Wirtschaft und Gesellschaft* (published annually since 1948, Düsseldorf), with important articles by F. Böhm, W. Eucken *et al.;* see also W. Röpke, article "Wettbewerb-Konkurrenzsystem," *Handwörterbuch der Sozialwissenschaften*.

3. (p. 238) *The Crisis of Collectivism and the Problem of Economic Order*

The ideas outlined in the text have been developed at greater length by the author in his short papers *Die Krise des Kollektivismus* (1947) and *The Problem of Economic Order* (Cairo, 1951) and in his book *Mass und Mitte* (Zurich, 1950). On the problem of order see also: L. Robbins, *The Economic Problem in Peace and War* (London, 1947); J. M. Clark, *Alternative to Serfdom, op. cit.;* John Jewkes, *Ordeal by Planning* (London, 1948); Henry C. Simons, *Economic Policy for a Free Society* (Chicago, 1948).

4. (p. 243) *The Soviet Economy*

The pioneer works studying the claims and realities of the Soviet economy are: G. Warren Nutter, *The Growth of Industrial Production in the Soviet Union,* (Princeton, 1962); Colin Clark, *The Real Productivity of Soviet Russia,* (printed for the use of the Internal Security Subcommittee, Committee on the Judiciary, U. S. Senate, Washington, 1961); Naum Jasny, *Soviet Industrialization 1928-52,* (Chicago, 1962); and Abram Bergson, *The Real National Income of Soviet Russia Since 1928,* (Cambridge, [Mass.], 1962).

5. (p. 243) *Western Aid to the Soviets*

A fascinating study of the Western contribution to the construction of the Soviet industrial and agricultural base has been made by Werner Keller in his book, recently translated from the German, *East Minus West Equal Zero,* (New York, 1961).

6. (p. 248) *The Example of the West German Economic Revival*

The German experiment in monetary discipline and economic freedom may be studied in detail in the following works: Ludwig Erhard, *Prosperity through Competition* (New York, 1958); *The Mainsprings of the German Revival* (New Haven, 1955); David McCord Wright, *Post-War West German and United Kingdom Recovery* (Washington, D. C.: American Enterprise Association, 1957); Egon Sohmen, "Competition and Growth: West Germany" in *American Economic Review,* December 1959, and the subsequent discussion thereon, *American Economic Review,* December 1960; W. Röpke, "Das deutsche Wirtschaftsexperiment—Beispiel und Lehre" in the Symposium *Vollbeschäftigung, Inflation und Planwirtschaft* (Erlenbach-Zurich, 1951; W. Röpke, *Ein Jahrzehnt sozialer Marktwirtschaft in Deutschland und seine Lehren* (Cologne, 1958); W. Röpke, *Ist die deutsche Wirtschaftspolitik richtig?* (Stuttgart, 1950). On the technique of the monetary reform of 1948 see: F. A. Lutz, "The German Currency Reform and the Revival of the German Economy" in *Economica,* May 1949.

7. (p. 256) *Scientific Directives for Economic Policy*

In the text the author has remained true to his early thoughts on this topic as developed in his article "Staatsinterventionismus," *Handwörterbuch der Staatswissenschaften,* 4th ed., supplementary volume, (1929). There too an outline of a theory of economic policy may be found. See also: A. C. Pigou, *The Economics of Welfare* (4th ed., London, 1932); M. St. Braun, *Theorie der staatlichen Wirtschaftspolitik* (Leipzig-Vienna, 1929); L. Mises, *Planned Chaos* (Irvington-on-Hudson, N. Y., 1947); O. Morgenstern, *The Limits of Economics* (London, 1937); H. Laufenburger, *L'intervention de l'État en matière économique* (Paris, 1939); C. Bresciani-Turroni, *Economic Policy for the Thinking Man* (London, 1950); Th. Pütz, *Theorie der allgemeinen Wirtschaftspolitik und Wirtschaftslenkung* (1948); William A. Orton, *The Economic Role of the State* (London, 1950); W. Eucken, *Grundsätze der Wirtschaftspolitik* (1952).

8. (p. 257) *The Third Road*

For a complete statement of the author's program of a "third road," ranging far beyond the purely economic factors see: W. Röpke, *The Social Crisis of Our Time, op. cit.;* W. Röpke, *Civitas Humana, op. cit.;* W. Röpke, *International Order and Economic Integration* (Dordrecht, Holland, 1959); W. Röpke, *Mass und Mitte, op. cit.;* W. Röpke, *A Humane Economy* (Chicago, 1960).

9. (p. 258) *Essence and Method of Economics*

Instead of defending economics in detail against the attacks to which it is continuously being subjected, the author has preferred in this book to let economics speak for itself and thus to give the reader the opportunity of making his own judgment as to whether this science is really as impractical, unmodern, reactionary, socially noxious, or rationalistic as its despisers so untiringly declaim. The economist must learn not to be dissuaded from his real task by such attacks, and to recognize that he will remain unloved by the special interests and political adventurers. On methodological problems see: W. Eucken, *The Foundations of Economics, op. cit.;* L. Robbins, *An Essay on the Nature and Significance of Economic Science* (2nd ed., London, 1935); O. Morgenstern, *op. cit.;* L. von Mises, *Human Action* (New Haven, 1949); A. Rüstow, "Zu den Grundlagen der Wirtschaftswissenschaft," *Revue de la Faculté des Sciences Économiques de l'Université d'Istanbul,* 1941; L. v. Mises, *Grundprobleme der Nationalökonomie* (1933); W. Röpke, *A Humane Economy, op. cit.*

INDEX

INDEX OF PERSONS

INDEX OF SUBJECTS